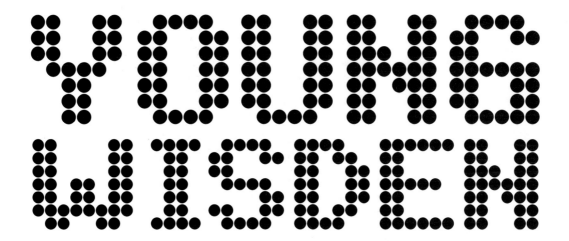

YOUNG WISDEN

A NEW FAN'S GUIDE TO CRICKET

by

TIM DE LISLE

A&C Black • London

First published 2007 by
A & C Black Publishers Ltd
38 Soho Square, London W1D 3HB
www.acblack.com

Copyright © Tim de Lisle 2007

ISBN-13: 978 0 7136 8719 4

A CIP catalogue record for this book is available from the
British Library.

Designed and typeset by Nigel Davies
Pre-press production by James Bunce

Cover photographs © Getty Images

Photographs on pages 46, 47, 48, 124 and 125 © Philip Brown;
pages 39, 47, 48, 51 and 117 © PA Photos; page 49 © BBC
Publicity; page 82 and 83 © ECB Hit Squad; page 85 ©
Rob Tucker; page 89 © Bridgeman Art Library; page 110 ©
Clare Skinner/MCC; page 115 © Billy Bowden; page 116 ©
Moviestore Collection; page 125 © Crazy Catch.
All other photographs © Getty Images.

This book is produced using paper that is made from wood
grown in managed, sustainable forests. It is natural, renewable
and recyclable. The logging and manufacturing processes
conform to the environmental regulations of the country of origin.

Printed and bound in China by C&C Offset Printing Co. Ltd

CONTENTS

4   Introduction
5   How to use the book

PART 1 — basics

6   The aim of the game
8   The 11 ways of being out
12   The four possible results
14   How to read a scorecard
16   Pitch, toss and weather
18   The fundamental things apply
20   Kit
22   Laws and umpires
24   A matter of time
26   The language: a crash course
28   **storytime: Shane Warne** – from beach bum to legend

PART 2 — types of cricket

32   International: Test, one-day and Twenty20
34   County: the 18 teams and the four competitions
38   Women's: the battles they have faced and five great women
40   **storytime: Andrew Flintoff** – from fat lad to heavyweight champion

PART 3 — players in general

42   The qualities cricketers need
44   Cricketers' body shapes
46   A day in the life of Mark Ramprakash
50   **storytime: Don Bradman** – the best batsman ever

PART 4 — skills and roles

52   Batting: attack and defence
54   Batting: the four choices
56   Bowling: fast
58   Bowling: slow
60   Being an allrounder
62   Wicketkeeping
64   Fielding
66   Captaincy
68   Setting the field
70   **storytime: Sachin Tendulkar** – cricket's biggest star

PART 5 — the world of cricket

72   Planet cricket
74   Test teams: Australia and England
76   Test teams: India, Pakistan, Sri Lanka, South Africa
78   Test teams: New Zealand, West Indies, Bangladesh, Zimbabwe
80   My world XI
82   England team profiles
84   The great grounds
86   **storytime: Botham's Ashes**

PART 6 — history

88   The eight ages of cricket
94   The greatest … everything, from coach to personality
96   Three great rivalries: the Ashes, India v Pakistan, Yorkshire v Lancashire
98   Extreme matches
100   **storytime: Wisden** – from a tiny fast bowler to a fat yellow book

PART 7 — fun and figures

104   The magic numbers: most, best, biggest
106   The tragic numbers: least, worst, smallest
108   Statistics and how they work
110   Hundreds, five-fors and ducks
112   Sixes and hat-tricks
114   Unusual occurrences
116   Quotes

PART 8 — how to …

118   Go and see
120   Follow in the media
122   Read about the game
124   Have a go yourself

126   Index
128   Acknowledgements

INTRODUCTION

Welcome to **Young Wisden**, the first book for younger readers in the 144-year history of John Wisden and Co.

The book is a guide to cricket – how it works, why it's fun, who plays it best, how it has grown. It's not a coaching manual, although there are dozens of tips that you can apply to your own game if you wish. Wisden doesn't do coaching manuals, preferring to concentrate on following the game, recording, reporting, appreciating and appraising it. With its tradition of independence and intelligence, it is a wonderful place for a sportswriter to work.

Unlike big *Wisden*, this is not an annual either. It is topical, using current and recent players to shed light on the workings of the game, but it is not a record of what happened over the past year. Of the dispiriting 2007 World Cup, you will find few mentions here.

But the book is like its much older sister in one crucial way: it is driven by a love of cricket. In many offices, there are jokeys mugs saying you don't have to be mad to work here, but it helps. Well, you do have to be cricket-mad to work at Wisden.

Almost any sport is a good thing for a child to get into, a bridge into the adult world. Even football, overbearing as it is at the moment, has many good points – it's simple, accessible, global, a constant source of news, debate and human interest. But cricket has dimensions that football doesn't have. It's subtle and sophisticated. The captain needs to be a tactician and strategist. It goes on for ages, which sounds like a drag but turns out to be a strength, allowing suspense to build up over five days.

It is a game of great contrasts. It can be fast and furious or slow and artful. It demands brain as well as brawn; some of its stars are not even athletic (see page 44). A great player can be huge or tiny, clever or thick, dashing or dogged. It's both a small world – only 10 major nations – and a wide one, spanning many races and creeds and climates. This book tries to capture some of that flavour.

Some guides to the game offer nothing to disagree with. That's understandable but not very cricket-like. Cricket fans love disagreeing with each other. They love arguing about who's the greatest spinner of all, Shane Warne or Murali, or whether the present Australian team would have beaten the great West Indies side of the 1980s, or exactly how many English county competitions need to be abolished. **Young Wisden** doesn't expect you to agree with everything it has to say.

I've tried to write the book I would have loved when I was 12, to convey the pleasure to be had from the game and its finer points. If a teacher ever tells you off for reading this book, you could point out to them – very politely – that it's actually quite educational. There is history in here, and maths, a little bit of science, plenty of geography and a fair amount of drama. You will learn new words, get your head round complicated concepts, and be given a reading list. Without even noticing, you will pick up vital skills – concentration, close observation, and powers of analysis. But that makes it sound a bit dry, which is something we have tried hard to avoid – especially through Nigel Davies's outstanding designs.

Until quite recently, cricket was often stuffy and impenetrable. Now it is getting better all the time, with exciting new developments from Twenty20 to Chance To Shine. With a bit of luck, **Young Wisden** will be part of that process. On page 23, you'll find a summary of the Spirit of Cricket, as laid down by MCC. It's an admirable document with just one glaring omission. It doesn't say anything about enjoying the game. So let's say it loud and clear here: have fun.

Tim de Lisle
Islington, June 2007

The structure: eight parts

The book consists of 60 double-page spreads, divided into **eight parts**. The parts were listed in **the contents** on the previous page. The coloured strip at the top of each page tells you which part you're in, and so do the words on it. But nearly all the spreads are self-contained, so this is a book you can **dip into** if you want.

Between the parts

Between the parts, like the ad break in a TV show, comes **a story**. Each one is true although they read like fiction. They are about some of cricket's extraordinary characters, starting with **Shane Warne** on page 28. For the stories, the design changes so the page looks like a book within a book.

Now, what are you – a total beginner?

Begin at the very beginning. The first section, **basics** (pages 6 to 29), is for you. If you can't find what you need to know, try **The fundamental things apply** (page 18). If that doesn't work, try the **Index** (page 126).

... already quite keen?

You could skip the first few pages, although I've tried to put stuff on every page that is aimed at you. Here's a test: if you already know the **11 ways of being out** (page 8) and the **four possible results** (page 12), you can go straight to page 14. If not, maybe you should glance at them. It would be a shame to find younger kids knowing more than you.

... or mildly obsessed?

Welcome to the club. Most introductions to the game don't have much for you, but I hope this one will. You can compare and contrast the **three types of international cricket** on page 32. Check out **how long things take** in cricket, from under half a second to 30 years, on page 24. Ponder all **the qualities cricketers need** on page 42, or **the body shapes** they tend to have on page 44. Hear all about **Mark Ramprakash's day** (page 46), or go to the section on **skills and roles** (page 52) to find **the four choices** a batsman has to make (page 54) and the **five strong points** of the leading fast bowlers (page 56). Study the form and foibles of **the Test teams** on pages 74-79, or get a quick tour of **the history of the game** on pages 88-93. For light relief, try **the six wacky dismissals** (page 10), **the tragic numbers** (page 106) or **the unusual occurrences** (page 114). If you have tickets for a big game, there's a guide to **pacing your day** on page 118. If not, find the best of **the cricket media** on page 120 and **11 good books** on page 122. If all this is making you want to **have a go yourself**, turn to page 124.

Abbreviations

Test teams in orange. For a guide to cricket language, see page 26. For a guide to the scorecard, see page 14

A or Aus	Australia
ave	average
B in batting stats	balls faced
B or Bang	Bangladesh
BB	best bowling figures by that player
capt	captain
Ch'ship	Championship
D	drawn
dec	declared
div	division
E or Eng	England
ft	feet
hrs	hours
HS	highest score by that player
I or Ind	India
ICC	International Cricket Council
in after a number	inches
inns	innings
mins	minutes
L	lost
LBG	legspinner (the G stands for googly)
lbw	leg before wicket
LFM	left-arm fast-medium bowler
LHB	left-handed batsman
LM	left-arm medium-pace bowler
m after a number	million
M in bowling figures	maidens
MCC	Marylebone Cricket Club
mph	miles per hour
No	number, in batting order
NR	no result
NZ	New Zealand
O	overs
OB	offspinner
ODI	one-day international
P	played
P or Pak	Pakistan
R	runs
RF	right-arm fast bowler
RFM	right-arm fast-medium bowler
RHB	right-handed batsman
RM	right-arm medium-pace bowler
SA	South Africa
secs	seconds
SL	Sri Lanka
SLA	slow left-armer
T	tied
T20	Twenty20
W in bowling figures	wickets
W in results stats	won
WI	West Indies
WK	wicketkeeper
yps	yards per second
Z or Zim	Zimbabwe

Web links

These are given without the http:// so most begin with www. They were working as the book went to press, but may have changed in the meantime.

Genders

Most of the pronouns in the text are masculine, which is just because most top-class cricket is played by men, and more boys than girls become fascinated by the game. I'm not suggesting for a moment that this should be the case.

The Aim Of The Game

The object of the game is to score more runs than the other side – but you also need to bowl them out. So the currency of cricket is runs and wickets

Runs

A run is what you get when you and your partner each run to the opposite end of the pitch before the fielders can get the ball to the stumps. You get more runs for a better shot (or, sometimes, a lucky one): if you steer the ball away from the fielders, you get two or three, and if the ball reaches the boundary, you get four. If it flies over the boundary without touching the ground, you get six. A good team will score plenty of fours, but also loads of ones and twos. **Running between the wickets** is a vital skill. It's just one of the areas where Australia are currently better than everyone else.

Wickets

There's a famous **tea towel**, often found in Christmas stockings, which explains how cricket works. "You have two sides, one out in the field and one in," it begins. "Each man that's in the side that's in goes out, and when he's out he comes in and the next man goes in until he's out. When they are all out, the side that's out comes in and the side that's been in goes out and tries to get those coming in, out …" Quite fun but not very helpful.

The tea towel is right to concentrate on the business of being out. It's the key to cricket. When a wicket falls, the game moves forward. There are a surprising number of ways of getting out – see page 8.

This is why bowling ultimately matters more than batting. If a team with great bowlers meets a team with great batsmen, the team with the bowlers will usually win. Australia's rise to the top in the 1990s came when one great bowler, Shane Warne, was joined by another, Glenn McGrath. Their batsmen

CRICKET
(as explained to a foreign visitor)

You have two sides, one out in the field and one in.

Each man that's in the side that's in goes out, and when he's out he comes in and the next man goes in until he's out.

When they are all out, the side that's out comes in and the side that's been in goes out and tries to get those coming in, out.

Sometimes you get men still in and not out.

When both sides have been in and out including the not-outs

That's the end of the game!

HOWZAT!

were very good too, but not awesome. A team with great batsmen and average bowlers, like today's India, will only be quite good.

One innings or two?

Each team has the same number of innings – ie, goes at batting. In a one-day match, they have one innings each. In a match of three or four days, known as first-class, they have two innings each. Same in a Test match, which takes five days. In an 11-a-side match, an innings consists of 10 wickets.

Why 10 wickets, not 11?

Because batsmen have to bat together. The team's innings ends when the last pair are parted, with one of them left not out. So batting always happens in partnerships. This is vital. When you bat yourself, you may feel very much alone – but there's always someone at the other end, and it helps to think about them too.

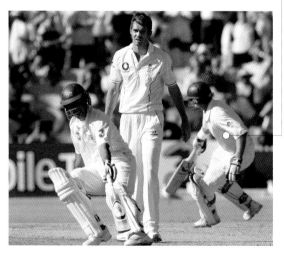

◄ Two more
Ricky Ponting left and Mike **Hussey** running in the second Ashes Test at Adelaide, 2006-07. The bowler is James Anderson

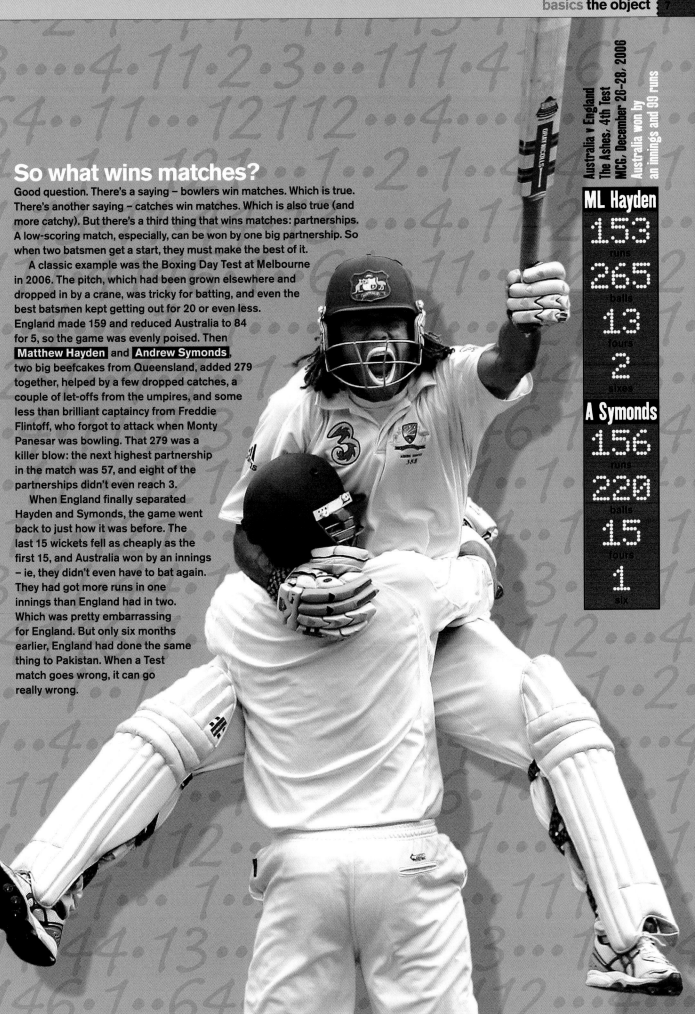

So what wins matches?

Good question. There's a saying – bowlers win matches. Which is true.
There's another saying – catches win matches. Which is also true (and
more catchy). But there's a third thing that wins matches: partnerships.
A low-scoring match, especially, can be won by one big partnership. So
when two batsmen get a start, they must make the best of it.

A classic example was the Boxing Day Test at Melbourne
in 2006. The pitch, which had been grown elsewhere and
dropped in by a crane, was tricky for batting, and even the
best batsmen kept getting out for 20 or even less.
England made 159 and reduced Australia to 84
for 5, so the game was evenly poised. Then
Matthew Hayden and Andrew Symonds,
two big beefcakes from Queensland, added 279
together, helped by a few dropped catches, a
couple of let-offs from the umpires, and some
less than brilliant captaincy from Freddie
Flintoff, who forgot to attack when Monty
Panesar was bowling. That 279 was a
killer blow: the next highest partnership
in the match was 57, and eight of the
partnerships didn't even reach 3.

When England finally separated
Hayden and Symonds, the game went
back to just how it was before. The
last 15 wickets fell as cheaply as the
first 15, and Australia won by an innings
– ie, they didn't even have to bat again.
They had got more runs in one
innings than England had in two.
Which was pretty embarrassing
for England. But only six months
earlier, England had done the same
thing to Pakistan. When a Test
match goes wrong, it can go
really wrong.

Australia v England
The Ashes, 4th Test
MCG, December 26–28, 2006
Australia won by
an innings and 99 runs

ML Hayden
153 runs
265 balls
13 fours
2 sixes

A Symonds
156 runs
220 balls
15 fours
1 six

THE 11 WAYS OF BEING OUT

Being out is the most miserable moment in cricket, for the batsman: it has even been described as a little death. And there are a surprising number of ways to perish. They fall into three groups…

THE BiG THREE

Bowled

For a batsman, it's the worst sound in the world – shrill, chilling, and horribly final. You play a shot, the ball somehow passes your bat, and clink! You're gone. While the fielding side gather for a noisy group celebration, you set off in silence on a long, lonely walk.

Being bowled is the simplest dismissal. You missed a straight one – or maybe edged it (known as "played on"), because if the ball touches your bat, pad or body on the way, it still says "bowled" in the scorebook. The only thing that can save you is if the umpire calls "no-ball!". Or if the stumps are brushed so faintly that the bails stay on. Don't bank on it.

▲ **Bowled** above **Justin Langer of Australia is out played on, which counts as bowled, against South Africa**

▶ **LBW** **Shoaib Akhtar of Pakistan appeals for the wicket of New Zealand's Craig MacMillan**

▶▶ **Run out** **Ricky Ponting falls short against England in 2006-07**

Caught

This is the most likely way for a good player to be out. More than half of all Test dismissals are catches. Ricky Ponting has been caught 93 times in Tests, and dismissed in other ways 65 times – LBW 31, bowled 19, run out nine, and stumped six.

Catches win matches, and sometimes start arguments. There are two common bones of contention: did the bat or glove touch the ball, and was the catch taken cleanly? The definition of a fair catch is quite fiddly. Here are the crucial bits:

LBW

Leg before wicket is the thing that stops you saving your skin with your pad. If the fielding side **appeal**, and the umpire feels sure the ball was going to hit the stumps, you're out, as long as:

- the ball didn't pitch outside leg stump (this is to stop boring defensive medium-pace bowling from round the wicket).
- you didn't play a shot if it hit you outside the line of off stump.
- you didn't hit it first with your bat or glove. This saves you from an LBW, even though it doesn't stop you being bowled.

LBW is slightly more common than bowled: in Tests since 2000, there have been 1763 players bowled and 1844 LBW. Some of them shouldn't have been given out – though others should have. This is why we have Hawk-Eye, the tracking technology.

The fielder CAN ...

- touch the ground with his hand, as long as the ball doesn't touch the ground too.
- lean over the boundary, as long as he doesn't touch it or the ground beyond it. (This is rough on the batsman, who was just thinking he had hit a six.)
- catch the ball via another fielder (or an umpire).
- hug the ball to his body: hands are not strictly necessary.
- catch the ball by accident in his clothes, or, if he is keeping wicket, in his pads.

The fielder CAN'T ...

- catch the ball in his cap or helmet, or via one of his team-mates'.
- lose control of the ball while still on the move. "The act of making the catch," says Law 30, rather solemnly, "shall start from the time when a fielder first handles the ball and shall end when a fielder obtains complete control both over the ball and over his own movement."

▲ Caught Ian Bell snaffles Adam Gilchrist
▼ Stumped AB de Villiers of South Africa stumps Robert Key of England

THE NEXT TWO

Stumped

You're not trying to run, but your stroke takes you out of your crease, you miss the ball, and the keeper **whips the bails off** before you can scramble back. Warning: you may look quite silly. On the other hand, dancing down the pitch to a slow bowler is a good way to play him, so you'll probably score lots of runs too.

The top stumping victim of all time is Wasim Akram, of Pakistan, with 21 in international cricket. The top eight are all captains. Are these people fit to tell everyone else what to do?

Run out

You think there's a run there, or your partner does, but it turns out there isn't, as the fielding side get the ball to the set of stumps you're running to, before you arrive. You depart kicking yourself. Run-outs are traditionally accompanied by cries of "Yes! No! Wait! Sorry!" Mostly, it's not the decision to run that does for the batsman: it's the indecision, the moment of hesitation.

The current king of run-outs is widely believed to be Inzamam-ul-Haq, the magnificently slow-moving ex-captain of Pakistan, who has been run out 46 times in all internationals. But even he is out-done by Marvan Atapattu of Sri Lanka, who is on 48. And keep an eye on Rahul Dravid, the captain of India, who's on 43, despite starting years later than the others. Again, the top seven worst runners are all captains past or present.

A run-out doesn't count as a wicket to the bowler. It's also the only dismissal that allows you to score runs at the same time – if you are out going for, say, a third run, you get to keep the first two.

THE SIX WACKY ONES

Hit wicket

Back in 1975, the first World Cup final was held at Lord's. I was there, aged 12, with my dad, and the atmosphere was electric. Dennis Lillee of Australia, a big, fierce fast bowler, opened the bowling to Roy Fredericks of the West Indies, a small, stylish left-hander. At first Fredericks played quite carefully. Then Lillee tried a bouncer. Fredericks swivelled and played a perfect hook shot, right off his nose. It sailed over the boundary. Most of us didn't even notice that he had trodden on his stumps. He was out, hit wicket bowled Lillee, for only 7. It was quite a way to go – defeated by the force of his own rotation. At least he finished on the winning side.

Hit wicket – dislodging your own bails, whether with the bat or your body – is the most common of the wacky dismissals. There have been 14 cases in Tests this decade. The all-time champion is **Denis Compton**, a much-loved England batsman of the 1940s, famous for playing the sweep shot, which may explain why he hit his wicket five times.

▲▶ **Hit wicket** Ian Botham above attempts to avoid a bouncer from Curtly Ambrose, but dislodges a bail while stumbling over his wicket playing for England v West Indies at The Oval, 1991. Denis Compton right falls on his wicket in the Trent Bridge Test against Australia in 1948

Handled the ball

You're out handled the ball if you "wilfully" (ie deliberately) touch the ball, while it is in play, with a hand that is not holding the bat, unless you have the "consent" (agreement) of the other side. In practice, this means you can throw the ball back to the bowler if you've finished playing your shot and you're not running. What you can't do is try to push the ball away as it trickles towards your stumps. Seven men have been out this way in Test history, and the last three were Test captains – Graham Gooch and Michael Vaughan of England (though Vaughan wasn't captain at the time), and Steve Waugh of Australia. They all disappeared shaking their heads.

Obstructing the field

This is defined as "wilfully obstructing or distracting" the fielding side "by word or action". In practice, this means hitting the ball after it has been touched by a fielder – eg deliberately blocking a throw to save yourself being run out. And batsmen usually get away with it, because it is hard to prove the deliberate bit.

Only once has a Test batsman been given out this way: Len Hutton, one of England's all-time greats, against South Africa in 1951. He top-edged the ball, and then tried to stop it hitting the stumps with the bat, which is allowed, but in the process prevented the wicketkeeper, Russell Endean, from taking the catch, which isn't. Another time, Hutton was out hit wicket. Perhaps he was trying to collect the set.

Hit the ball twice

You're allowed to hit the ball twice if it looks like hitting the stumps. You can even kick it away. Otherwise, you're out if you deliberately take a second bite of the cherry. It just hasn't ever happened in an international.

▲ **Kick it** Ricky Ponting stops the ball from hitting his stumps with his foot

Timed out

Technically, you can be out if you take three minutes to reach the middle at the start of your innings. In practice, this is often talked about but never happens at international level. It happened to AJ Harris of Nottinghamshire against the students of Durham in 2003 (he had a groin strain, and simply couldn't move fast enough), and it nearly happened to India's Sourav Ganguly in a Test at Cape Town in January 2007. Ganguly, who had sometimes been late for the toss when he was India's captain, took SIX minutes to appear, but got away with it as the delay was the result of a debate about whether Sachin Tendulkar was allowed to go in. He was padded up ready to go, but when the relevant wicket fell at 10.43am, the fourth umpire told Tendulkar he wasn't allowed in until 10.48, because he had spent some time off the field earlier. One of the on-field umpires, Daryl Harper, asked the South African captain, Graeme Smith, not to appeal for timed out, and he sportingly agreed. South Africa still had time to win the match by five wickets.

Retired out

If you are finding the game so easy it's boring, you can stop batting and let someone else have a go. In 2001, Bangladesh went to Sri Lanka as part of the short-lived Asian Test Championship. Bangladesh, playing only their fifth Test, were all out for 90, skittled by Murali. Two Sri Lankans, Marvan Atapattu and Mahela Jayawardene, made 201 and 150 respectively, and then lost the will to bat, so they went down as "retired out" – the only two such dismissals in Test history. It should really have said "retired bored". If they had retired hurt, claiming to have cramp, they would have gone down as not out and improved their average, so they get marks for honesty. And they still won by an innings.

Conclusion

Keep the ball down, cover your stumps, run without hesitation, and the only serious risk you're taking is being LBW, so if you take a big step forward, which makes most umpires reluctant to give you out, you will never be out at all. In theory.

4

THE POSSIBLE RESULTS

When a match gets exciting, you hear the commentators say "all four results are possible here". What they mean is: one team can win, so can the other, it could be a draw, and it could be a tie.

Winning batting first

You make lots of runs, then bowl the other side out for fewer. This is how most captains prefer to do it. Bowlers often do better with a big score behind them – it's like a strong wind. And batting last, especially in a two-innings game, is mysteriously difficult. The pitch gets a bit uneven or cracked, and the weight of history bears down on the batsmen, who know that few big scores have been made batting fourth. Then again, batting second is often easier than batting first, because the pitch has flattened out. The pitch, you see, is crucial. More on that on page 16. The win is expressed as being "by X runs".

Winning batting second

Often easier at lower levels. You go in to bat knowing exactly how many you have to get. You may not even have to bat better than your opponents. In a one-day game, they might have made 220 for five from their 50 overs. As long as you get to 221 in your 50 overs, it doesn't matter if you have lost six, seven or even nine wickets. Bit unfair, isn't it? The win is expressed as "by X wickets" – X being the number you had left.

Whether batting first or second, a team can win by an innings. This means making more runs in one innings than your opponents do in two (completed) ones. If you bat first, you can ask your opponents to bat twice in a row – or "follow on" – if you have a big first-innings lead. In a Test, the lead has to be 200 runs; in a county or similar match, 150. The win is expressed as being "by an innings and X runs".

The draw

This is the one non-cricket lovers, especially Americans, find hard to understand. A game can go on for five whole days and not produce a winner? Bizarre, but true. If the side batting last doesn't reach its target, but isn't bowled out either, then the match is drawn. This can be very dull, or it can be exciting – if all four results were possible till the end. Draws used to happen a lot in Test cricket. Nowadays, thankfully, they are rarer, as batsmen are much more enterprising.

The tie

This is when the team batting last is all out with the total scores level. It is very rare in two-innings matches: out of the first 1830 Tests, only two were tied. (See page 98.) Ties are more common in shorter games: in one-day internationals, there were 22 in the first 2567 matches, including the classic cliffhanger between Australia and South Africa in the 1999 World Cup semi-final and the meeting between Ireland and Zimbabwe in the 2007 World Cup.

If the scores finish level in a two-innings match but the team batting last is not all out, that's technically not a tie. It is known, rather longwindedly, as a draw with the scores level. The only time it has ever happened in Test cricket was in England's first meeting with Zimbabwe, at Bulawayo in 1996-97, when the England captain was Mike Atherton. Chasing 205, England finished on 204 for 6 with their star performer, Nick Knight, run out for 96 off the last ball. The England coach, David Lloyd, was furious because the Zimbabweans had been allowed to get away with bowling deliberately wide. He came out with a famous quote: "We flippin' murdered 'em." This had a grain of truth, but wasn't very gracious. Lloyd is now a Sky TV commentator, making better use of his gift for a colourful phrase. So is Atherton, and so is Knight.

Winning batting first

widest margin in a Test

England (903 for 7 declared) beat Australia (201 and 123) by an innings and 579 runs at The Oval, 1938.

Len Hutton left made 364, a new world record. Australia were missing two batsmen in each innings including their superstar, Don Bradman, who had broken his ankle in a freak accident – his foot got stuck in a foothold while he was bowling. But England's mammoth victory was not enough to win the Ashes: the series was drawn 1-1, so the Ashes remained with the holders, Australia.

narrowest margin in a Test

West Indies (252 and 146) beat Australia (213 and 184) by one run at Adelaide, 1992-93.

The series hinged on that one run. If Australia had won the match, they would have taken an unbeatable 2-0 lead with one Test to go. As it was, West Indies pulled it back to 1-1 and went on to win the fifth Test and with it the series. It was almost the end of an era. Australia haven't lost a Test series at home since; West Indies now seldom win one away.

▼ **Narrow squeak** Courtney Walsh celebrates getting the final wicket of Craig McDermott to win the Test

HOW TO READ A SCORECARD

They're in the papers, on the web, on the telly, and in your hand if you go to a game. But they don't always explain themselves very well. Here's what they would say if they did, using a scorecard from a cliffhanger of a Test match

Batting side

England are first because they batted first – and if you look at **Toss**, you'll see that was Australia's choice. Bad decision, Ricky

Key men

The captain and wicketkeeper are identified by their own little symbols – usually an asterisk for the captain and a cross or dagger for the keeper

Not out

At least one batsman is always left not out. For England, it was their No 11, Simon Jones, in both innings, which is how it should be. For Australia, a very good player and a decent one were left, as they say, high and dry. And Jones helped Flintoff add an absolutely crucial 51 in the second innings

Bowling figures

Usually four of them per bowler. In this order: overs, maidens (overs without a run conceded by the bowler), runs conceded, wickets taken. So Brett Lee managed only one maiden in the first innings, and he went for more than six runs per over – very expensive by Test standards

Batsmen

Traditionally shown with initials rather than first names. Often have numbers too, so an old-fashioned scoreboard can call them "1" rather than "Trescothick"

Balls faced

Ground scorecards don't give the number of balls a batsman faced, but the media increasingly do. They are highly revealing. Here, in the first innings, they tell you that Trescothick rattled along, Pietersen and Flintoff matched him, Geraint Jones struggled, Hoggard stonewalled as usual and Harmison slogged. In Australia's first innings, you can see that Hayden got a golden duck, and Martyn set off at high speed before being run out

Number of bowlers

Keep an eye on the number of bowlers used. Australia picked four as usual, and Ponting didn't bother with any part-timers like Clarke, Katich or himself, all of whom have taken Test wickets. In the first innings he used his bowlers fairly evenly, but in the second he lost faith in Gillespie and Kasprowicz. Warne bowled for almost the whole innings, as you expect with a great spinner on a wearing pitch, and Ponting favoured Lee as his partner even though he was expensive. England picked five bowlers and used them all, but in a short innings, some get under-used, which happened here. Vaughan didn't think Matthew Hoggard was worth risking once the shine had gone off the new ball. He used Giles as his stock bowler at one end and rotated his three fast men at the other, with a bias to the most reliable of them – Flintoff

2nd Ashes Test
England v Australia
Edgbaston, August 4-7, 2005

England won by 2 runs. Five-Test series level 1-1

ENGLAND			R	B	4/6			R	B	4/6
ME Trescothick	c Gilchrist	b Kasprowicz	90	102	15/2	c Gilchrist	b Lee	21	38	4/0
AJ Strauss		b Warne	48	76	10/0		b Warne	6	12	1/0
MP Vaughan*	c Lee	b Gillespie	24	41	3/0		b Lee	1	2	0/0
IR Bell	c Gilchrist	b Kasprowicz	6	3	1/0	c Gilchrist	b Warne	21	43	2/0
KP Pietersen	c Katich	b Lee	71	76	10/1	c Gilchrist	b Warne	20	35	0/2
A Flintoff	c Gilchrist	b Gillespie	68	62	6/5		b Warne	73	86	6/4
GO Jones†	c Gilchrist	b Kasprowicz	1	15	0/0	c Ponting	b Lee	9	19	1/0
AF Giles	lbw	b Warne	23	30	4/0	c Hayden	b Warne	8	36	0/0
MJ Hoggard	lbw	b Warne	16	49	2/0	c Hayden	b Lee	1	27	0/0
SJ Harmison		b Warne	17	11	2/1	c Ponting	b Warne	0	1	0/0
SP Jones	not out		19	24	1/1	not out		12	23	3/0
Extras	lb 9, w 1, nb 14		24			lb 1, nb 9		10		
Total	79.2 overs, 356 mins		407			52.1 overs, 249 mins		182		

Fall of wickets (1st): 1-112, 2-164, 3-170, 4-187, 5-290, 6-293, 7-342, 8-348, 9-375

Fall of wickets (2nd): 1-25, 2-27, 3-29, 4-31, 5-72, 6-75, 7-101, 8-131, 9-131

Bowling (1st): Lee 17-1-111-1, Gillespie 22-3-91-2, Kasprowicz 15-3-80-3, Warne 25.2-4-116-4

Bowling (2nd): Lee 18-1-82-4, Gillespie 8-0-24-0, Kasprowicz 3-0-29-0, Warne 23.1-7-46-6

How out

That little b does a lot of work: it tells you who the bowler was. Bowlers get a credit for any of the common dismissals except a run-out – Vaughan's name on that one shows he was the fielder, and the absence of a second name suggests he pulled off a direct hit (a rare thing). Even hit wicket counts to the bowler's tally.

A b without a c means the batsman was bowled, either cleanly or played-on. A c means the batsman was caught, st stumped; lbw, as you know, means leg before wicket

Extras

This could be really confusing. In the Extras line, b changes its meaning, from bowled to byes – runs taken when the ball hit neither bat nor pad (and the wicketkeeper couldn't gather it). There are four types of run that don't come off the bat and they are given in this order

b – byes
lb – leg-byes (ball went off the pad or, less often, the body)
nb – no-balls (bowler overstepped; run awarded automatically)
w – wides (ball out of batsman's reach)

In a match as close as this, extras could make all the difference. But they didn't. Australia collected 71, England only 34

Overs per innings

The typical Test innings lasts 100 overs, and the fielding side get a new ball after 80. In this match, no innings made it to 80 overs, a sure sign that it was frenetic – and entertaining. And England's fast scoring, which was actually criticised on the first day by Geoff Boycott and others, was vital – Australia lasted almost as long in their first innings, but scored 99 fewer runs

Fall of wickets

The number of runs the batting side had when each wicket fell. You can use this to trace the partnerships – which win matches, remember. Trescothick and Strauss put on 112 for the first wicket – excellent. Vaughan helped Trescothick add another 52 – handy. But then three wickets fell in quick succession, so Australia were back on level terms. Pietersen and Flintoff put on 103 for the fifth wicket (ie after four wickets had gone down), so England were back in charge. And although one wicket then led to another, the tail wagged merrily to add 114 from the entrance of Ashley Giles at 293 for 6. Contrast that with England's top four wickets in the second innings, which fell in the space of six runs to Warne and Lee – horrible

Umpires

The two on-field umpires are given first. They have to be from countries other than those playing, so there's Billy Bowden from New Zealand and Rudi Koertzen from South Africa. After the semi-colon you get the third or TV umpire, Jeremy Lloyds. He can be local (and is – he's English). His job is to sit in the stand with a TV monitor and rule on tight run-outs and stumpings whenever his two colleagues make the telly sign. The match referee is the umpires' boss, sort of – though there have been cases where he failed to do much

Fours and sixes

Another media innovation, and a good one. Edgbaston is a small ground and the 4/6 column shows how England made full use of it in the first innings, smashing 54 fours and 10 sixes. Australia managed 39 fours and no sixes. England even hit six sixes in their second innings, although wickets fell; only Shane Warne had the confidence to follow suit. Australia, for once, were out-slogged

The nightwatchman

The numbers in brackets show that Australia varied their batting order, sending Gillespie in ahead of Warne and Lee, as a so-called nightwatchman – blocking out the last few overs to preserve better batsmen for the next morning. On this occasion, it didn't work – Gillespie was trapped lbw by Flintoff second ball. But he made up for it later: against Bangladesh in 2006, Gillespie batted for a day and a half to make the highest score ever by a Test nightwatchman – 201 not out

AUSTRALIA – First innings

Batsman	How out	R	B	4/6
JL Langer	lbw b S Jones	82	154	7/0
ML Hayden	b Hoggard	0	0	0/0
RT Ponting*	c Strauss b Giles	61	76	12/0
DR Martyn	run out Vaughan	20	18	4/0
MJ Clarke	c G Jones b Giles	40	68	7/0
SM Katich	c G Jones b Flintoff	4	18	1/0
AC Gilchrist†	not out	49	69	4/0
SK Warne	c Flintoff b Giles	8	14	2/0
B Lee	lbw b S Jones	6	10	1/0
JN Gillespie	lbw b Flintoff	7	37	1/0
MS Kasprowicz	b Flintoff	0	1	0/0
Extras	b 13, lb 7, w 1, nb 10	31		
Total	76 overs, 346 mins	308		

AUSTRALIA – Second innings

Batsman	How out	R	B	4/6
JL Langer	b Flintoff	28	47	4/0
ML Hayden	c Trescothick b S Jones	31	64	4/0
RT Ponting*	c G Jones b Flintoff	0	5	0/0
DR Martyn	c Bell b Hoggard	28	36	5/0
MJ Clarke	c Trescothick b Harmison	30	57	4/0
SM Katich	c Flintoff b Giles	16	21	3/0
AC Gilchrist†	c Flintoff b Giles	1	4	0/0
SK Warne	(9) hit wicket b Flintoff	42	59	4/2
B Lee	(10) not out	43	75	5/0
JN Gillespie	(8) lbw b Flintoff	0	2	0/0
MS Kasprowicz	c G Jones b Harmison	20	31	3/0
Extras	b 13, lb 8, w 1, nb 18	40		
Total	64.3 overs, 307 mins	279		

Fall of wickets

(1st) 1-0, 2-88, 3-118, 4-194, 5-208, 6-262, 7-273, 8-282, 9-308

(2nd) 1-47, 2-48, 3-82, 4-107, 5-134, 6-136, 7-137, 8-175, 9-220

Bowling

Harmison 11-1-48-0, Hoggard 8-0-41-1, S Jones 16-2-69-2, Flintoff 15-1-52-3, Giles 26-2-78-3

Harmison 17.3-3-62-2, Hoggard 5-0-26-1, Giles 15-3-68-2, Flintoff 22-3-79-4, S Jones 5-1-23-1

Toss Australia
Umpires BF Bowden (NZ), RE Koertzen (SA); JW Lloyds
Match Referee RS Madugalle (SL)
Man of the Match A Flintoff

PITCH, TOSS AND WEATHER

◄ Heads I lose
Andrew Flintoff
won the toss
at Adelaide in
2006-07, chose
to bat first,
and England
declared on
551-6. And went
on to lose the
match ...

It's not all about runs and wickets. The earth, the air and the toss of a coin make a big difference too

Batsmen and bowlers bicker about which of them really rules the game. In fact, neither lot does. It's the pitch.

The pitch dictates what a good score is. You can see this by looking at the scores through a Test series. In one Test, both teams may make 500, and the game peters out into a draw. In the next, both may struggle to reach 300, and the game is over in three or four days. The difference is in the conditions. It's in the lap of the gods – and the groundsman.

A good pitch ... but who for?

A good pitch for batting is flat, hard, dry and light-brown. Flat means the bounce will be even. Hard means the ball will come onto the bat and ping off it. Dry and brown mean the ball won't sink into the surface and move off the seam.

A good pitch for bowling has a touch of greenness or damp or both, which gives sideways movement. Or, it's dry, but has cracks, which will open up as the game goes on, producing some uneven bounce. If it's very dry, there will be turn for the spinners and sometimes reverse swing for the fast bowlers.

A good pitch for cricket will help the bowlers and the batsmen at different times. It will be bouncy throughout. It will have a touch of moisture early on to help the seamers; then it will dry out and help the batsmen for a couple of days; then it will start cracking or roughing up, giving help to the spinner and the reverse swinger.

It's a toss-up

Some matches are decided in a single moment, by a curious little event which happens before 20 of the 22 players even take the field: the toss. The home captain flips a coin, the away captain calls heads or tails, and the winner has the choice of batting first or second.

The toss itself is pure luck, a 50-50 chance, but the choice is judgment. Again, this depends on the pitch. Normally, the winning captain bats first. There's a quote about this from Colin Cowdrey, who captained England in the 1960s and ended up being made a Lord. "Nine times out of ten," he said, "you should automatically bat first. The other time, you should think about fielding, then bat." He was as good as his word: as England captain, he won the toss in 17 Tests and batted every time.

But that was the 1960s, when most captains were cautious.

These days they are bolder. England won the toss and fielded 70 times in their first 130 years in Test cricket (1877-2007), and 42 of those 70 came in the last 30 years. Lately bowling first has led to more wins than losses, but when it doesn't, it can be a big blow. ▪▪▪▪▪▪▪▪▪▪▪▪▪▪▪▪▪▪▪▪

Sometimes the captain's choice is really tricky. "A good toss to lose," say the commentators – because it's a 50-50 decision and the team winning the toss is expected to do well. But that expectation isn't entirely logical. Several Test teams actually do better when losing the toss. In the 10 years to April 2007, Australia, Pakistan, New Zealand and West Indies all won more of their matches when losing the toss than when winning it. South Africa, England and Sri Lanka did better when winning the toss, and with India it made no difference. So perhaps it's less crucial than we think.

When bowling first goes wrong, it can go very wrong. Just look at two recent Ashes series. The 2002-03 Ashes began with Nasser Hussain of England putting Australia in to bat on a belting pitch at Brisbane. Australia strolled to 364 for two on the first day and England never recovered, losing 4-1. The Ashes series of 2005 hinged on the toss for the second Test, when Ricky Ponting, already 1-0 up, opted to bowl first. England responded by slamming 400 in a day, won the match by a heart-stopping two runs, and went on to a famous series victory.

Some like it hot ... some don't

The weather can play a big part. Sometimes one side bats in blazing sunshine, while the other bats under thick cloud. Here's why it matters:

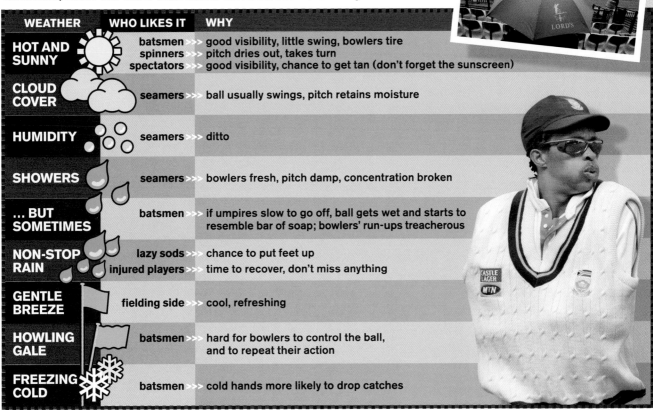

WEATHER	WHO LIKES IT	WHY
HOT AND SUNNY	batsmen >>>	good visibility, little swing, bowlers tire
	spinners >>>	pitch dries out, takes turn
	spectators >>>	good visibility, chance to get tan (don't forget the sunscreen)
CLOUD COVER	seamers >>>	ball usually swings, pitch retains moisture
HUMIDITY	seamers >>>	ditto
SHOWERS	seamers >>>	bowlers fresh, pitch damp, concentration broken
... BUT SOMETIMES	batsmen >>>	if umpires slow to go off, ball gets wet and starts to resemble bar of soap; bowlers' run-ups treacherous
NON-STOP RAIN	lazy sods >>>	chance to put feet up
	injured players >>>	time to recover, don't miss anything
GENTLE BREEZE	fielding side >>>	cool, refreshing
HOWLING GALE	batsmen >>>	hard for bowlers to control the ball, and to repeat their action
FREEZING COLD	batsmen >>>	cold hands more likely to drop catches

THE FUNDAMENTAL THINGS APPLY

A few very basic basics. You, of course, know them already, but your younger brother or sister may not …

How many players?

Each team has 11, but only two batsmen are out in the middle at once. The rest of the batting side are in the pavilion, either watching nervously, reading the paper, playing cards, having a shower, sending text messages, using their laptops, or exchanging amusing remarks. The fielding side are all out there. They don't get to do any of these things except the remarks.

Overs and ends

A bowler can only bowl six balls in a row (plus any no-balls or wides). This is called an over. All six balls are bowled from the same end, then someone else has a go from the other end. A bowler can bowl all day from one end, in theory. In practice, bowlers bowl spells, then have a rest. A fast bowler's spell will last anything from two to 10 overs, typically six or seven. A spinner's spell will usually be longer, more like 10 to 12 overs. But in one-day cricket, all bowlers are limited to a fifth of the total overs available for the innings – ie 10 in a 50-over game – and they often bowl them in several short spells.

The best place to bowl

At the top of off stump. That way, the batsman has to play a shot (in case the ball hits the stumps); he can't swing his body into it, as he can with a ball on his legs; he can't free his arms and swing the bat, as he can if the ball is wide of off stump; and there is a chance of an edge to the wicketkeeper or slips if the ball moves away from the bat.

Are subs allowed?

Yes, up to a point. A substitute can replace an injured player, but only as a fielder: he can't bat or bowl. He appears on the scorecard as "sub", with his name in brackets afterwards if he's lucky.

Batsmen can't just be good at batting

As well as batting, a batsman should also be good at running between the wickets. This is a skill in itself, in fact three skills: you have to be a good judge, a clear caller, and a fast runner. A good runner calls "Yes!" or "No!" early and decisively. A bad runner calls "Yes – no – wait – sorry". Some people will never be a fast runner, but everyone should be able to become a good judge and a clear caller.

What a team consists of

An international team usually consists of five or six specialist batsmen, one wicketkeeper, and four or five bowlers. If there is a genuine allrounder, the team gets six batsmen and five bowlers at the same time. This is often referred to as a balanced side. But some of the greatest teams have had only four bowlers – Australia in recent years and West Indies in the 1980s. A team also needs two or three good slip catchers, and one or two outstanding ground-fielders. These are usually batsmen, which allows the bowlers to head off into the long grass for a rest.

Team or individual?

Cricket is a team game made up of a series of little individual duels. Each ball is a battle between batsman and bowler, with everyone else a bystander – unless or until the ball goes to them.

The balance between team and individual is continually fascinating. Sometimes one great player makes all the difference; other times he is powerless in the face of a more united and determined team. For an example of the first, check out Brian Lara of West Indies against Australia in 1998-99: he won two Tests almost single-handed, and the series finished 2-2. For an example of the second, look at most of the series he played in after that. During his long and highly distinguished career, West Indies went from great, to good, to bad, to worse.

The two sides of a cricket field

The leg side is the whole half of the ground that is behind the batsman as he stands at the crease. This is one of cricket's more sensible names: it's so called because that is where the batsman's legs are. The other side is the off side. Which side is which depends on whether the batsman is right-handed. If the batsman is left-handed, what was the leg side becomes the off. If a right-hander and a left-hander are batting together, the bowler has to adjust his line each time they take a single. This can mean lots of free runs, and explains why selectors like to pick a left-and-right-hand opening combination. The last one to do well in Tests for England was Michael Vaughan and Marcus Trescothick in 2003.

OFF LEG

OVER ROUND

Over the wicket, or round?

If the bowler is using his left arm rather than his right, that doesn't change off and leg, which are dictated solely by the batsman. But it does change the meaning of over and round rhe wicket. A bowler is bowling over the wicket if he is a right-armer coming past the umpire's left shoulder, or a left-armer coming past the umpire's right shoulder. A simple way to remember it is: if he goes round the umpire, he is bowling round the wicket. Over the wicket is the norm for most bowlers except slow left-armers, who naturally come round, angle the ball in and turn it away (see page 58). When a new bowler comes on, he has to tell the umpire what sort of stuff he bowls – "right arm over," etc. The umpire then relays this in a louder voice to the batsman.

ARMED ... AND EXTREMELY SAFE

No major team game requires more equipment than cricket. Even a player as good as this one needs plenty of protection

BAT

For a long time, bats looked like hockey sticks.

Then overarm bowling came along, and they turned into planks with handles. Now they are more like clubs with springs. **Kevin Pietersen** has a lifetime deal with Woodworm, a company that was only founded in 2001 and doesn't even make its own bats, preferring, like Nike, to out-source the manufacturing. The bats are built for big hitting – Andrew Flintoff uses them too – and cunningly designed to fire your imagination. Like other bat companies, Woodworm stick big, bold, bright graphics on the back. Unlike other companies, they don't use the language of war or the jungle for their bat names. They prefer the language of magic or fire: first there was the Wand, then the Flame and the Torch. Their latest bat, produced for the 2007 World Cup, is the slightly less exciting Globe, which has to be one of the odder names ever given to an oblong piece of wood. Here KP is wielding the Torch. Remember: you won't spend long looking at your bat – that's the fielders' job. What matters is how it feels and how it plays.

made of willow, with Irish linen to bind the handle, and rubber to cover it; the handle itself may be made of polycarbon

limits length 38 inches (965mm), width 4¼ inches (108mm); strangely, there is no limit on weight, but 2lbs 7oz or less is considered light for a grown man, 2lbs 8oz to 2lbs 10oz is medium, and 2lbs 11oz or more is heavy

price £40-£240

BATTING GLOVES

Once they had spikes. For a brief time in the mid-1970s they were flat, like little thigh pads for the hands. Now gloves nearly always have sausages. Even so, fingers get broken. Nasser Hussain, England captain from 1999 to 2003, got so many breaks he was known as Poppadom Fingers. Some top players have them customised: Hussain's predecessor Alec Stewart, after getting a few fractures in mid-Test career, wore a little plastic scabbard over the forefinger of his bottom hand, which seemed to work – he went on to become England's most capped player, appearing in 133 Tests. He was also famous for having the neatest corner of the dressing-room.

made of palm cotton, nylon or leather; panels may be suede or leather **limits** practicality – need a flexible grip on the bat **price** £8-£60

HELMET

Generations of cricketers batted in caps or even went bare-headed, but nasty accidents did happen occasionally and since the late 1970s, when helmets caught on, almost everyone (except Viv Richards) has worn one. England players used to be allowed white ones but now they have to wear navy blue ones, which almost match their caps. KP's helmet let him down in the Old Trafford Test against West Indies in 2007: struck by a bouncer from Dwayne Bravo, it did its job of protecting his head, but came off in the process and fell on to the stumps. Instead of collecting another hundred, he was out hit wicket for 68.

made of shell **ABS (acrylonitrile-butadiene-styrene) plastic; lining foam; visor titanium or steel; strap: nylon and lycra**

limits nobody wants much weight on their head **price** £37-£100

THIGH PAD

If you've ever been hit there, you'll want one. Nearly everyone wears one on their front thigh; KP also has one on the back, which makes sense because he has ended up, as he often does, bringing his right leg forward into the shot as well as his left. The most famous thigh pad in the game belonged to Mark Waugh, the stylish Australian batsman of the 1990s, who drew a stick figure on it every time he hit a first-class hundred. This meant he had to keep using the same thigh pad. It outlived more than 30 bats, before finally succumbing to old age – or sweat. It had helped him make 59 hundreds.

made of high-density foam

limits space in trousers

price £9–£28

PADS

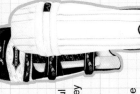

The manufacturers call them leg-guards. Nobody else does, but all cricketers are grateful for the broken legs they prevent. Remember to tuck in the straps – then they are less likely to nick the ball and make the umpire think you're out.

made of mainly foam and cane with some leather **limits** practicality – need to be able to run **price** £16–£80

BOX

You can't see it, but it's definitely there, unless KP is crazier than we thought. No male cricketer over the age of 13 leaves home without one. The Woodworm box is orange – easy to find when wickets are tumbling and you have to get kitted up in a hurry. Boxes are a source of reassurance and humour. Once, a Wisden XI were playing at Wormsley, a beautiful ground – way too good for the likes of me – owned by our then boss, Paul Getty. One player had taken along his five-year-old son and showed him his kit as he got changed. As the man walked out to open the innings, the boy yelled after him, "Dad! Have you got your willy protector?" Mostly, boxes get given more elaborate names by manufacturers who seem reluctant to face the simple truth of what they do. "Abdo guard" is a favourite, as if it was your tummy muscles that were in danger. When leading batsmen get hit in the box, the commentators tend to resort to euphemism too. "And he's hit amidships!" is a favourite, along with "And he's hit in the most painful part of the anatomy." One Test physio had no such qualms. A West Indian tail-ender, who might prefer not to be named, was hit in the box, and ended up in hospital. The physio helpfully explained to the press that the box hadn't quite been in the right place when it was struck – one testicle was inside, and one out. Seldom has a cricket story inspired so many sympathetic winces.

made of plastic **limits** only the size of your trousers, but no point wearing one that's too big **price** £2–£4

ARM GUARD & CHEST GUARD

KP seems not to be wearing these. Many batsmen prefer not to, but you may notice your favourite fast bowler looking a little bulkier as he potters out to bat against a fellow paceman.

made of high-density foam

limits length of forearm, volume of shirt

price £7–£20

BALL

Red, shiny, hard and hand-stitched, a top-quality cricket ball is a beautiful thing – when new. Eighty overs later, it will be pinkish, dull, soft and hideous. It takes cows, sheep, trees and dozens of human beings to make a cricket ball. The human beings are alive; the other ingredients are dead. Most of the balls for Test matches are made by Dukes or Kookaburra. Dukes are used in England, have a proud seam and swing a lot. Kookaburra are used more elsewhere, especially in Australia, have a flatter seam and tend to swing only for the first hour.

made of people say leather, but actually the ball is made of at least four materials – the core is cork or a cork-rubber mixture, then there's a layer of wool string, then the leather skin, some more string (sometimes made of flax) to form the seam, and finally a layer of lacquer

limits weight 5½ oz to 5¾ oz (155.9g to 163g), circumference 8¹³/₁₆ inches to 9 inches (224mm to 229mm); seam 78 to 82 stitches

price £5–£65

FIND OUT ABOUT

the right bat size www.thecricketstore.net/html/cricket_bat_advice.html

bat-making salixcricketbats.com/manufacturing.html

ball-making content-usa.cricinfo.com/wac/content/story/210922.html

NOTE Prices taken from online stores, June 2007. They may vary, as may the materials used

THE LAWS AND THE MEN WHO ENFORCE THEM

Cricket is like school – there are a lot of rules. They are even called the Laws, as if they were made in Parliament. There are so many that they take up 46 pages in the *Wisden Almanack*. We don't have 46 pages to spare, so here are some of the main points

THE UMPiRES

There are two of them, one at each end. The one whose end the bowling is from stands a few yards behind the stumps, enjoying the best view in the house. The other stands sideways on, 20 yards back, usually at square leg, sometimes at square cover if there is a fielder in the way. They are on the field for longer than anyone else.

The bowler's-end umpire is the busy one. He has to watch out for no-balls, then instantly switch his focus to the far end, so he can make crucial decisions about lbws, edges to the keeper, and bat-pad catches to the close fielders, as well as less vital ones about wides, byes and leg-byes. He also counts the number of balls in the over, usually by moving six pebbles across from one pocket to the other, and makes the majority of the signals. These are addressed to the scorers, of whom there are also two (cricket is like Noah's Ark: the animals come in two by two). The scorers raise a hand to show that they have seen the signal.

6 KEY PiECES OF ETiQUETTE

Etiquette is a funny word which makes things sound rather … twiddly. But it just means accepted behaviour, which helps to make things happen. Here are some dos and don'ts.

All Do accept the umpire's decision – it may be wrong but he's not about to change it.

Fielding side Don't celebrate till the umpire's finger goes up.

Bowler Don't follow through close to the stumps.

All Don't run on the pitch.

Fielders Don't appeal for a catch if you're not sure about it.

Fielders Do applaud the batsmen when they reach 50 or 100, or get out for plenty.

6 TOP TEST UMPiRES

Steve Bucknor
WI, 61, 117 Tests
Slow decision, hand goes out as well as up

Rudi Koertzen
SA, 58, 82 Tests
Slow hand, getting slower

Daryl Harper
A, 55, 65 Tests
Mixes good decisions with baffling ones

Simon Taufel
A, 36, 41 Tests
Sideburns, three times ICC Umpire of the Year

Billy Bowden
NZ, 44, 40 Tests
Crooked fore-finger, general eccentricity

Aleem Dar
P, 39, 38 Tests
Solid judgment and calm way with players

3 KEY LAWS

Bowl with a straight arm. If you straighten your elbow as you deliver the ball, you are not bowling – you're chucking, which gives you an unfair advantage. Quite a lot of bowlers do this occasionally as they strain for extra pace or bounce. Some observers, mostly in Australasia, think Muttiah Muralitharan does this all the time. Others agree with the game's bosses that his action is unusual but within the rules. The rules have been relaxed recently – bowlers are now allowed 15 degrees of flexion, as video evidence suggested that many of them were breaking the old rule.

Don't tamper with the ball. You can dry it, polish it, and apply saliva or sweat to it. But you can't do anything else.

Don't distract or obstruct the batsman. Once the bowler runs in, the fielders can walk in, but they can't change position or do anything to put the batsman off.

7 DODGY PRACTiCES CRiCKETERS GO iN FOR

Claiming catches when they're not sure the ball has carried.

Time-wasting when playing for a draw.

Taking the light when they're in no danger.

Moving or running after being struck on the pad to distract the umpire and get away with an LBW.

Rubbing their arm to trick the umpire when the ball has actually flicked the glove.

Selective walking when they have edged the ball to the keeper. Walking means giving yourself out without waiting for the umpire's decision. Some think it's honourable; others think it's crazy. But the important thing isn't whether you walk – it's whether you are consistent about it. By walking most of the time, you may con the umpire into giving you not out.

Sledging – talking to or about the batsman in a way that you hope will help get him out. It's clearly against the spirit of the game, so it shouldn't be tolerated. Any winning team, whether they're Australia or the 2nd XI at St Cake's, would be more impressive if they didn't sledge. Often it is just bullying, which, as you know from school, is a sad and cowardly thing to do. But umpires meekly put up with it – and sometimes, sledging almost redeems itself by being quite witty. See page 117 for a few examples.

12 UMPIRING SIGNALS

Out!	Refer to TV umpire	No ball (also spoken)	Wide
Bye	Leg-bye	Four	Six
One run short	Dead ball	New ball	Penalty runs*

***PENALTY RUNS**	Right arm resting on left shoulder – five runs to fielding side
	Right arm tapping left shoulder – five runs to batting side
OTHER	Each hand touching opposite shoulder – I've changed my mind (quite rare)

4 KEY AREAS FOR THE UMPIRES

1 The weather
Should rain stop play? It's up to the umps. At the first drop of drizzle, they play on. If the rain gets harder, they confer, and play on again, hoping the shower will pass. Then they confer again, or exchange a knowing glance, and remove the bails. Everyone trots back to the pavilion.

2 The light
The sky darkens, the light meters come out, and often the light is offered to the batsmen – ie, they are given the chance to come off. Test umpires tend to offer the light too readily, and batsmen tend to take

it too readily. When play does continue in the gloom, the batsmen's eyes adjust amazingly well. It's actually the fielders who struggle, because they don't know when to expect the ball.

3 Intimidatory bowling
It means designed to frighten. A lot of pace bowling does this a bit. The umps step in when it becomes a relentless bombardment.

4 Ball-tampering
The ball suddenly starts swinging again when it's old. This could be perfectly legal – the fielding side have polished one side, the other

has been roughed up by the turf, and the bowlers have the skill to whip it in at the batsmen's toes. Or they may have worked on it illegally, by lifting the seam. The umps have to decide. They can award five penalty runs against the fielding side – but the only umpire ever to do this, Darrell Hair, who penalised Pakistan in a Test in England in 2006, paid a heavy price. The Pakistanis refused to play on, so Hair ruled that they had forfeited the match. He was technically right, but inflexible and undiplomatic. He has not umpired a big international match since.

THE SPIRIT OF CRICKET
For more than 200 years, the spirit of the game was something talked about but not written down. Then, in 2000, the guardians of the laws – MCC – put it on paper and attached it to the laws as a preamble. The full text can be found at **www.lords.org/laws-and-spirit/laws-of-cricket/preamble-to-the-laws,475,AR.html** but it 's a bit long-winded, so here are the main points:

Cricket is a game with a special appeal. It should be played not only within its Laws but also within the spirit of the game – fair play, basically. If you abuse this spirit, you damage the game. The umpires are the sole judges of fair and unfair play, but it's up to the captains to make sure their players keep to the spirit. If a player behaves badly, the umpire concerned should report him to the other umpire and to his captain, and tell the captain to do something about it.

The spirit of the game means respecting:
● your opponents
● your captain
● the authority of the umpire
● the game's traditional values.

It is against the spirit:
● to dispute the umpire's decision by word, action or gesture
● to swear at an opponent or umpire
● to go in for any cheating or sharp practice, such as:
  ● to appeal knowing that the batsman is not out
  ● to advance aggressively towards the umpire when appealing
  ● to try and distract an opponent, either verbally or with persistent clapping or unnecessary noise disguised as motivation of your own side.

There is no place for any act of violence on a cricket field.
Captains and umpires set the tone for the match, but every player is expected to contribute.

FIND OUT MORE
The full Laws of Cricket can be found:
● in *Wisden Cricketers' Almanack* 2007, pp1449-1495
● in the Lord's shop, as a **booklet** to buy (£2.50)
● online, at **www.lords.org/laws-and-spirit/laws-of-cricket/**

The leading book on how to apply and interpret the Laws is Tom Smith's *New Cricket Umpiring and Scoring* (Weidenfeld, 2004, £9.99).

TICK TOCK

0.79 SECONDS

Time the ball takes to reach the batsman, if bowled at 50mph – the pace of Monty Panesar on a good day (*Calculation: 50mph = 24.44 yps. Time taken = 19.33/24.44 = 0.79 seconds*)

0.44 SECONDS

Time the ball takes to reach the batsman, if bowled at 90mph – the pace of Andrew Flintoff on a good day. (*Calculation: 90mph = 1.5 miles per min = 0.025 miles per second = 44 yards per second. Distance from bowler to batsman: = 22 yds – 8ft = 58ft = 19.33 yds Therefore time taken = 19.33/44 = 0.44 seconds*)

3 MINUTES

Time allowed for a new batsman to get into position, from the fall of the previous wicket – otherwise he can be timed out (see page 11)

4 MINUTES

Recommended length of a Test-match over. A fast bowler tends to take five minutes, a slow bowler three. Teams are supposed to bowl 90 overs in a six-hour day

11 MINUTES

Fastest genuine fifty ever made in first-class cricket, by Big Jim Smith of Middlesex against Gloucestershire at Bristol in 1938. It is thought to have taken him only 12 balls. Although mainly a fast bowler, Smith was also "a batsman whose entry always roused a hum of excitement," according to his obituary in the 1980 *Wisden Almanack*. "His principal stroke (perhaps his only one!) was to advance the left foot approximately in the direction of the ball and then swing with all his might. If the ball was well up (and the foot on the right line) it went with a low trajectory an astonishing distance." A fifty was made in eight minutes by Clive Inman of Leicestershire against Nottinghamshire at Nottingham in 1965, but the bowlers were deliberately bowling badly to hasten a declaration, so *Wisden* mentions it only in a footnote and the record still belongs to Big Jim.

20 MINUTES

Time allotted for tea break in Test and most first-class cricket. Many players say it is too short – especially those who have to bowl straight afterwards with a cucumber sandwich and two Jaffa Cakes in their gullet

28 MINUTES

The fastest Test fifty in terms of minutes, made by Jack Brown of England against Australia at Melbourne in 1894-95. "All the reports of the match agreed," noted *Wisden*, "that his innings was absolutely free from fault." And it really made a difference: Brown, a stumpy Yorkshireman with a powerful cut shot and a good sense of humour, made 140, England cantered to their target of 297, and they won the series 3-2. The match was timeless, but Brown was a young man in a hurry. Perhaps he sensed that he would not live long: he died of heart failure ten years later, aged only 35

35 MINUTES

The fastest hundred in first-class cricket, by Percy Fender of Surrey against Northamptonshire at Northampton in 1920

40 MINUTES

Time allotted for lunch break in Test and most first-class cricket

1 HOUR 6 MINUTES

Time the ball is actually in play in a six-hour day, according to one study

1 HOUR 41 MINUTES

The slowest-ever duck in Tests, by Geoff Allott of New Zealand against South Africa at Auckland in 1998-99. He faced 77 balls and couldn't prevent the follow-on but did help his team draw the match. The series, appropriately if not very excitingly, finished 0-0

1 HOUR 53 MINUTES

The fastest double-century in first-class cricket, by Ravi Shastri of Bombay against Baroda in 1984-85. Shastri became only the second player ever to hit six sixes off an over (see page 113)

2 HOURS 45 MINUTES

Time allowed for a Twenty20 match. Each innings is 20 overs, to be bowled in 75 minutes, and there is a 15-minute break between innings

3 HOURS 1 MINUTE

The fastest triple-century in first-class cricket, by Denis Compton for MCC against North Eastern Transvaal at Benoni, South Africa in 1948-49. MCC (Marylebone Cricket Club) was what the England team were called in those days when they were touring abroad and playing warm-up matches between Tests

3-4 HOURS

Typical time taken to make a Test century

6 HOURS

Official length of a Test-match day – normally three sessions of two hours each. In practice, the fielding side usually get behind with the over rate, so the day runs to about 6½ hours

7 HOURS 45 MINUTES

Official length of one-day international match – two innings of 50 overs, lasting 3 ½ hours each, and a lunch or supper break of 45 minutes

9 HOURS 17 MINUTES

The slowest Test century of all, by Mudassar Nazar of Pakistan against England at Lahore in 1977-78. As if they hadn't suffered enough, the crowd were tear-gassed by the police following disturbances provoked by the appearance of the wife and daughter of the deposed prime minister Zulfikar Ali Bhutto

4 DAYS

Length of a first-class match between English counties or Australian states

5 DAYS

Length of a Test match if it goes the distance

10 DAYS

Length of the longest match ever – the Timeless Test at Durban in 1939. South Africa made 530, England (who were 1-0 up in the series) 316, and South Africa 481. All of that took six days. England finished the sixth day on 0 for none, needing 696 to win. They nearly made it, reaching 654 for five towards the end of the tenth day (not counting two rest days and one day lost to rain). But then it rained again, and there couldn't be an 11th day as England had to catch the boat home

47 DAYS

Length of the 2007 World Cup. Even the man in charge, Chris Dehring, admitted that this was too long. The football World Cup takes a month

10 YEARS

Typical length of a successful international career

17 YEARS

Length of international career, so far, of Sachin Tendulkar. He made his Test debut for India at 16, in November 1989, and is now 34. He is the first person to play 500 times for his country – 137 Tests, 385 ODIs and one Twenty20 match to June 25, 2007 – and the only one to score 25,000 international runs (see page 70)

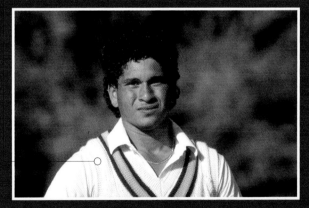

30 YEARS

Span of the longest international career – that of Wilfred Rhodes, the Yorkshire slow left-armer, who played 58 times for England from 1899 to 1929-30. He made his Test debut in 1899, aged 21, alongside WG Grace, who was playing his last Test at the age of 50. Grace was the oldest Test cricketer – until Rhodes played at 52

THE LANGUAGE

Every sport has its own vocab, and cricket more than most. Here are 101 terms you need to know, not including the fielding positions (see page 68) – plus a few extras

101 EVERYDAY TERMS

appeal 🔴 ⚪ ask the umpire if the batsman is out by saying "Howzat?"

arm ball 🔴 a ball from a spin bowler that goes on with the arm rather than turning

back-of-a-length 🔴 just short of a traditional good length

beamer 🔴 full-toss heading for the batsman's head. Usually followed by a gesture of apology

blockhole 🏏 part of the crease where the batsman taps his bat, and which the bowler aims for with a yorker

bouncer 🔴 fast short-pitched ball aimed at batsman's head

boundary 🔴 the rim of the outfield, or a shot that reaches it ("Afridi's got 48, all of them in boundaries")

bump ball 🏏 shot that looks like a catch but isn't because the ball hit the ground just after the bat

carry your bat 🏏 to open the innings and still be there when all 10 of your colleagues are out

chance ⚪ possible catch

chuck 🔴 bowl with a less than straight arm ("Bloggs definitely chucks his bouncer")

close (of play) 🔴 (aka stumps) the end of the day's play

crease 🔴 a line across the pitch. The crease usually means the batting or popping crease, 4ft from the stumps. The bowling crease means the line the stumps sit on. The return crease is the line joining the two

cross 🏏 (of batsmen) to pass each other before a catch is taken, so the man who was the non-striker becomes the striker, and the new batsman starts at the bowler's end

dead bat 🏏 a shot with no follow-through and usually no scoring intent

death 🔴 the closing overs of a one-day innings: usually frenetic

declare 🏏 to decide you've got enough runs and would rather bowl now

the deep ⚪ part of the outfield near the boundary, usually occupied (or patrolled) by resting bowlers

dolly ⚪ easy catch

doosra 🔴 legbreak bowled by an offspinner to fox the batsman

dot ball 🔴 a ball that is not scored off, going down as a dot in the scorebook

duck 🏏 a completed innings of 0. **Golden duck:** out for 0 first ball (see page 111)

extras 🏏 runs that didn't come off the bat – either byes, leg-byes, wides or no-balls

false stroke 🏏 a mis-hit, edge or otherwise unintended shot

first-class 🔴 type of cricket – professional or equivalent, and not one-day

fish 🏏 to play with the bat well away from the body, which tends to be perilous

five-for 🔴 haul of five wickets by the same bowler in one innings

flight 🔴 (of a slow bowler) the trajectory of the ball, especially if he gives it air

follow on 🏏 to have your second innings straight after your first, because you've done so badly. The fielding captain can ask his opponents to follow on if they are a certain number of runs behind – 200 in a Test

full-toss 🔴 delivery that doesn't bounce before it reaches the batsman. Traditionally considered a bad ball, but now sometimes used deliberately at the death to flummox the batsman

gardening 🏏 patting the pitch down to make it flatter. Curiously, batsmen are allowed to do this

gate 🏏 the gap between bat and front pad. Technically, there shouldn't be one

give the ball air 🔴 (of a slow bowler) to bowl in a loop rather than fire it in

go back 🏏 to move your back foot (the right, if you're right-handed) towards the stumps

go down the pitch 🏏 to take a couple of steps out of your crease to meet the ball, usually to a slow bowler, although Kevin Pietersen does it to the quicks too

go forward 🏏 to move your front foot (the left, if you're right-handed) down the pitch to meet the ball

googly 🔴 offbreak bowled by a legspinner to fox the batsman

guard 🏏 place where a batsman habitually puts his bat as the bowler runs in

half-volley 🔴 ball that lands a yard or less in front of the batsman's front foot – usually the easiest ball to hit. Curiously, volley is not a cricket term – it belongs in tennis, football and volleyball

hat-trick 🔴 three wickets in successive balls by the same bowler in the same match (p113)

in 🏏 currently batting, or seeing the ball well ("I was just getting in, when I was out")

innings 🏏 a go at batting, either for an individual or team

inswing 🔴 movement through the air, in towards the right-hander's legs

jaffa 🔴 perfect ball, usually pitching on off stump and leaving the batsman

leading edge 🏏 shot that goes to the off side when aimed towards leg

leg (side) 🔴 the half of the ground behind the batsman as he stands at the crease

length 🔴 how close to the batsman the ball lands

length ball 🔴 ball on a good length, making the batsman unsure whether to go forward or back

---

KEY

🔴 mainly to do with bowling

🏏 mainly to do with batting

🔴 to do with both

⚪ mainly to do with fielding

23 TERMS THAT ARE NOT ESSENTIAL, BUT ENTERTAINING

agricultural 🏏 ungainly or primitive, of a shot that probably goes to cow corner

bits-and-pieces 🔴 player who can bat a bit and bowl a bit, but is sometimes a bit useless

buffet bowling 🔴 so poor that batsmen help themselves

castled 🏏 bowled

chin music 🔴 hostile, short-pitched bowling

corridor of uncertainty 🏏 channel just outside off stump, making batsmen unsure if it's safe to leave the ball

cow corner 🏏 deep mid-wicket, where agricultural shots go

dasher 🏏 (old-fashioned) fast-scoring batsman

dibbly-dobbly 🔴 medium-paced bowling ("Collingwood's just a dibbly-dobbly merchant")

do the hard part 🏏 get to 20 or so – usually mentioned if the batsman then gets out

donkey drop 🔴 a comical delivery which goes high in the air before approaching the batsman almost vertically

A CRASH COURSE

line ⚫ lateral position of the ball as it reaches the batsman. A good line is usually just on or outside off stump

line-and-length ⚫ sustained accuracy

long hop ⚫ a short ball that sits up and begs to be hit for four

maiden ⚫ an over in which no run goes against the bowler's name, ie there are no runs off the bat, no wides and no no-balls (byes and leg-byes allowed, as they are not considered his fault)

middle 🏏 (verb) to hit the ball with the middle of the bat, or time it well; (noun) the crease or pitch

nip back ⚫ to move into the right-handed batsman off the seam

no-ball ⚫ improper delivery, usually because the bowler has overstepped the crease

non-striker 🏏 batsman who is in but not facing

not out 🏏 either still batting ("at lunch, Sehwag was 99 not out") or left unbeaten at the end of the innings ("Lara 400 not out")

nurdle 🏏 to deflect the ball rather than whack it

off (side) 🏏 the half of the ground the batsman faces when standing at the crease

off the mark 🏏 no longer on 0

on a pair 🏏 still on 0 in your second innings, when you made 0 in the first

one short 🏏 when the batsmen have run two or more, but one of them hasn't grounded his bat properly, so the umpire deducts one from the tally

out 🏏 dismissed; no longer batting; back in the hutch

outfield 🎩 outer part of the ground, further from the bat than the men in catching positions

outswing ⚫ movement through the air, away from the right-handed batsman

over ⚫ set of six balls bowled by the same bowler from the same end. He can't bowl the next six.

over rate ⚫ average number of overs bowled per hour – 15 is meant to be par in Tests, but 13 is the norm

overthrows 🎩 extra runs taken by the batsmen when the ball is thrown at the stumps, misses, and eludes anyone who is backing up

pad up 🏏 to get your batting kit on, or, once batting, to play with the pad rather than the bat

a pair 🏏 two ducks in the same match by the same player – short for a pair of spectacles. King pair: two first-ball ducks in the same match

pitch ⚫ (verb) to bounce (of a ball bowled); 🏏 (noun) the 22-yard strip on which the batting and bowling takes place

play and miss 🏏 to play a shot but not connect with the ball – a moral victory for the bowler

played on 🏏 bowled out via the edge of the bat

rough 🏏 the part of the pitch that has been roughed up by the fast bowlers' follow-through. Usually outside the left-hander's off stump. Can provide huge turn, as when Shane Warne was bowling to Andrew Strauss

run-up ⚫ bowler's approach to the wicket, even if he prefers to walk it, like Shane Warne

seam ⚫ sideways movement off the pitch; the stitching on the ball, which enables this; type of bowler – the faster kind, even including bowlers who use swing rather than seam

short (of a length) ⚫ pitching a few yards in front of the batsman, giving him time to go back and pull or cut

shoulder arms 🏏 to play no stroke

sightscreen 🏏 screen on the boundary, behind the bowler, that allows the batsman to pick up the ball. White if the ball is red; black if the ball is white

sitter 🎩 easy catch. Strangely, the word is only used if it is dropped

6-3 or 7-2 field 🎩 having six or seven fielders on the off side and only two or three on the leg

sledging 🎩 chat from fielders, designed to put a batsman off or get under his skin. Unsporting, but usually allowed

slog 🏏 a big hit disapproved of by the coaching book

slog-sweep 🏏 lofted sweep, not in coaching book but increasingly vital ploy for batsmen facing spinners

slower ball ⚫ delivery from a fast or medium-paced bowler which is deliberately bowled a lot slower to trick the batsman into playing too early and being bowled or caught. Usually achieved by switching to a spinner's grip

spell ⚫ bowling stint by one bowler, consisting of anything from one to 40 or even 50 overs, but usually about six for a quick and nine or ten for a spinner

square 🏏 the mown area (more often a rectangle) in the middle of the ground, containing the pitches

stance 🏏 the batsman's posture as he waits for the ball – often distinctive, like somebody's walk

stock bowler ⚫ one who is expected to keep runs down more than take wickets

the strike 🏏 being at the end facing the next ball ("Boycott takes a single, so he keeps the strike, and that's over")

strike bowler ⚫ one who is expected to take wickets

sundries 🏏 Australian word for extras

swing ⚫ sideways movement through the air

tail-ender 🏏 batsman who has been picked as a bowler, normally down at No 9, 10 or 11

time it 🏏 to hit the ball sweetly

two 🏏 guard between middle and leg stumps

the V 🏏 area between mid-off and mid-on where a classical strokeplayer likes to hit the ball – although the idea rather takes it for granted that the bowling will be of full length

walk 🏏 to give yourself out without waiting for the umpire's decision. Considered sporting by some people in the game, and mad by others

wicket 🏏 a dismissal; the pitch; the stumps ("and he's at the wicket now")

wrong'un ⚫ Australian name for a googly

yorker ⚫ ball that lands in the blockhole, near the batsman's toes

---

ferret 🏏 hopeless No 11 batsman, so called because he goes after the rabbits

filth ⚫ terrible bowling ("I have to say Harmison has bowled some absolute filth today")

Harrow cut 🏏 (or Chinese cut) inside-edge which diverts the ball close to the stumps – often for runs

heavy ball ⚫ a delivery that slams into the shoulder of the bat

milk 🏏 to help yourself to singles, usually off a spinner

Nelson 🏏 a score of 111, or its multiples, often considered unlucky in England. Named after Horatio Nelson, because he had one eye, one arm, and one ... what was the third thing?

play around 🏏 to go for your shots while one of your team-mates anchors the innings ("Colly was looking very solid so the rest of us played around him")

rabbit 🏏 inept tail-ender

shirtfront 🏏 a ridiculously flat pitch

stonewall 🏏 to block the ball or score very slowly ("dear old Hoggard, stonewalling as usual")

streaky 🏏 unconvincing or lucky ("he edges it, and that's a streaky way to get off the mark")

the yips ⚫ heebie-geebies that can afflict bowlers, making them unable to land the ball in the right place. Left-arm spinners are especially prone to them, although the most glaring example among recent England players was a right-arm medium-pacer, Gavin Hamilton. His fate was to go back, after a single Test, and play for his previous international team – Scotland

SHANE WARNE
FROM BEACH BUM
TO LEGEND

O nce there was a little boy who grew up in a place called Ferntree Gully, a suburb of Melbourne, the most sports-mad city in Australia (and possibly the world). The boy was blond, cheerful, chubby and rather accident-prone. One day he was playing with a boomerang, didn't realise it would come back to him, and got a cut on his forehead that needed stitches. Another time, a boy at school jumped down on him and he broke both legs. His legs were put in plaster and he had to spend a year on a special low trolley, lying on his tummy and wheeling himself around with his arms. Later, he wondered if all that wheeling had built up strength in his shoulders and wrists.

The boy spent hours playing cricket in the garden with his brother Jason. Aged nine, he played for his primary school, East Sandringham Boys. He wanted to be a fast bowler like Dennis Lillee, Australia's most exciting player of the time, but he was also intrigued by how spin bowlers could make the ball turn. He was shown how to bowl a leg-break by his school coach, Ron Cantlon. A useful club legspinner himself, Cantlon had noticed that the West Indies, then the world's best team, were not great players of spin. "Keep at it," he told the boy, "because in 10 years' time they'll be scouring the country for a leggie." He had just shown Shane Warne how to do the thing that was going to make him a legend.

At secondary school, Shane preferred batting, and often went in in the top four for the 1st XI. He was also naughty enough to get several canings from the headmaster. "I guess I could have paid more attention to my studies," he said. A rough translation of this is: "I didn't do any work at all." Picked to play for Victoria Schools against New South Wales Schools, he travelled all the way to Sydney, 500 miles away, and took five wickets. Aged 19, he spent a summer in England, playing club cricket in Bristol. He drank so much beer, he put on three stone. He was a beach bum first and a cricketer second.

Back home, he won a place at the Australian Cricket Academy – but he didn't do well there and they chucked him out. He played a few games for Victoria and the Australian Test selectors, who hadn't had a major spin bowler for decades, decided to take a punt on him. They picked him in a Test against India, whose batsmen are probably the best players of spin. Warne took one wicket – for 150 runs. The next three innings he bowled in, he took none for 185, so his Test average was now 335.

The Academy invited him back. He went, and studied legspin under Terry Jenner, a

fine coach and what Aussies call a larrikin – someone who doesn't always obey authority. Warne was picked for the tour of Sri Lanka and the Australian captain, Allan Border, trusted him to bowl as Australia pressed for victory on the last day. He took three for 11, and turned a corner.

In the 1992 Boxing Day Test in his home town of Melbourne, he faced the mighty West Indies, the world's No 1 team. He took seven for 52 to bowl Australia to victory. Shane Warne had arrived. He took more wickets in New Zealand and then went to England for his first taste of the Ashes. The Manchester groundsman generously prepared a turning pitch. Australia were all out for 289, a poor score. England were a comfortable 80 for one when Warne came on to bowl to Mike Gatting, a skilful player of spin. His first ball was spun so hard that it dipped and curled to leg before pitching well outside leg stump and then turning a full 18 inches past a startled Gatting and clipping the off stump. It soon became the most famous ball ever bowled in the Ashes: the wonderball.

Warne destroyed England in that series with 34 wickets. Australia won 4-1 and he was chosen as one of *Wisden*'s Five Cricketers of the Year. He was getting wickets all the time, and conceding few runs, unlike most legspinners. So he gave his captain everything: control and a cutting edge. In the next Ashes series, he did even better, and in the Boxing Day Test, 1994, he took a hat-trick against England. All three deliveries were leg-breaks, but he spun them different amounts. The only team who could cope with him were India.

He became a superstar. He was also a handy, fearless No 8 batsman, and a very good slip fielder. But the naughty boy never quite went away. He has smoked throughout his career, even though he once accepted money to give up. In September 1994, at a Sri Lankan casino, he made a more serious misjudgment. He was introduced by a team-mate, Mark Waugh, to an Indian bookmaker known only as John. John said he was a person who bet on cricket. He offered Warne 5,000 US dollars (about £3,000) in return for information on pitches and weather, and Warne took the money.

When Australian officials heard about this from reporters, they fined Warne 8,000 Australian dollars (also about £3,000) and Waugh 10,000 – but kept the fines secret until a reporter got hold of the story four years later. After that, an independent report by a leading lawyer concluded that the fines were too small and the two players should have been banned. "They must have known it is wrong," the lawyer said.

It could have been worse. The very worst thing a cricketer can do, in cricket, is match-fixing – agreeing to try to lose, in order to make money – and Warne hadn't done that. But it looked as if that was what he was being set up for. He accepted that he had been "naïve and stupid".

The 1998-99 season was a bad one on the field too, as Warne, returning from shoulder surgery, took only four wickets in four Tests. People wondered if he might be losing it. But then Australia bounced back from a poor start to win the 1999 World Cup, with Warne taking vital wickets, and in 2000 he received a huge honour: he was named as one of *Wisden*'s Five Cricketers of the Century. He was the only current player among them, and the only one without a knighthood: the others were Sir Don Bradman, Sir Garry Sobers, Sir Jack Hobbs and Sir Viv Richards.

In 2003, he planned to retire from one-day cricket after the World Cup. But then he was caught taking a banned drug, a diuretic. He reacted like a little kid: he blamed his mum, saying she had given him the pills to help him lose weight. He was banned for a year, and the World Anti-Doping Agency said it should have been more.

He turned this disgrace into a bonus by coming back refreshed in 2004. He soon reached 500 Test wickets, only the second man to do so after Courtney Walsh. Then, after Muttiah Muralitharan had pinched Walsh's world record, Warne nipped past him. But the drugs scandal, and a few other stories alleging that he had been unfaithful to his wife, meant that he missed out on the Australian captaincy. He has often been described as "the best captain Australia never had". His wife got fed up too: they separated in 2005, although two years later they were rumoured to have got back together, and in April 2007 their three kids moved to schools in England, where Warne was captaining Hampshire.

Warne carried on eating Englishmen for breakfast and in the 2005 Ashes, at the grand old age of 35, he took 40 wickets, and made plenty of runs, yet finished on the losing side. He became the first man to 600 Test wickets and set a new record for most Test wickets in a calendar year (96). In the 2006-07 Ashes, he started badly again, but in the second Test he led Australia's charge to a victory so astonishing that England never recovered from it. They lost every match in the series.

He announced that he would retire from Tests, and from cricket in Australia, at the end of the series. This gave him two last Tests, in Melbourne and Sydney, to say goodbye and reach 700 wickets. He finished with 708, and many fond farewells were said – not least by England players who were delighted not to have to face him

Shane Warne waves goodbye to the fans at the Sydney Cricket Ground, after his last Test

again. Just about the only thing he hadn't achieved was a Test century. His top score was a tantalising 99. "The one statistic that does annoy me," he said in 2006, "is having the most Test runs in the history of the game without a hundred. I don't like that."

Many people said he was the best bowler ever. That is hard to prove, as the game has changed so much from one era to another. He may not even have been the best bowler of his time (Murali is amazing too, with a lower average and a better strike rate), or the best in his team (Glenn McGrath, in a quieter way, was a genius too). But Warne has certainly been a fantastic bowler, a fascinating character and a great entertainer. And he has changed the game, making legspin fashionable again.

If he stays fit, he is planning to play one last season for Hampshire in 2008. Go and see him if you possibly can.

THE LONG AND THE SHORT OF IT

Why is international cricket like a Mars bar? Because it comes in three different sizes. Here's a quick guide to them all

TEST

Full name?	Test match
How long does it last?	Five days, 90 overs a day
How many innings per side?	Two
And matches per series?	Two to five, most often three
What does it look like?	Traditional – red ball, white kit, no names or numbers
Any special rules?	New ball after 80 overs
Any meal breaks?	Lunch and tea
What's a big score?	500 (though you can still lose)
What's a good scoring rate?	Four an over
Team scoring record?	952 for 6 dec by Sri Lanka v India, Colombo, 1997 (see page 105)
Individual scoring record?	400no by Brian Lara, West Indies v England, Antigua 2003-04 (see page 104)
Best bowling in a match?	19 for 90 by Jim Laker, England v Australia, Old Trafford, 1956 (see page 104)
What's so good about it?	Ebb and flow Full canvas, wide variety High drama Scope for tactics
When did it start?	1877
How many matches so far?*	1830
How is it for batsmen?	Ultimate examination, takes great skill and patience
How is it for bowlers?	Tough, as pitches tend to be flat, but there is time to relax and settle in
How is it for fielders?	Tough for catchers, but places to hide for the donkeys
What's not so good?	Dull if too slow or high-scoring
Who's best at it now?	Australia, by far
Where are England?	2nd in the table
Who's the best team ever?	West Indies in the 1980s (the scariest, thanks to fearsome pace attack) or Australia under Steve Waugh in 2000-03 (the fastest-scoring)
Overall verdict?	The highest form of the game. Not called Tests for nothing. But there need to be more five-Test series for maximum drama

◄ **Three outfits, one star**
Ricky Ponting, captain of Australia, in a Test, a one-dayer and a Twenty20

*all figures to May 1, 2007

ODI

Full name?	One-day international
How long does it last?	1 day – 50 overs a side
How many innings per side?	One
And matches per series?	Usually three, five or seven
What does it look like?	Football with long trousers. – names, numbers, white ball
Any special rules?	Fielding circles, powerplays, umpires strict on wides, rain delays in 2nd inns mean target revised using Duckworth-Lewis system (don't ask)
Any meal breaks?	Lunch or tea
What's a big score?	300
What's a good scoring rate?	Six an over
Team scoring record?	443 for 9 by Sri Lanka v Holland, Amstelveen, 2006
Individual scoring record?	194 by Saeed Anwar, Pakistan v India, Chennai, 1996-97
Best bowling in a match?	8 for 19 by Chaminda Vaas, Sri Lanka v Zimbabwe, Colombo, 2001-02
What's so good about it?	Exciting if close Draws big crowds Often a feast of runs Fairly fast-moving Sometimes floodlit
When did it start?	1970-71
How many matches so far?*	2581
How is it for batsmen?	Easy – loaded in their favour, but expectations are high and run-chases hard on the nerves
How is it for bowlers?	High pressure – short spells, no leeway
How is it for fielders?	Tougher – quick singles taken all the time, nowhere to hide
What's not so good?	Dull if one-sided or too low-scoring
Who's best at it now?	Australia, by so far that it's embarrassing
Where are England?	7th in the table
Who's the best team ever?	Australia, now – 23 World Cup wins in a row, super-powerful top order, varied and accurate attack, great ground-fielding
Overall verdict?	Has given fine entertainment, but now a bit tired. Too many games, not enough possibilities. Powerplays have helped, more tweaks needed

T20

Full name?	Twenty20 international
How long does it last?	Three hours – 20 overs a side
How many innings per side?	One
And matches per series?	Usually one, sometimes two
What does it look like?	ODIs, but colours may vary
Any special rules?	Same as ODIs but players in dug-out, not pavilion
Any meal breaks?	No – 15 minutes between innings
What's a big score?	200
What's a good scoring rate?	Ten an over
Team scoring record?	221 for 5 by Australia v England, Sydney, 2006-07
Individual scoring record?	98no by Ricky Ponting, Australia v New Zealand, Auckland, 2004-05
Best bowling in a match?	4 for 22 by Paul Collingwood, England v Sri Lanka, Rose Bowl, 2006
What's so good about it?	Fits in with school and work Draws big crowds, new fans Often a feast of runs Very fast-moving All over by suppertime
When did it start?	2005
How many matches so far?*	14
How is it for batsmen?	They have a ball, as long as they get on with it
How is it for bowlers?	Medium pressure – only four overs each, and expectations very low
How is it for fielders?	Toughest of all – every single gets turned into a two
What's not so good?	Dull if one-sided or too low-scoring
Who's best at it now?	Too early to say, but Sri Lanka are pretty handy
Where are England?	There isn't a table, luckily
Who's the best team ever?	Too early to say, but England were brilliant in their first match, reducing Australia to an incredible 31 for 7. Then they didn't win for two years …
Overall verdict?	Sparkling entertainment and a great introduction to the game. Has worked far better than expected. Maybe not so surprising – many schools and clubs play 20-over matches

COUNTY CRICKET

Why is county cricket like a maze?
Because it's very confusing … but also fun.
Here is the lowdown on every trophy and team

KEY = Test venue; **(Eng, 3)** = has played 3 Tests for England; **Ch'ship** = Championship; **Form** shows how the teams have done up to 2006

THE FOUR COMPETITIONS

	LV COUNTY CHAMPIONSHIP	FRIENDS PROVIDENT TROPHY	NATWEST PRO40	TWENTY20 CUP
started life as	County Championship, 1890 (only 8 teams)	Gillette Cup, 1963 (60 overs per side)	John Player League, 1969	Twenty20 Cup, 2003
type of cricket	first-class, four-day	one-day, 50 overs per side	one-day, 40 overs	one-day, 20 overs
structure	two divisions of nine, all play all twice	two divisions of 10, all play all once, winners meet in final	two divisions of nine, all play all once	three groups of six, then quarter-finals, semi-finals, final
how is that decided?	on merit – two up, two down	geographically – North and South	on merit – two up, two down plus one play-off	geographically – North, South and Mids/West/Wales
extra teams?	no	Ireland and Scotland	no	no
time of year	whole season – April to September	early summer – April to June, final in August	late summer – July to September	midsummer – June to July, final in August
days of the week	mostly Wednesdays to Saturdays	mostly Tuesdays, Thursdays, Sundays	any, but mainly Sundays	weekday evenings
flood-lights	never – no evening play	sometimes	sometimes	seldom needed
TV	Sky do the odd game	Sky do plenty	Sky do plenty	Sky do plenty
prestige	high	medium	low	medium-high
crowds	low with the odd high	medium	medium	record-breaking
looks	traditional	colourful	colourful	colourful
feels	like a museum	like a school outing	like a picnic	like a party

SOMERSET

home County Ground, Taunton – bags of runs, and now the headquarters of England Women

captain Justin Langer (Aus, 105 Tests), nuggety nurdler

stars Marcus Trescothick (Eng, 76), stiff-legged blaster; **Andy Caddick** (Eng, 62), bang-it-in seamer; **Cameron White** (Aus, 16 ODIs), big-hitter

form poor since 2nd in Ch'ship 2001

heyday 1970s – great one-day side

legends Ian Botham, Viv Richards and **Joel Garner,** 1970s superstars

strange but true Botham walked out after Somerset's then captain, Peter Roebuck, ousted Richards and Garner

GLOUCESTERSHIRE

home Nevil Road, Bristol – slow, seaming

captain Jon Lewis (Eng, 1), big-haired opening bowler

stars Lewis, classical medium-pacer; **Hamish Marshall** (NZ, 13), corkscrew-haired stylist

form poor in Ch'ship – never won it

heyday 1999-2004, seven one-day trophies

legends WG Grace, captain 1870-98 – the first celebrity cricketer; **Wally Hammond**, master batsman of 1930s

strange but true champion county three times in the 1870s, before the Ch'ship officially started

GLAMORGAN

home Sophia Gardens, Cardiff (down for an Ashes Test in 2009) – low and slow

captain David Hemp (Bermuda, 17 ODIs), stylish left-hander

stars Jimmy Maher (Aus, 26 ODIs), punchy left-hander; **Simon Jones** (Eng, 18), ace reverse swinger

form poor since Ch'ship win in 1997, but won 40-over league in 2002 and 2004

heyday 1948 and 1969 – champions

legend Wilf Wooller, 1948 captain and great believer in fielding

strange but true the only first-class county in Wales

FIRST-CLASS COUNTIES IN THE SOUTH

SURREY

home **The Oval, London** – historic, flat, takes spin

captain **Mark Butcher** (Eng, 71), laid-back batsman and guitarist

stars **Mark Ramprakash** (Eng, 52), run machine (see page 46); **Ally Brown** (Eng, 16 ODIs), one-day biffer

form **patchy** – relegated 2005, promoted 2006

heyday **1952-58**, seven Ch'ships; **1999-2002**, three Ch'ships

legend **Sir Alec Bedser**, immaculate seamer; **Peter May**, elegant batsman; **Sir Jack Hobbs**, master opener

strange but true the coach, Alan Butcher, is the captain's dad

MIDDLESEX

home **Lord's, London** – majestic setting, flat pitch (apart from the slope)

captain **Ed Smith** (Eng, 3), writer and thinker about the game

stars **Owais Shah** (Eng, 2), one-day master; **Ed Joyce** (Eng, 17 ODIs), stylish left-hander; **Chris Silverwood** (Eng, 6), persevering paceman

form **poor** – relegated 2006

heyday **1976-93** – seven Championships

legend **Denis Compton**, debonair batsman, 1940s

strange but true they wore pink one-day shirts in 2007, to support a breast-cancer charity

ESSEX

home **County Ground, Chelmsford** – flat, with short straight boundaries

captain job vacant in mid-2007 as **Ronnie Irani** (Eng, 3), cheerful extrovert, was forced to retire by injury

stars **Alastair Cook** (Eng, 14), cool-headed opener; **Danish Kaneria** (Pak, 43), erratic legspinner

form **good at Pro40** – won it 2005 & 2006

heyday **1983-92**, five Ch'ships

legend **Graham Gooch**, majestic opener, now their batting coach

strange but true after 83 years with no trophies, they won 12 in 14 years

HAMPSHIRE

home **Rose Bowl, Southampton** – handsome, seamers' paradise

captain **Shane Warne** (Aus, 145), legspin legend and bold tactician (see page 28)

stars **Warne**; **Kevin Pietersen** (Eng, 23), big-hitting celebrity

form **good** – 2nd in 2005, 3rd 2006

heyday **1961** and **1973** – champions

legends **Barry Richards**, South African opener, perhaps the best player to play only four Tests; **Malcolm Marshall**, West Indian fast bowler

strange but true they built the ground without providing enough roads, so the traffic is terrible

SUSSEX

home **County Ground, Hove** – sea breezes and swing

captain **Chris Adams** (Eng, 5), inspirational leader

stars **Mushtaq Ahmed** (Pak, 52), tireless legspinner

form **top** – champions 2003, 2006

heyday **now**

legends **KS Ranjitsinhji**, Indian prince and England batsman; **Tony Greig**, controversial England captain; **John Snow**, pace ace; **Adams**

strange but true in 1611, two men from Sidlesham in Sussex missed church to play cricket. They were fined a shilling (5p) each

KENT

home **St Lawrence Ground, Canterbury** – attractive, flat

captain **Rob Key** (Eng, 15), hard-hitting batsman and ace poker player

stars **Martin van Jaarsveld** (SA, 9), correct batsman and ace slip fielder

form **solid** – top five, six years running, but nothing special

heyday **1973-78**, eight trophies

legends **Frank Woolley**, lordly left-hander; **Tich Freeman**, tiny legspinner; **Colin Cowdrey**, regal cover-driver; **Alan Knott**, master keeper

strange but true for decades, a lime tree stood inside the boundary; only four men ever hit the ball over it for six

FIRST-CLASS COUNTIES IN THE NORTH

LANCASHIRE

home Old Trafford, Manchester – excellent pace, bounce and turn

captain Mark Chilton, good sort

stars Andrew Flintoff (Eng, 67), superstar allrounder; Muttiah Muralitharan (SL, 110), world's best spinner

form nearly men – 2nd five times since 1998

heyday 1970s and late 90s – two great one-day teams

legends Brian Statham, pinpoint seam bowler; Clive Lloyd, West Indies captain; Wasim Akram, sultan of swing; Mike Atherton, blocker

strange but true they blame their near misses on the Manchester rain

YORKSHiRE

home Headingley, Leeds – green seamer on dank days, can turn flat

captain Darren Gough (Eng, 58), elderly but ebullient swing bowler

stars Matthew Hoggard (Eng, 62), king of the outswingers; Adil Rashid (Eng, soon), feisty legspinning allrounder

form up-and-down – went down in 2004, up in 2005, 6th in 2006

heyday 1893-1968 – champions 29 times in 76 years

legends dozens: Lord Hawke, Wilfred Rhodes, Sir Len Hutton, Fred Trueman, Geoff Boycott …

strange but true they're always arguing with each other

DURHAM

home Riverside, Chester-le-Street – seamers' paradise

captain Dale Benkenstein (SA, 23 ODIs), respected tactician

stars Steve Harmison (Eng, 50), nasty fastie; Paul Collingwood (Eng, 20), self-made batsman

form improving fast from miserable beginnings

heyday still to come

legend Ian Botham – helped start them off

strange but true they only entered first-class cricket in 1992

DERBYSHiRE

home County Ground, Derby – low and slow

captain Simon Katich (Aus, 23), new to the job

stars Katich, dogged left-hander; Ian Harvey (Aus, 73 ODIs), inspired slogger and crafty medium-pacer

form poor – usually low in Div 2

heyday 1936 – their only Ch'ship

legend Dean Jones, dynamic captain and one-day batsman of the 1990s

strange but true in one-day games, they're called the Phantoms

NOTTiNGHAMSHiRE

home Trent Bridge, Nottingham – much-loved, especially by swing bowlers

captain Stephen Fleming (NZ, 104), astute man-manager

stars David Hussey (Aus, 0), big-score specialist and brother of Mike; Chris Read, best keeper in England

form like a yo-yo – champions 2005, relegated 2006

heyday 1980s – won Ch'ship under Clive Rice and …

legend Sir Richard Hadlee, master seamer

strange but true ball swings more since they built a new stand in 1998

LEiCESTERSHiRE

home Grace Road, Leicester – low and slow

captain in one-dayers Jeremy Snape (Eng, 10 ODIs), sports psychologist; in Ch'ship, Darren Robinson, solid opener

stars Stuart Broad (Eng, 6 ODIs), promising fast bowler

form poor since 2002

heyday 1996-98 – champions twice

legends Ray Illingworth, canny captain who led them to first Ch'ship; David Gower, dreamy left-hander

strange but true Broad played for England in 2006 while still growing – and he was already 6ft 6

WORCESTERSHiRE

home New Road, Worcester – green and pleasant, next to cathedral

captain Vikram Solanki (Eng, 51 ODIs), elegant strokeplayer

stars Graeme Hick (Eng, 65), monster run-maker at county level; Phil Jaques (Aus, 2), aggressive left-hander

form patchy; no trophies since …

heyday 1988-89, consecutive Ch'ships

legends Hick; Ian Botham, who joined for those Ch'ships

strange but true Botham gave his winner's medal to the dressing-room attendant

WARWiCKSHiRE

home Edgbaston, Birmingham – good sporting surface

captain Darren Maddy (Eng, 3), ace Twenty20 opener

stars Ian Bell (Eng, 23), elegant on-driver; Ashley Giles (Eng, 54), doughty spinner

form solid – champions 2004

heyday 1993-95 – six trophies including the triple in 1994

legends Brian Lara, record-breaking star of '94; Dennis Amiss, 1970s opener who made 35,000 runs

strange but true England often play better at Edgbaston, perhaps because the crowd make a lot of noise

NORTHAMPTONSHiRE

home Wantage Road, Northampton – spinners' paradise

captain David Sales (Eng U-19), beefy batsman

stars Lance Klusener (SA, 49), old master blaster; Monty Panesar (Eng, 13), crowd-pleasing spinner

form threadbare – never champions

heyday 1899-1904 – four Minor Counties Ch'ships

legends Colin Milburn, rotund 1960s big-hitter; David Steele, 1970s blocker who looked like a bank clerk

strange but true they have the smallest main ground of any county – capacity just 4000

THE LIE OF THE LAND

England and Wales have dozens of counties, but only these 18 can play first-class cricket. The rest can enter the Minor Counties Championship.

The 18 counties together form the England and Wales Cricket Board (ECB), which runs the game for them. Most of the ECB's income comes from television deals and ticket sales for the England team. The profits are divided up to give each county a hand-out of over £1m a year, and the ones that stage Tests get more than the rest. Counties also raise money from ticket sales and sponsorship, staging events like rock concerts, and subscriptions from members. The county with the most members is usually Lancashire.

Many people believe there are too many county competitions. In a poll published in May 2007, two-thirds of county players agreed that there should be three competitions, not four. In Australian domestic cricket, there are only two. The commonsense solution is obvious: drop one, which would probably be the Pro40, the one that has no counterpart in the international game. But commonsense doesn't always prevail in cricket ...

DURHAM

YORKSHIRE

LANCASHIRE

DERBYSHIRE

NOTTINGHAMSHIRE

LEICESTERSHIRE

WORCESTER-SHIRE

WARWICKSHIRE

NORTHAMPTONSHIRE

WOMEN IN CRICKET

For centuries, bowling was underarm. The first man to bowl round-arm at Lord's was John Willes of Kent in 1807. The umpire called no-ball and Willes is reported to have got on his horse and ridden away "in high dudgeon". Round-arm bowling was banned for 21 years, until finally MCC, the game's then rulers, saw that it was here to stay. Overarm bowling followed in 1864. You may be wondering why I'm telling you this on a page about women. The reason is that John Willes is thought to have got the idea from his sister, Christina. The story goes that he would get her to bowl at him in the barn, which may have been the world's first indoor net. She tried to bowl underarm but couldn't because her voluminous skirts got in the way. So she bowled round-arm, and changed the course of sporting history. (Willes also trained his dog to field. It was said that Willes, his sister and his dog "could beat any team in England".)

Women have been playing cricket for centuries. The first recorded county match between two female sides was Surrey v Hampshire in 1811. Women's Test cricket began in 1934. The first cricket World Cup was contested by women in 1973, two years before the men. There are women cricket writers, photographers, physios, scorers, press officers, committee members and administrators. Behind almost every promising young cricketer there is a long-suffering mum, equipped with a car, a washing machine, formidable powers of organisation and a shoulder to cry on after a golden duck. Yet some men still behave as if cricket was an all-male game. It's not just sexist – it's stupid.

In 1985, Lancashire CCC had a vote to decide whether to allow women into the pavilion at Old Trafford. "Let them in," said one member, "and the next thing you know, the place will be full of children." The sexists won that battle, but lost the war. Lancashire has had women members for years and the place is not full of children. In any case, why would it be a bad thing if it was?

Lord's was not much better. It did host a women's one-day international in 1976, and arranged for the dressing-room attendant to be replaced for the day by his wife. But the members, who enjoy the best views in the house at the best ground in the world, repeatedly refused to allow women to join the club. The only woman who could sit and watch a Test match from the pavilion was **the Queen**.

In 1989, the club secretary said there was "not a hope in hell" of the members voting to admit women. In 1998, they came up against an MCC president, Colin Ingleby-Mackenzie, who was determined to push the change through. He was a charming figure who had captained Hampshire and led his team to the County Championship after telling them, with a straight face, that they had to be in bed before breakfast.

He held a members' vote on the issue in February 1998. They voted in favour by 56 per cent to 44, but the rules required a two-thirds majority, so even though most members were now in favour of the change, it still didn't happen. He kept fighting, and some of his opponents helped him out by saying ridiculous

things. One man declared that women shouldn't become members because they wouldn't be able to afford the subscription, then around £300. Another said he liked to get to the Lord's Test early to bag a seat with his *Daily Telegraph*, and how would he be able to go on doing that when he had been brought up to give up his seat to a woman?

Ingleby-Mackenzie announced another vote for September, only seven months after the previous one. He sent the members a glossy brochure arguing the case and pointing out that they might suffer from "future legislation" if they continued to block women – a subtle reference to the fact that there was a Labour government for the first time in 18 years. On September 28, the members voted – 9,394 in favour of women, 4,072 against. The percentage was 69.8 and that was enough. "Life as we know it," said one disgruntled member, "is over."

A few honorary women members joined, and later, some playing members. Life went on. The Lord's pavilion is still overwhelmingly male, but at least it's possible for any cricket lover to apply for membership, regardless of their colour, creed or gender.

Women's cricket is now thriving. Junior forms of the game like Kwik cricket and inter cricket give more girls a chance to wield a bat. There are still not many women's Tests – England have played only 86 in 73 years – but they get more publicity than they ever have. England Women won the Ashes in 2005, like the men, and unlike the men, they haven't lost them yet.

▲ Not out any more Rachael Heyhoe-Flint left and Jackie Court were among the first women to become members of the MCC

5 GREAT CRICKET WOMEN

Martha Grace

Mother, and coach, of three Test cricketers. In 1859 she wrote to George Parr, who ran the England XI: "I … ask you to consider the inclusion of my son, E. M. Grace – a splendid hitter and most excellent catch – in your England XI. I am sure he would play very well and do the team much credit. It may interest you to learn that I have a younger son, now 12 years of age, who will in time be a much better player than his brother because his back stroke is sounder, and he always plays with a straight bat. His name is W. G. Grace."

Myrtle Maclagan

In any cricket, a bowler who can take wickets while keeping the runs down is a captain's dream. If they can also make runs, they are priceless. Myrtle Maclagan did all this for England against Australia in the first women's Test series ever played, in 1934-35. Opening the bowling in the first Test at Brisbane, she took 7 for 10 in 17 overs of offbreaks as Australia capitulated to 47 all out. Then she opened the batting and showed how it was done by making 72 out of England's 154. England cruised to victory, and in the second Test, at Sydney, she followed a tidy four-for with 119, the first women's Test century, to wrap up the series. Later, she served as a soldier. "At various times in her life," *Wisden* reported, "she won prizes for squash, tennis, badminton and knitting."

Rachael Heyhoe-Flint

Most male batsmen are either attacking or defensive. Rachael Heyhoe-Flint was both. She hit the first six by a woman in a Test, for England v Australia in 1963, in the 25th women's Test, and 14 years later she made 179 in nearly nine hours to save an Ashes Test and series. She captained England against Australia in the **first women's match at Lord's** in 1976: "I cried all the way to the wicket," she said. "We had arrived." She finally joined the MCC committee in 2004 and is still the biggest name in women's cricket – though not the longest. That honour has passed to the England allrounder Ebony-Jewel Cora-Lee Camellia Rosamond Rainford-Brent.

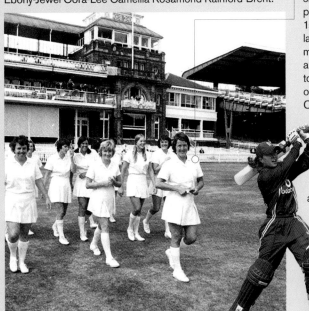

Belinda Clark

She didn't just captain the Australian team – she was chief executive of Women's Cricket Australia. A hugely consistent opener, she had been an international for eight years before she was dismissed in single figures. Her 229 against Denmark at Mumbai in 1997-98 was the first double-hundred in a one-day international by a man or woman. She was *Wisden Australia* Cricketer of the Year in 1998. She retired in 2005 with averages of over 45 in both Tests and ODIs.

Clare Connor

Clare Connor has been the Rachael Heyhoe-Flint of the 21st century, a pioneer who has got results and changed attitudes. An allrounder and slow left-armer, she captained England to the 2005 Ashes, their first series win over Australia for 42 years. But years before that, she had made waves by playing for Brighton College 1st XI, with 10 men. Years later, she commentated on men's cricket on Channel 4 and became the first woman to play in the public-school old-boys' tournament, the Cricketer Cup. She returned to Brighton as an English teacher, and although she retired as a player in 2006, she is now head of girls' cricket and one of her pupils, the slow left-armer **Holly Colvin**, has already been an England player for two years. At Brighton they even have a Clare Connor Scholarship; anyone who is interested is invited to apply to a Mrs C Connor.

ANDREW FLINTOFF
FROM FAT LAD TO
HEAVYWEIGHT CHAMPION

One day in 1987, Lancashire Under-11 cricketers were taking on Derbyshire. Lancashire's 12th man was a boy of nine from Preston, with fair hair, a toothy grin and big hands. It was raining. He fielded for about 10 overs. "I was over the moon just getting on," he said.

Two years later, Andrew Flintoff was the Under-11s' captain and star allrounder, leading them through an unbeaten season, making 1,000 runs and taking 50 wickets. A supply teacher asked his class to write about what they had done in the holidays. Andrew described his runs and wickets. "What a dream," wrote the teacher. It was left to some of the other children to tell her it was true. Later, the kids had to state their preferred careers. "Professional cricket," wrote Flintoff. A teacher told him to think again.

At 14, tall and skinny, he played grown-up club cricket for St Anne's, wearing a T-shirt under his whites to look larger. Playing for St Anne's Under-15s, he scored 232 in a 20-over match. At 15, he played for Lancashire 2nd XI. His dad, Colin, a club player, was delighted; Andrew himself was "bricking it" with nerves. He made 26 and 13, and the coach, John Stanworth, nicknamed him Freddie after Freddie Flintstone. The name stuck.

His school in Preston was "quite rough," he once said, and the other kids considered cricket posh. "In the evenings I went to play cricket, and they went to nick cars." He was bright enough to collect nine GCSEs and play chess for Lancashire. He left school at 16, went to work at Woolworths, in the CD department, where he became a big fan of Elvis Presley.

As a junior cricketer, Flintoff had only one weakness: his back. It didn't just hurt, it often stopped him bowling, threatening his chances of reaching the top. Captains needed him more than was good for him. Picked as a batsman for England Under-19 in West Indies in 1994-95, he ended up opening the bowling. "I got home, and my back just collapsed."

At 17 he played for Lancashire against Hampshire. He scored 7 and 0, took no wickets, held two catches but dropped another three, and barely spoke. He fared better with England Under-19, captaining them to victory in Pakistan. When a fast bowler called Steve Harmison got homesick, Flintoff handled him well and they became friends.

In 1998, Flintoff hit 34 off an over. He was picked for England against South Africa. He made 17, 0 and 0, and took only one wicket. The second duck reduced him to tears, but England won to seal a then-rare series victory. The cameras nosed into the dressing-room, where a sheepish Flintoff could be seen hastily removing a page-three pin-up from the wall. Despite the win, he was dropped. He returned for the 1999 World Cup in England, but the team flopped and he didn't get going.

He toured South Africa under England's new coach, Duncan Fletcher, and showed promise. But then came his lowest ebb. His back flared up again and his weight soared to 19 stone. *The Sun* called him a VAST BOWLER. He batted for England without his back support to look thinner – reversing his old T-shirt ploy. He made 42 and said: "Not bad for a fat lad."

He missed the 2001 Ashes because he was out of form. His managers gave him a severe talking-to. They suggested he ask to go on the Academy tour of Australia, which was run like a boot camp. He went, England summoned him to India, and he ended up opening the bowling. In New Zealand, he finally made a Test hundred. He had arrived.

In 2002, he fell in love with Rachael Wools, a marketing executive. He missed another Ashes with another injury, but in 2004 both Flintoff and England, under Michael Vaughan, got on a roll, winning all seven home Tests. Flintoff blasted 167 against West Indies. He was now a star – and a family man. Rachael gave birth to Holly and became Mrs Flintoff.

Finally, at Lord's in 2005, he played an Ashes Test. Gripped by nerves, he had a shocker. He took a week off and resolved to be himself. At Edgbaston, he got two fifties, nine sixes, and seven wickets, bowling the perfect over to remove Justin Langer and Ricky Ponting (for 0). England won by two runs. A nation throbbed.

England played out of their skins and just beat Australia 2-1 to regain the Ashes after 16 years. Flintoff was their best player, fit, disciplined, consistent. And then came the celebrations. The team paraded through London in an open-top bus. Flintoff, wearing shades but obviously pie-eyed, told the nation: "I've not been to bed yet. The eyes behind these glasses tell a thousand stories."

The perfect over: Flintoff bowls Langer, Edgbaston 2005

Six months later, he captained England in India, missing the birth of his son Corey to replace the injured Vaughan. He batted solidly, but England went 1-0 down. At lunch on the last day, he grabbed Matthew Hoggard's iPod, put on Johnny Cash's *Ring Of Fire* and led a team sing-song. They went out and won.

Back home, disappointment was waiting. England only drew with Sri Lanka and Flintoff overbowled himself. Injured again, he handed over to Andrew Strauss, who did better. The selectors narrowly chose Flintoff to captain the Ashes tour. It was a shambles. The Aussies were honed and hungry; England were rusty. They lost 5-0.

At the World Cup in the Caribbean, they lost their first match, to New Zealand. Several players stayed out late drinking, and Flintoff ended up at sea, in a pedalo, at 4am. He was sacked as vice-captain. England's World Cup fizzled out as usual. Afterwards, he needed yet another operation, this time on his ankle. The saga continued.

THE QUALITIES

	PATIENCE	**FOCUS**	**A GOOD EYE**	**GUTS**
BATSMEN	**loads** a big score will take three hours or more, and Test batsmen have to be able to bat all day	**loads** one mistake and you could be out. Must switch on and off	**very** must judge length and line of the ball in fractions of a second	**lots** the ball is hard and it may be coming at your head at 90mph
BOWLERS 	**lots** even the best will bowl 50 balls for each wicket	**lots** every ball must be on the spot. But they do get long breathers	**not very** some have been hopeless batsmen and fielders, like Phil Tufnell	**some** got to keep being yourself when all is going wrong
FIELDERS 	**some** could be out there all day	**loads** if fielding close, less if in deep	**very good** if close in, less so in the deep	**lots** if close in, especially when the bowling is slow – the ball comes at you from point-blank range 
CAPTAINS 	**less** always busy, but sometimes have to wait for a breakthrough	**loads** must notice everything	**no more** than other fielders	**lots** may have to make tricky decisions, tell mates they are dropped

CRICKETERS NEED

REFLEXES	BRAINS	ATHLETICISM	STOICISM	DEDICATION

fast you have half a second to make a decision and carry it out

some judgment, ability to read the conditions and know when to attack or defend

some can get away with little, but it helps, especially for running between the wickets

loads could get several low scores in a row

plenty most spend long hours in nets

none unless the ball is hit straight back at you

some same as for batsmen, plus a good memory – knowing how this batsman tends to get out

a lot unless bowling spin, in which case you can be portly or even elderly, and wreak havoc as long as your name is Shane

loads could get smacked around, and sure to get injured at some point

loads as for batsmen, but it's harder work and bowlers get more injuries

fast if fielding close or saving one, average in the deep

hardly any just need to decide which end to throw the ball to, and how hard

a little if catching, a lot if saving one, some in the deep

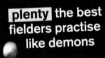

some could drop easy catch

plenty the best fielders practise like demons

none unless fielding close, but may need to react fast to changing situations

loads although it may be cricket intelligence rather than academic

none as shown by Inzamam-ul-Haq

loads could do everything right and still lose

loads must have big appetite for every facet of the game

CRICKETERS' BODY SHAPES

THE BEANPOLE

height	6ft 4 to 6ft 8
weight	12-13 stone
build	slim
job	fast bowler
current example	**Steve Harmison** (England)
past master	**Curtly Ambrose** (West Indies)

The beanpole looks as if he is built for basketball rather than cricket, but he is a key member of most teams. He opens the bowling, gliding to the wicket with a run-up which is rhythmic and deceptively mild, and getting the ball up into the batsman's ribs. His height means that the ball is 8 or 9ft above the ground when it leaves his hand; on some grounds, it is above the line of the sightscreen, which makes the batsman's task harder and gives the beanpole a touch of menace. He fields in the deep and bats at No 10 or 11, where he is either endearingly hopeless or a handy slogger. He gets called "lanky" by the press, and "streak of piss" by the coach (excuse his language). He becomes captain only if his team are a bit stuck and he has been around a long time, like Bob Willis of England in the 1980s and Courtney Walsh of West Indies in the 1990s.

THE HULK

height	6ft 2 to 6ft 5
weight	14-17 stone
build	hefty
job	fast bowler, batsman, or both
current example	**Andrew Flintoff** (England)
past master	**Ian Botham** (England)

The hulk has always found cricket easy because he was so much bigger than the other boys. His bowling has more than pace: it has weight, so that he delivers what the pros call "a heavy ball" – a delivery that seems to lose little of its pace when it pitches, so it slams into the top of the bat. As a batsman he can be unstoppably destructive, using his reach and muscle to strike the ball crisply off the front foot, but when things go wrong, they go very wrong. His movements become wooden and he mis-hits the ball into the hands of mid-off or mid-on. He fields well for a big man, standing at second slip and grabbing most of what comes his way, using what the papers call his big bucket hands. He may become captain by sheer force of personality ("larger than life," allegedly), but is no great tactician as he has never had to think much about his own game. He parties as hard as he plays, which can lead to trouble. Best kept away from pedalos.

6FT

5FT

4FT

3FT

2FT

1FT

MR AVERAGE

height	5ft 9 to 6ft 2
weight	11-13 stone
build	medium
job	batsman or slow bowler
current example	Andrew Strauss (England)
past master	Mike Atherton (England)

If you saw him in the street, you wouldn't guess he was a sportsman. Standing in a huddle with his team-mates, he may look a bit dull – he's Mr Middling, six inches taller than some of his mates and six inches smaller than others. But he is needed too. He either opens the batting or comes in at number five, as a canny accumulator and one-day finisher. He tends to have a normal personality: easy-going, level-headed, could make a great captain. If he bowls, he is probably a spinner, like Monty Panesar (6ft 1) or Shane Warne (variously described as 5ft 11 and 6ft). Extra height, producing extra bounce, helps spinners just as much as fast bowlers, but it's not essential: Murali is only 5ft 9. If the everyman is a batsman, he fields at slip or short leg. If he's a spinner, he is probably tucked away at square leg or mid-on, although a few spinners down the years, like Warne and Phil Edmonds, have been top-class catchers.

THE TITCH

height	5ft 3 to 5ft 7
weight	10-12 stone
build	wiry
job	batsman or wicketkeeper
current example	Sachin Tendulkar (India)
past master	Brian Lara (West Indies)

There's a saying, "Small is beautiful". And it is often true of batsmen. If you're one of the shorter ones in your class, don't worry – you can still be a giant of the game. You probably won't be a fast bowler, because you won't get enough bounce, but you can be a top batsman or keeper. Short players tend to be deft and well-organised, and they have the low centre of gravity which helps with most ball games because it gives good balance. They are nearly always back-footers, adept at the cut and the pull. Don Bradman, the greatest batsman of them all, was only 5ft 7. They usually field close in and may well become captain. They may not be so good at that: superstars like Tendulkar and Lara seldom make great leaders. But some little guys are a big hit as captain, like Mahela Jayawardene of Sri Lanka.

THE ROLY-POLY

height	5ft 8 to 6ft
weight	12-16 stone
build	comfortable
job	batsman or slow bowler
current example	Inzamam-ul-Haq (Pakistan)
past master	Mike Gatting (England)

One of the best things about cricket is that you don't have to be slim to play it. Or even athletic. There's a long tradition of cricketers with an ample frame. They are nearly always batsmen, although the first famous example, WG Grace, managed to combine a formidable waist measurement with a long career as an allrounder. These days, bowling is out, but the well-padded sportsman can still be a top-order batsman. Remember how important it is to get your weight into the shot? If he strikes the ball well enough, and stands at slip, he won't have to run much; if he is from the subcontinent, and has a lordly air about him, he can walk most of his runs. He often ends up as captain, and may have great success. Arjuna Ranatunga lifted the World Cup for Sri Lanka in 1996, combining the guile of a fox with the girth of a horse.

And England's last portly captain, Mike Gatting, led them to an Ashes win in 1986-87. Gatting also had the distinction of facing the ball of the century from Shane Warne in 1993. It swung into him, pitched outside leg stump, turned viciously the other way, and clipped the top of off. Martin Johnson wrote in *The Independent*: "How anyone can spin the ball the width of Gatting boggles the mind."

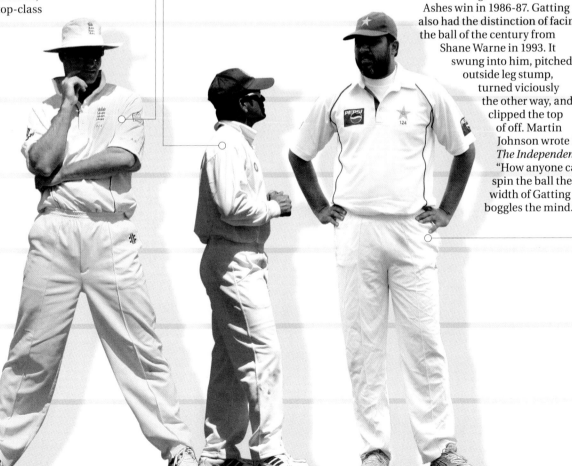

For a roll-call of roly-polies, go to www.cricinfo.com/columns/content/story/281064.html

A DAY IN THE LIFE OF

MARK RAMPRAKASH

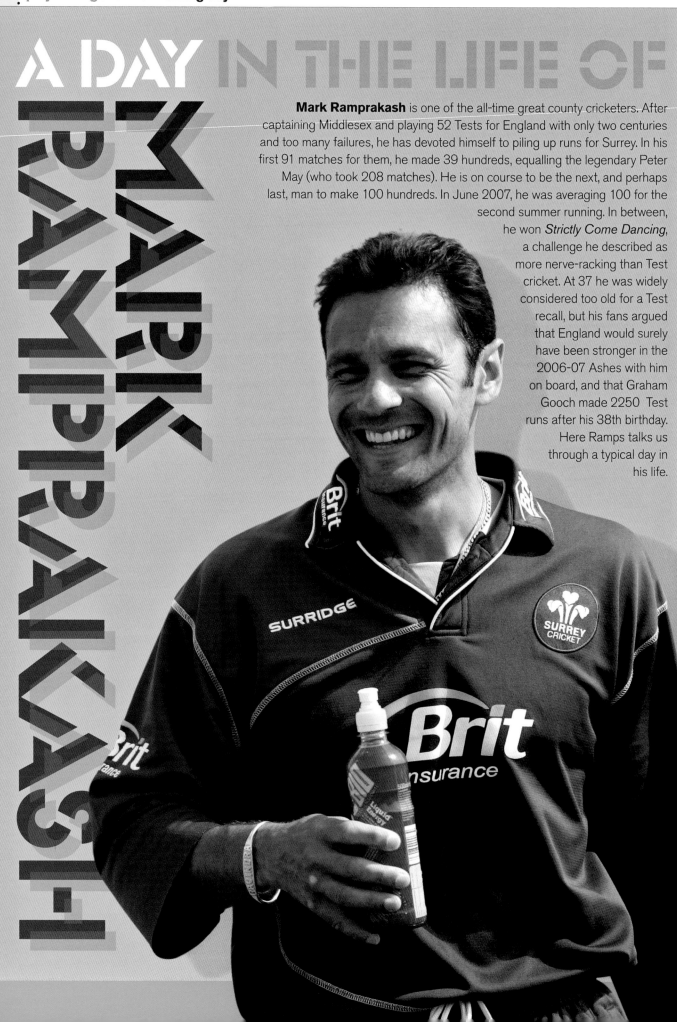

Mark Ramprakash is one of the all-time great county cricketers. After captaining Middlesex and playing 52 Tests for England with only two centuries and too many failures, he has devoted himself to piling up runs for Surrey. In his first 91 matches for them, he made 39 hundreds, equalling the legendary Peter May (who took 208 matches). He is on course to be the next, and perhaps last, man to make 100 hundreds. In June 2007, he was averaging 100 for the second summer running. In between, he won *Strictly Come Dancing*, a challenge he described as more nerve-racking than Test cricket. At 37 he was widely considered too old for a Test recall, but his fans argued that England would surely have been stronger in the 2006-07 Ashes with him on board, and that Graham Gooch made 2250 Test runs after his 38th birthday. Here Ramps talks us through a typical day in his life.

⏰ 6.45AM TO 8.30
getting up and out

For a home game, I set the alarm for about a quarter to seven. Quick shower, make my way down to the station by car – I did have a good intention to ride my bicycle down there, it's six or seven minutes by bike, but early season, it was often wet, so I ended up taking the car. I go to the Metropolitan Line station near where I live in north-west London. If it's a weekday, I always take the train. The journey takes around an hour. I read the paper or read a book, currently a Robert Ludlum thriller. I get to The Oval at half eight and go to the caff round the corner for baked beans on toast and scrambled egg.

🕘 9.00 TO 10.20
warming up

I get to the ground at nine. Quick change and then out to the nets with the bowling coach, Geoff Arnold, or another player, to do some throwdowns. It's not a full net, it's someone throwing balls off about 16 yards, seam up, different lengths, mixing it up. I like to get my batting out the way early. Sometimes I have a net, particularly early season. Surrey usually warm up as a team about 9.45 – a team stretch, led by one of our physios, then a five-minute game of football to get loose. I play now and again for the Arsenal charity side. Then some fielding, some catching. I like to go up to the dressing-room pretty early, about 10.20.

🕙 10.20
autograph time

When I come off the pitch, I'll often sign a few autographs. It really depends where you're playing. What we're finding at the outgrounds more and more is that people are in your face at every opportunity. I've noticed a big change in the last couple of years. Last week at Worcester, I arrived at the ground at five to nine, parked at the far end, a couple of guys came racing over to get autographs then, and it will happen constantly through the day, and I left quite late and three or four of them were still waiting at 7 o'clock at night. That's not just me, all the players are finding this – people bring books, pictures, four or five things each often – I don't quite know what they're doing with them. *Going on eBay, maybe?* Yes, possibly. *Do you still sign?* I certainly try and do all the kids that I can. It depends a little bit on what time of day you catch me. If I'm in the car park at the end, I'm a bit reluctant, my working day is done, I'm not so inclined to sign them as I've started at nine in the morning. Unfortunately the players are getting a little bit more careful about it – we'll do them at 10.20, we'll do them at lunchtime, but not at the end of the day.

◀ **ready** a bit of stretching and football before the match to warm up
▲ **willing (top)** signing another autograph for a young fan
▶ **able** the first wicket falls and Ramps goes in at No 3

🕥 10.30
tea and thinking

I'll have a cup of tea and a few biscuits and get the mind right. The captain does the toss at half ten and we'll find out whether we're batting or bowling. I usually have a little think before about the bowlers. Obviously most of them you know, but if there's someone new I'll try and find out whether anyone knows about him and his style of bowling, if we've got anything on the computer, try and take in any information.

🕚 11.00
start of play

If we're batting, I pad up straightaway – as a No 3, I have to be ready from ball one. Whilst I'm waiting to bat I will often keep an eye on the cricket, but also perhaps be sitting around with some of the other papers or watching the TV: I want to get the balance right between being ready to go in and not losing energy. If there's an early wicket, I don't mind that – get in early, 'cause the opposition are attacking, there are gaps, as a No 3 you can't mind getting in early. Having said that, if the openers hang around, then great, because they see off the new ball

and when you go in, the ball may be doing less. There are probably only four or five top-class spinners playing county cricket at the moment, so if you can see off that burst when the ball is new, and if the pitch is good and you're concentrating well, you want to go on to a big score. *Are you playing differently the last couple of years? Different mindset, or playing different strokes?* A little bit of both, I think. On the mental side, I saw John Crawley [an England contemporary] play yesterday and I heard Shaun Udal [Hampshire and England spinner] say that he may be 36 or whatever but he doesn't stop learning about the game. That's true. The last three or four years, my balance has been a lot better at the wicket, you're constantly tinkering with bits and pieces, constantly exploring the best way to do it for you.

I've never been a slip fielder. For Middlesex I was always at square cover. Now I've managed to find my way into the gully. I've always liked square of the wicket and at gully you do have to be quite sharp, quite on the ball. I like to make sure I've had a few flat catches, make sure the hands are ready. As the day wears on, I'll be anywhere around the outfield. I find with the long days in the field, I'm having to stretch constantly, you're out there for three sessions of two hours, it's easy to get stiff. You may have not much to do for half an hour, then suddenly you have to chase a ball. *Is your fielding as good as ever?* No. I've lost some pace, and diving is quite hard work, the grounds are hard, the back gets a little stiff, getting down is a little harder.

 1.15PM
lunch

Lunch is generally very good, we get a choice of perhaps fish, pasta or a lamb shank, something like that. The food at The Oval is excellent and we get treated very well. If I'm batting, I don't tend to eat as much – a bit of fruit or ice cream. If we're fielding, I pile it on.

after batting

If I've made runs, I'm happy to sit down, have a rest and recover, and I'll be in a good mood. If I've had a long day, I have the dreaded ice bath. It's very refreshing for the legs, I'm a convert to it. If I've missed a straight one, as can happen, I will perhaps have a gym session, working on either core stability or a bit of strength work or aerobic work. It's important to take any opportunity you can to keep ticking over. As you get older you've got to work hard at trying to stay in shape. You work very hard in the winter to get in shape and

then in the summer you're trying to maintain it. I'm lucky with my weight, I'm probably slightly lighter than I was at 18 – not for lack of trying, I've got a very sweet tooth. I don't drink alcohol, so that may help. When I did *Strictly Come Dancing*, I wasn't in the gym for about 14 weeks so I was losing strength. It's a different type of fitness. Dancing is mainly balance.

 **4.10**
tea

The sandwiches are quite good but I often have to bring in my own tea. I often go along to the caff and get a couple of chocolate chip cookies. I've really made an effort to cut down on cups of tea, it's not very good for you, it can dehydrate you, so I just have two or three in a day. As I've got older, I've paid much more attention to my nutrition and fluid intake. I try and drink the required amount of water, and if we've had a particularly tough day there is a powdered mix of stuff to rehydrate us. They say we should drink between 1.5 and 2 litres of water. If you can get close to that, you're doing pretty well.

Does that mean you have to think about when you can get to the loo? (laughs) In the morning is when I try and drink as much as I can, 500 mls of water. While I'm waiting to bat, I often have to go, because I'm trying to get hydrated for the day. Only last week I was actually in the gentlemen's room when a wicket went down. It didn't make me late but it was close. I don't know how other sports people handle it, footballers and that, they seem to

◄▲ "Quite hard work" fielding against Hampshire at the Rose Bowl; ▲ "Constantly exploring" (top) facing Kent at Whitgift School, where he made his fifth century of 2007

be drinking all the time, but I suppose they've only got to spend 90 minutes out there.

6.30
close of play

I don't really do warm-downs, it's a long enough day as it is. We come off at 6.30 or sometimes later, slow change, possibly an ice bath, then a shower, looking to leave around 7ish. Usually get a lift with Nayan Doshi [Surrey spinner] to Finchley or one of the Metropolitan stations so that saves me a bit of walking, and hopefully I'm back to the station near my house at 8.15, home by half eight. It's a long day but it was my choice to go to Surrey and not to move house. My journey is not dissimilar to a lot of players'. Sometimes it's a relief when we're playing away because you stay [in a hotel] a lot closer to the ground. We don't tend to go for drinks, because everyone's got journeys. When I started, at Lord's, we'd go to the Tavern, but that really doesn't happen now unless you have a very good friend that you've been touring with over the years. At Worcester Ian Salisbury [Surrey and England spinner] and I went out for dinner with Graeme Hick [England contemporary] and his wife. Players are more inclined to get back to their families, I've got two young girls and I want to see them, I value my time at home.

8.30
home again

The girls are in bed, but they come running down, so I have a chat with them for five to ten minutes. My wife will have already eaten. I'll have my dinner and we'll watch something like an episode of CSI. Then to bed about 10.15 and the whole thing starts again. *If anyone reading this wants to be a cricketer, would you recommend it?* Oh yeah, without a doubt. I can't express how lucky I've been to be a professional cricketer. I've travelled all over the world, Australia, the Caribbean, Asia, and in the English summer, I'm not stuck in an office. Of course, it is a job, and you have to work very hard at it, because it's a competitive life and the results are there for all to see. But it is a great life. I'm 37 and making the most of the years I've got left.

Ramprakash's purple patch, score by score

2006

67
v Durham UCCE, The Oval, Apr 5-17

71, 12
v Derbys, The Oval, Apr 19-22

113, 22
v Leics, Leicester, Apr 26-29

292
v Gloucs, The Oval, May 3-5

118
v Worcs, The Oval, May 17-20

14, 48
v Essex, Whitgift School, May 31-June 3

73
v Leics, The Oval, June 7-10

87no, 51
v Somerset, Bath, June 14-16

20, 156
v Glamorgan, Swansea, June 20-23

51, 155
v Northants, Northampton, July 14-17

167
v Somerset, Guildford, July 19-22

301no, 30
v Northants, The Oval, Aug 2-5

196
v Worcs, Worcester, Aug 8-10

77, 31
v Glamorgan, the Oval, Aug 30-Sept 1

75, 51
v Gloucs, Bristol, Sept 6-9

CLOSE SEASON

not picked for England's Ashes tour, even when Marcus Trescothick flies home

- reluctantly persuaded by his wife and daughters to go in for *Strictly Come Dancing* on BBC1. Teams up with Karen Hardy and wins the series, collecting a perfect 40/40 from the judges for his salsa, wearing some very flouncy shirts, and making a few hearts flutter.

- named as one of *Wisden's* Five Cricketers of the Year

2007

115, 5
v Yorks, The Oval, Apr 18-22

107no, 43
v Hants, The Oval, Apr 25-28

13, 7
v Lancs, Old Trafford, May 2-4

128no
v Warks, The Oval, May 9-12

266no
v Sussex, Hove, May 16-19

35, 108
v Kent, Whitgift School, May 30-June 2

84, 33
v Worcs, Worcester, June 6-9

YEAR	MAT	RUNS	HS	AVE	100/50	4s/6s
2006	15	2278	301*	103.54	8/9	316/20
2007	7	936	266*	104.00	5/1	122/10

Scores (first-class only) from Cricinfo.com, to June 10, 2007, before the break for the Twenty20 Cup

DON BRADMAN
THE BEST BATSMAN EVER

Click! Clack! Click! Clang! The noise rang down the street, all day long. It was made by a small boy, a golf ball, a cricket stump, a water tank and a brick stand. The tank stood on the stand, behind the boy's home. Hour after hour, under a harsh sun, the boy would hit the ball with the stump against the stand, which was curved, so the ball would bounce back at odd angles. Hitting it with the stump took patience, concentration, and an amazing eye.

Without knowing it, the boy was giving himself a great training for Test cricket. After that stump, a bat always felt like a luxury. Donald Bradman was the fifth and youngest child, so he always had company and competition, but he liked solitude too. Destiny was designing the perfect character for a team game with a strong individual element.

The Bradmans lived in Bowral, outside Sydney. In 1920, aged 12, Don made his first hundred for Bowral school. His uncle played for the town team and Don became their scorer. Once, they let him bat, at No 10, and he made 37 not out. He was given his first bat, a battered old thing, as a thank-you. It was too big, so his father cut 3in off the bottom. His dad also took him to Sydney to see a Test match – Australia v England. Australia were 4-0 up and wanted a whitewash. They got it. "I shall never be happy," Don announced, "until I play on this ground." His father smiled "with affectionate tolerance".

By 14, Don had left school and gone to work for an estate agent. Pressed for time, he spent one summer playing tennis, not cricket. When he picked up his bat again, he made 234 for Bowral against Wingello. In a district final against Moss Vale, a match spread over five Saturdays, Bradman made 300.

He joined a Sydney team, St George, and made a hundred on debut, but went back to Bowral to make 320 not out in another final against poor Moss Vale. On debut for his state, New South Wales, he made 118. He moved to Sydney, faced England for the first time in a tour match, and made 87 and 132 not out. At 5ft 7, he wasn't big, but he was quick, nimble, crafty, attacking … and insatiable.

Picked for Australia aged 20, he surely couldn't fail. But he did. He made 18 and 1 as England inflicted a humiliating 675-run defeat. He was dropped; Australia lost again. He was recalled; Australia lost yet again, but he starred with 79 and 112 – the youngest man to make a Test hundred. He added another as Australia won a consolation victory. A year later, against Queensland, he made 452 not out, a world first-class record. He mostly evaded the field, but once, batting against Victoria, he announced "a round-up" and hit the ball to each fielder in turn, going anti-clockwise from slip to fine leg.

Touring England in 1930, the prodigy became a legend. In the Tests, he made 8, 131, 254, 1, 334, 14 and 232, and Australia won back the Ashes. The 334 at Headingley, then a Test record, is still famous because he made 309 in a day, but Bradman himself preferred the 254 at Lord's as "practically … every ball went where it was intended to go". A businessman sent him £1000, worth £30,000 today; his team-mates noted that he still didn't buy them a drink. The Australian public didn't mind. To them, he was a hero and a symbol of national strength.

In 1932 Bradman married Jessie Menzies in what he called the best partnership of his life. Under pressure to make huge scores, he usually succeeded, although his health suffered. The English, desperate to stop him, hatched a dastardly plan: to bowl at the batsman's body with a slip cordon on the leg rather than the off. It was labelled Bodyline. Bradman missed the first Test because of a row over his newspaper column, then returned to a standing ovation – and was out first ball. But he made a hundred in the second innings and Australia were level at 1-1. He kept making runs, but his series average of 56 was the worst of his Test career. England won the series and lost the goodwill of the cricket world. Bodyline was outlawed.

Bradman practises at Lord's in 1948

The Bradmans moved to Adelaide and Don became a stockbroker. Even a genius couldn't be a full-time cricketer in those days. Back in England in 1934, he made 244 and 304 to win back the Ashes, but then fell ill. After having his appendix out, he got peritonitis, a dangerous disease of the gut. Jessie set off for England not knowing if he would be alive when she got there. King George – of Australia as well as Britain – asked to be kept informed. Bradman pulled through.

He became Australia's captain. They went 2-0 down in the 1936-37 Ashes, and he shocked his fans by making consecutive ducks. But then he piled up 270, 212 and 169 to engineer a fairy-tale 3-2 win. In 1939, he took up squash to keep fit – and won the South Australia Open Squash Championship. His glittering career was rudely interrupted by the Second World War: he tried to serve as an airman, then a soldier, but was thwarted by a bad back. The army even said he had poor eyesight. Just think how well he might have batted if he'd been able to see properly.

In 1948, aged 40, Bradman led the Australians on one last Ashes tour. They were so good, they were labelled The Invincibles. "Next to Mr Winston Churchill," said *Wisden*, "he was the most celebrated man in England." In his final innings, at The Oval, he needed just four runs to keep his Test career average above 100. The crowd gave him a thunderous ovation and the England team gave him three cheers. A modest legspinner, Eric Hollies, bowled a googly, and Bradman, who (some said) had a tear in his eye, missed it. He was out for 0; his average was 99.94. No other man has managed more than 60 over a complete career. He wasn't just the best batsman ever: he was the best by miles.

Find out more at www.bradman.org

BATTING
ATTACK AND DEFENCE

The art of batting comes down
to two things. Do make runs;
don't get out. So a batsman must
be able to attack and to defend

Attack

When lions are stalking a herd of antelope, they bide
their time until one of the weaker ones gets separated
from the rest. Many batsmen take a
similar approach. They wait for the
bad ball, then pounce.

The weakness may be the
ball's length – either too short or
too full. The batsman shifts his
weight accordingly, rocking back
or stepping forwards. Or it may be
the line – either wide of off stump,
or heading for the batsman's pads.
That allows him to swing the bat.
Result: the short ball, or long hop,
gets cut past cover, pulled through
midwicket, or hooked to deep square
leg. The full ball, or half-volley, gets
driven through the covers, down
the ground ("in the V"), or flicked
through square leg.

The best batsmen can attack
good balls too, if their eye is in and
the pitch is trustworthy. They treat
a good-length ball like a half-volley,
hitting through the line as the pros
say. That really freaks the bowler out.
If the good balls are going for four,
what should he do? Bowl a bad one?

Defence

These days most batsmen are strokeplayers who prefer to attack, which makes cricket more fun to watch. But every batsman has to do some defending, and even a great attacking innings will contain dozens of defensive shots.

Traditionally, most teams have had at least one blocker, someone who doesn't fret if the runs come slowly. Often he's an opener, because the fast bowlers are most dangerous early on – fresh, hungry and armed with a shiny, hard ball.

The last blocker to open for a major Test team was **Mark Richardson** of New Zealand, who retired in 2004. He plodded along with a strike rate (runs per 100 balls) of 37. It worked for him: his batting average was 44.

He was a slow runner too, so he started a tradition whereby, at the end of a Test series, he would challenge his least athletic opponent to a charity race. Richardson would squeeze himself into a bodysuit which was tight, beige and hideous. That's the thing about slow scorers: they're not bothered about looking good.

The last England star in the same mould was **Mike Atherton**, who played 108 Tests, retiring in 2001, and also had a strike rate of 37. At Johannesburg in 1995-96, England had to bat for 10 hours to save a Test – so that's what Atherton did. He survived for 643 minutes, faced 492 balls and made 185 not out. He wore the same kit throughout, thinking it might be bad luck to change. "I must have smelt like a polecat," he wrote in his autobiography, "but superstition was stronger than the smell or the discomfort."

Between attack and defence

Between attack and defence lies nudging and nurdling. A batsman may have a short backlift and no follow-through, but he is picking out the gaps, so the runs tick over. Remember, four runs an over is a good scoring rate. A strokeplayer like Michael Vaughan will get them with one handsome shot. A nudger like **Paul Collingwood** might get them with a scampered two and a single and another single if his partner gives him back the strike. The end result is just the same – except that Collingwood is a lot sweatier.

Beyond attack and defence

Attack and defence are not quite the opposites they seem. There are times when attack brings hardly any runs – say if the ball is moving around a lot and you can't middle it. And sometimes defence brings quite a few – say if there is no third man, and you have a solid defensive technique, keeping the ball down even when you edge it. Or when a player of great strength, like Andrew Flintoff, blocks the ball and it goes for four.

Attack can be an effective form of defence. Imagine you're facing a spinner who has three men round you, waiting for the bat-pad catch, like dogs hoping for a piece of cheese from the table. If you **hit a few fours**, those men will go back into run-saving positions. And then you'll be able to edge the ball into your pad and get away with it.

▲ Attack Jacques Kallis of South Africa makes Andrew Strauss of England leap out of the way during the third Test at Cape Town in January, 2005 ⟩⟩⟩

BATTING THE 4 CHOICES

A batsman is forever choosing between pairs of opposites

PLAY OR LEAVE

Illustrations by Major
JA Board, from the
*MCC Cricket Coaching
Book*, 1952

Sometimes, especially early on, the batsman won't play a stroke at all. It's usually because the ball is wide of off stump, and he would have to reach for it, which might mean edging a catch to the wicketkeeper or slips.

Leaving isn't as passive as it sounds. It tells the bowler he is wasting energy bowling wide, which makes him bowl straighter. Then the batsman can tuck the ball off his legs, a shot most top players find easy. But the key to leaving it is choosing the right ball. If the ball moves in and clips the off stump, it looks horrible.

BACKWARD OR FORWARD

When we first play cricket, we think batting is all about hitting, so we swing the bat. And we often miss the ball, because we haven't moved our feet. A good shot needs your weight in it as well as your hands, and it's your feet that carry your weight. You need to decide: am I playing back or forward? You may take a small step, like Marcus Trescothick, or a giant one, like **Kevin Pietersen**. The choice hinges on the length of the ball. If it is short, you need to be on the back foot; if it is pitched up, the front. Come to think of it, Pietersen hardly ever goes back. Maybe he should try it.

STRAIGHT BAT OR HORIZONTAL

Defensive shots are usually played with a straight bat. That's because the ball is usually straight – ie, probably hitting the stumps. By playing with an upright bat, you have the best chance of making contact. You can afford to misjudge the length a bit: it will just mean that the ball arrives higher or lower on the bat, which may jar (because it will hit solid wood, not the springs) but won't get you out. Most batsmen would rather be in pain than back in the pavilion.

A horizontal bat is mostly for short deliveries. If they're wide as well, you cut them. If they're aimed at your body, you pull them. If they're at your head, you hook them. If they're over your head, you leave them and hope the umpire signals wide.

The other horizontal-bat shot is the sweep, normally played to a spinner. You stretch forward to meet the ball on the half-volley or close to it, and sweep it towards square leg or finer. You have to get your head low. **Mal Loye**, of Lancashire and England, likes to sweep fast bowlers, which makes for a thrilling sight when it works, and a nasty bruise when it doesn't.

4 OFFSIDE OR ONSIDE

Little kids having their first go at cricket often try to hit everything to leg, because that's a natural swing. Pushing out, away from your body, comes less naturally, but the top players have to master it. Most players end up stronger on one side or the other, just as some prefer the back foot or the front.

Of course the direction of the shot depends on where the bowler bowls. Anyone facing South Africa needs to be strong on the off side, as the South Africans love to bowl eight inches outside off stump. Facing Shane Warne, you need to be able to play on the on side, as he lands the ball on or outside leg stump. Only two shots, the pull and the sweep, normally involve going from off to leg, although the best players of the on-drive, like Sachin Tendulkar of India, can do it from off stump. Only the reverse sweep goes from leg to off, and not many players try it.

One of the most classical shots, the straight drive, is played straight down the ground. As well as delighting elderly coaches, it is a winner in one-day cricket, because there is never a fielder directly behind the bowler. Don't go too straight, though: you'll hit the other set of stumps, and if the bowler has got a fingertip to the ball, your partner could be run out.

CONCLUSION

If you can make all these decisions in half a second and get most of them right, you'll be a top batsman. If not, you may have a future as a bowler. Or an antelope.

FAST BOWLING

It is one of the most
stirring sights in sport: a fast bowler
racing in off a long run-up and hurling the
ball at 90mph towards the batsman's feet, chest
or head. It gets the heart pumping even if you're
just watching from the safety of the sofa. But there is a
lot more to fast bowling than brute force. It's an art that
consists of five separate strengths ...

Pace

90 mph

Most top batsmen are comfortable facing bowling at 80-85mph. If a bowler can get past 90, that comfort evaporates, and the batsman can be hurried or unnerved, which is a polite word for terrified. Duncan Fletcher, the England coach from 1999 to 2007, was always looking for that extra few mph, and was prepared to select a bowler like Sajid Mahmood, who offered pace without much control. The ploy backfired: Mahmood became the most expensive one-day bowler England had ever had. But pace has its place – it's great for blasting out tailenders.

The fastest bowlers in the world today are **Shaun Tait** of Australia, around 94mph; Brett Lee, also of Australia, around 92 with the odd ball going up to 96; Shane Bond of New Zealand, around 93 when fit; and Shoaib Akhtar of Pakistan. Akhtar is one of cricket's bad boys, always getting into trouble, whether for alleged ball-tampering, alleged drug-taking, or for not playing through the pain. But he is highly gifted and when he is fast, he is very fast. At Cape Town in the 2003 World Cup, with a strong wind behind him, he bowled the first 100mph ball ever recorded, to Nick Knight of England. I was there and although it did seem lightning-fast, it wasn't very eventful. Knight played it easily enough, nudging it to square leg. The trouble was that it didn't have any ...

Movement

A ball that goes straight, however fast, is a ball a good batsman can usually handle. If it moves sideways, it's another story. Fast bowlers move the ball in one of three ways: seam, swing, or reverse swing.

Seam means keeping the seam upright and landing the ball on the seam, which makes it deviate a little or a lot depending on the pitch (see page 16). If it seams away, the batsman may edge the ball for a catch behind the wicket. If it seams in, he may be bowled or LBW. The new ball moves most because the seam sticks out less once the ball gets bashed around. The leading seamers in the world today are Stuart Clark of Australia and Mohammad Asif of Pakistan – tall men with upright actions, who get lift (see far right) as well as movement.

Swing achieves the same effect through the air. Late swing is especially dangerous. Orthodox swing happens with the new ball, which is shiny on both sides, or with a ball which is shiny on one side: the ball swings away from the shiny side. And it is helped by cloud cover. A leading swing bowler is Matthew Hoggard of England, who naturally moves the ball away from the right-hander and into the left-hander, but has an excellent variation, the nip-backer, which gets right-handers LBW or left-handers caught at slip. Reverse swing happens with the old ball, when it has been roughed up by an abrasive surface. The swing comes later in the ball's trajectory and it is usually inswing, homing in on the batsman's feet. Lasith Malinga of Sri Lanka (Malinga the Slinger)

produced a fabulous spell of reverse swing against South Africa in the 2007 World Cup, taking four wickets in successive balls with what appeared to be laser-guided missiles. Unfortunately South Africa spoiled the story by clinging on to win by one wicket. Somehow, despite bowling round-arm, **Malinga** has developed plenty of …

Control

Even pace and movement are not much use without control. Control means making the ball pitch where you want. It comes with experience, and often increases as pace fades. Some bowlers use control to land the ball in the same place again and again. Andrew Flintoff of England is like that. When Hawk-Eye shows his pitch map, all the blobs are in a cluster, in what Geoff Boycott famously called the corridor of uncertainty: around off stump, on a good length, or in Flintoff's case, a touch shorter – back of a length, as the players call it.

Other bowlers use control to create variations. In one-day cricket, a bowler can't just keep putting the ball in the same place. If he has movement and control, a bowler may not need pace. **Glenn McGrath** of Australia became almost medium-paced in his mid-thirties, but kept on taking wickets. He ended up with 563 of them in Tests, more than any other seamer, and was also the leading wicket-taker in the 2007 World Cup. It helped that he had …

Lift

If the ball stays low, the batsman can get his head over it and control it. If it bounces, it is much harder to keep down. Lift comes from two things: a bouncy pitch, and a tall bowler. If you ever bump into a cricket team at an airport – quite likely, as they do a ridiculous amount of flying – you'll notice that a third of them are giants. Mainly fast bowlers.

Tall bowlers are lethal on uneven pitches, when some balls scuttle through at ankle height, because the difference between that and their normal delivery is that much greater, so it's as if the batsman is playing on a trampoline one moment and an ice-rink the next. Steve Harmison of England gets a lot of lift. He is quick too, but he has a drifty action, and the ball slows down a lot after bouncing. His friend Flintoff doesn't have this flaw: he bowls a so-called heavy ball, which seems to retain its pace all the way into the top of the bat (ouch). And Flintoff has an extra helping of …

Heart

Fast bowling may be glamorous, but it's also hard work. In each spell, the bowler has to run 25 yards or so, 30 to 50 times, and walk back the same distance. It takes perseverance and determination. A bowler with a big heart will keep steaming in even late in the day when he has taken none for plenty. **Merv Hughes** of Australia (1985-94) was a prime example. In fact, he seemed to consist entirely of a big heart and a moustache to match. But he took 212 Test wickets and some of them were superstars.

FLING IT LIKE FLINTOFF
Five fast-bowling tips from the man himself

1 **Develop a comfortable, rhythmic run-up** but not necessarily longer – it won't make you any quicker

2 **Accelerate through your run-up** so you explode into the crease

3 **Keep your wrist steady behind the ball** a hard trick to learn, but it gets easier with practice

4 **Bowl at 90% pace most of the time** save the extra 10% for the big effort balls – yorkers and bouncers

5 **Develop variations** to become a bowler your captain can call upon in any conditions

Adapted from the website of Andrew Flintoff's agents, ISM. For full text, see www.cricketism.com/ism/sites/cricketism/tips.shtml

SLOW BOWLING

It's not fast, but it is clever.
And it can tie even the best
batsmen in knots

About 25 years ago, spin bowling was heading
for the rubbish dump. The cricket world was
ruled by West Indies, who often didn't even
pick a spinner – they just had four top-class
fast bowlers pounding in all day at the
hapless batsman. But spin never died out
on the Indian subcontinent, and soon a
legspinner, **Abdul Qadir**, was winning
matches for Pakistan. Australia went
through years of very ordinary spinners,
but then along came Shane Warne, who
would become the biggest wicket-taker
of all. He made spin bowling fashionable
again, and was soon joined on his pedestal
by **Muttiah Muralitharan**, the world's
weirdest bowler, with his double joints, his
huge turn and his bulging eyes, forever
expressing astonishment at how many
wickets he is taking. Thanks to these two,
there is now a healthy balance between slow
bowling and fast, between guile and force. In
fact, if anything, we could do with some more
fast bowlers.

Spin bowling is one of the best things about
cricket. It looks gentle and friendly and hittable, yet it
can be devastating. It comes from either the wrist or the
fingers. Usually, it is hard for wrist-spinners to control
the ball, so they go for a lot of runs, but Warne changed that.
Finger-spinners have more control, but less turn.

Both types of spinner need more than spin. They need
flight, also known as loop or dip – something to sow doubt in
the batsman's mind about whether to play forward or back. The
young Warne even brought swing into it – his leg-breaks would
swerve into the batsman before spinning the other way, which

▲ **Warne's trailblazer** Abdul Qadir
gets the wicket of Allan Lamb at
Karachi in 1983-84. He picked up
eight wickets in the match, helping
Pakistan to a three-wicket win, and
18 in the three-match series

was a fabulous trick. Spinners also need a variation ball (see table below), sometimes called a mystery ball. And they may even vary their stock ball, changing their pace and making it turn more or less. When **Warne** took a hat-trick against England at Melbourne in 1994-95, all three balls were leg-breaks, but they all had different amounts of spin on them.

To bat against spin, you need to be able to read it, ie spot which way the ball is spinning. Some batsmen can do that from the hand, by noticing a change of action. Others do it off the pitch, which means they usually have to play back, to give themselves time to adjust.

As bats gets heavier and boundaries shorter, spin bowling keeps being written off. But it always bounces back. And a great spinner can keep going for longer, both on the day, and through a career. The biggest Test wicket-taker of all time is Warne, and the only men with any chance of catching him are two fellow spinners – Murali and Anil Kumble. This is one race in which the tortoise really does beat the hare.

▲ **Hat-trick** Melbourne, 1994-95: Shane Warne gets his third wicket in three balls, Devon Malcolm caught by David Boon. The other two wickets were Phil DeFreitas lbw, and Darren Gough caught by Ian Healy. England were all out for 92

TYPE OF SPIN	BOWLED WITH	COMES FROM	TURNS FROM	VARIATION/S	COMMON?
Leg spin	right arm	wrist	leg to off	googly – off to leg flipper – shoots straight on	not very
Off spin	right arm	fingers	off to leg	(trad) arm ball – gentle outswinger (modern) doosra – leg to off	very
Slow left-arm	left arm	fingers	leg to off	arm ball – gentle inswinger	quite
Chinaman	left arm	wrist	off to leg	wrong'un – leg to off	not at all

TYPE OF SPIN	INCISIVE?	EXPENSIVE?	BEST EXPONENT TODAY	BEST EVER
Leg spin	can be very	can be very	Anil Kumble (I) – 547 wkts* at 28, though he is more of a topspinner	Shane Warne (A) – 708 wkts at 25, and a phenomenal ability to rise to the occasion. Not so hot against India though
Off spin	moderately	not very	Muttiah Muralitharan (SL) – has made off spin far more dangerous	Murali – 674 wkts at 21, turns it on almost any surface. Of the old school, Jim Laker (E) – 193 at 21, one-tenth of them in one Test (see page 104)
Slow left-arm	moderately	not very	Daniel Vettori (NZ) – 229 wkts at 34 and often in the top five ODI bowlers	Bishan Bedi (I) – 266 at 28, and top marks for style. But it could end up being another man in a patka: Monty Panesar (E) – 42 at 33
Chinaman	occasionally	can be very	Brad Hogg (A) – wily one-day bowler with two World Cup medals	Probably **Johnny Wardle** (E; 102 at 20), who used to switch from normal slow left-arm when the mood took him. He was also rather a good cartoonist

*all figures are for Tests

ALLROUNDERS

Cricket is designed so that everybody gets a breather – except the umpires, and one type of player. The allrounder. He is the only person expected to be a frontline batsman and a frontline bowler.

He needs bags of energy and two completely different sets of skills. He may even show two different sides of his personality. Sir Richard

Hadlee, New Zealand's greatest player, batted like a millionaire and bowled like a bank manager.

Captains and selectors love allrounders for the same reason that your mum or dad likes special offers at the supermarket: they're getting two for the price of one. When Andrew Flintoff plays, Michael Vaughan has five bowlers to play with, which means it doesn't matter if one of them is having an off day.

You don't have to have one. In fact, two of the best teams of all time didn't bother with allrounders. The West Indians of the 1980s just picked six batsmen, a wicketkeeper, and four fast bowlers.

And the Australians of the past decade played six batsmen, a wicketkeeper, three fast bowlers, and Shane Warne. But both those teams did have sort-of allrounders, because their wicketkeepers, Jeffrey Dujon and Adam Gilchrist, were also frontline batsmen.

Different teams have different habits when it comes to allrounders. Pakistan produce lots of them, India very few. South Africa and New Zealand produce more than Australia, although Australia almost always have the better team. West Indies haven't had many allrounders over the years, but they did have Garry Sobers, probably the greatest of them all.

The traditional test of a true allrounder is this: is his batting

KEY
✎ batting style
● bowling style
⚠ point of interest

2 JACQUES KALLIS
SA 1995-, 106 Tests

✎ rock-solid No 3 or 4
● beefy fourth seamer
⚠ greedy against minnows – average v Bang and Zim is 223

8430 runs at `55.09`
213 wickets at `31.71`
difference `+ 23.38`

3 IMRAN KHAN
Pak 1971-92, 88 Tests

✎ correct No 8 who rose to 5
● top-class inswing
⚠ a great captain as well, now a politician

3807 runs at `37.69`
362 wickets at `22.81`
difference `+ 14.88`

1 GARRY SOBERS
WI 1954-74, 93 Tests

✎ left-hander, great power
● left-arm, both fast and slow
⚠ born with a sixth finger on each hand, swiftly removed

8032 runs at `57.78`
235 wickets at `34.03`
difference `+ 23.75`

4 AUBREY FAULKNER
SA 1906-24, 25 Tests

✎ gritty, unorthodox battler
● leggie with a quicker ball
⚠ became a famous coach but ended up killing himself

1754 runs at `40.79`
82 wickets at `26.58`
difference `+ 14.21`

5 KEITH MILLER
Aus 1946-56, 55 Tests

✎ classical No 5
● genuine quick
⚠ ex fighter pilot. "Pressure," he said, "is a Messerschmitt up the arse"

2958 runs at `36.97`
170 wickets at `22.97`
difference `+ 14.00`

6 SHAUN POLLOCK
SA 1995-, 107 Tests

✎ elegant No 8 or 9
● immaculate swing
⚠ 26 Tests as captain, when his averages were 41 and 21

3781 runs at `32.31`
416 wickets at `23.19`
difference `+ 9.12`

average higher than his bowling average? Flintoff, after a tough Ashes series in 2006-07, was on 32 for both batting and bowling, but that's deceptive because he had a poor start. If you look at his figures since January 2004, he averages 38 with the bat and 27 with the ball – top stuff.

The one problem with this yardstick is that it favours batsmen who don't bowl much. It's not hard to have a bowling average of 35 if you only bowl a bit. Here are the top allrounders in Test history, using the averages yardstick, but with two qualifications. I've left out those who have played fewer than 25 Tests, as stamina is a big part of being an allrounder – although this is harsh on Willie Bates, the England offspinner of the 1880s,

whose career was cut short after 15 Tests because he was hit in the eye by a ball. I've also left out those who have taken two wickets per Test or fewer. Jacques Kallis just sneaks over that line.

There should really be extra marks for being a successful captain, which would bring Imran Khan and Monty Noble up the list, and to some extent Shaun Pollock and Tony Greig. An allrounder-captain is three players in one, which is an amazing, gravity-defying achievement. There should also be an extra credit for being a genuine fast bowler, like Imran, Miller, Gregory and Flintoff. Anyone who can do that and make a hundred as well is a genius. So the greatest allrounder of all time is Sobers … but Imran is right up there too.

THE MOST AMAZiNG ALL-ROUND TEST MATCH
Ian Botham
England v India, Bombay, 1979-80

⚠ First he took **6 for 58** as India scored 242.

⚠ Then he went in with England wobbling at 57 for 4 and made **114** to see them to 296.

⚠ Then he took **7 for 48** and India were all out for 149.

⚠ Then he put his feet up as England's openers knocked off the 96 they needed.

⚠ **A hundred and a five-for** in the same Test has been done 26 times.

⚠ Botham has done it more than anyone else – **five times**.

7 TREVOR GODDARD
SA 1955-70, 41 Tests

✎ correct, left-handed opener
● accurate left-arm swing
⚠ "a walking coaching manual," Cricinfo says. Later an evangelist preacher

2516 runs at `34.46`
123 wickets at `26.22`
difference `+ 8.24`

8 TONY GREiG
Eng 1972-77, 58 Tests

✎ No 6, aggressive front-footer
● third seamer and offspinner
⚠ grew up in SA, captained England and recruited for Kerry Packer

3599 runs at `40.43`
141 wickets at `32.20`
difference `+ 8.23`

9 JACK GREGORY
Aus 1920-28, 24 Tests

✎ left-handed blaster, didn't use gloves
● hostile quick
⚠ giant who played "like a nuclear explosion," as Neville Cardus wrote

1146 runs at `36.96`
85 wickets at `31.15`
difference `+ 5.81`

10 MONTY NOBLE
Aus 1898-1909, 42 Tests

✎ adaptable No 1, 2, 3, 4, 5 …
● medium-pacer and offspinner
⚠ also a shrewd captain. His nickname was Mary Ann

1997 runs at `30.25`
121 wickets at `25.00`
difference `+ 5.25`

11 iAN BOTHAM
Eng 1977-92, 102 Tests

✎ hard-hitting No 6
● king of the swingers
⚠ superstar, charity walker, now a commentator

5200 runs at `33.54`
383 wkts at `28.40`
difference `+ 5.14`

12 RiCHARD HADLEE
NZ 1973-90, 86 Tests

✎ left-hander, useful slogger
● immaculate seamer
⚠ so good that he was knighted before he retired

3124 runs at `27.16`
431 wickets at `22.29`
difference `+ 4.87`

Bubbling under
Chris Cairns (NZ 1989-2004) + 4.13
Kapil Dev (Ind 1978-94) + 1.41
Trevor Bailey (Eng 1949-59) + 0.53
Andrew Flintoff (Eng 1998-) +0.48

▲ **Best in the world** – but not
in the Test side. Chris Read
of Nottinghamshire stumps
Mansoor Amjad of Leicestershire
in a Championship match at
Trent Bridge, 2007

WICKETKEEPING

In most groups of people, there's somebody who is busier than everyone else. They are always in the thick of things, making things happen, knowing what's going on, chatting, bustling, oozing energy. In a cricket team, it's nearly always the wicketkeeper.

The keeper is different. He is the only fielder wearing gloves and pads. He is the busiest person on the field, touching the ball about four times an over. He has the best view of anyone apart from the umpire. He is seldom the captain – he's just too busy – but he is the hub of the team.

Three jobs in one

The keeper needs three distinct sets of skills. When the fast bowlers are on, he is a goalie, throwing himself sideways – except that he is not supposed to tip the ball round the post, and he should probably refrain from punching it. When the spinners come on, he has to be an artist, standing up to the stumps, reading the spin, whipping the bails off if the batsman wanders out of his crease. And all day long, he has to be a cheerleader, bossing the fielders, praising the bowlers ("Like it, Monty!"), and holding the whole show together. Matt Prior, who took over as England keeper in May 2007, talks about trying to create "bubble and intensity". Paul Nixon, who kept for England in the 2007 World Cup, said he tried "to drip-feed negativity into the batsman's ear".

He also has to bat, so that's a fourth job. For decades, keepers were allowed to average about 27 in the lower order. Then along came Adam Gilchrist of Australia, who averaged 50 and destroyed attacks. So now most teams want a batsman-keeper rather than the other way round. The best keeper in the world is probably **Chris Read**, of Nottinghamshire and England, who has immaculate soft hands. But whenever he gets into the England team, he gets dropped again, because he doesn't make many runs.

THE WACKY WiCKY

Many wicketkeepers become quite eccentric. **Jack Russell**, the Gloucestershire and England keeper in the 1990s, wore the same hat through his whole career from 1981 to 2004. It needed repairing at regular intervals and the only person allowed to do the mending was Russell's wife, Alison. Russell was also very particular about what he would eat for lunch: two Weetabix, soaked in milk for exactly 12 minutes, and a mashed banana. He drank about 20 cups of tea a day, all made with the same teabag, which he would hang on a nail in the dressing-room, ready for the next cup. But he was a fantastic keeper, who could stand up to fast-medium bowlers and take stumpings down the leg side, and he was a big reason why Gloucestershire were the best county one-day team of the early 2000s. He is now a successful painter, specialising in cricket scenes.

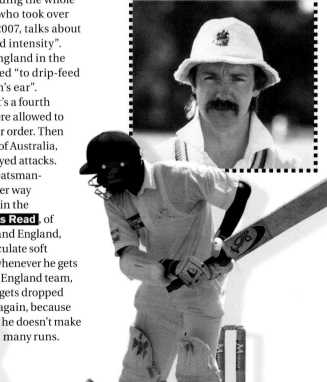

FIELDING

Fielding is almost the opposite of wicketkeeping. A fielder may have very little to do, and he could be miles from the centre of the action. But when the ball comes to him, he has to be wide awake and ready to catch it, stop it, chase it, dive for it, and fire it into the stumps. Fielding is a measure of a team's spirit, because 90 per cent of it doesn't show up on the scorecard. It is really four different arts:

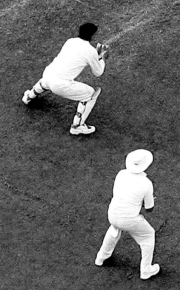

Slip catching

The good news for slip fielders is that they get to stand around all day and there's always someone to talk to. The bad news is that the ball comes at them like a bullet, without warning, and out of a bobbly background made up of distant spectators in their summer clothes. Oh, and if they drop it, everyone blames them for all the runs that the batsman concerned goes on to make.

A good slip fielder is a great thing. The best ones go either at first slip, deeper than the keeper, or at second, level with the keeper. First slips tend to be calm, no-fuss types, and can even be portly, like Shane Warne and his predecessor Mark Taylor. Second slips are usually more athletic and extrovert, like Ian Botham and Andrew Flintoff. Third slips can be either type – quietly efficient like Andrew Strauss, or brilliantly gymnastic like Paul Collingwood. The best slip of recent years is reckoned to be Mark Waugh of Australia, who was wonderfully consistent and apparently effortless. He holds the world Test record of 181 catches, although Stephen Fleming of New Zealand (159) is creeping up on him.

Outfielding

The best outfielders normally go at cover or midwicket in Tests, and at backward point in one-day games, although modern captains will move them to counter the strengths of a particular batsman. They're a magnificent sight, prowling the covers with an animal presence, so that the batsman feels hunted and trapped. Andrew Symonds of Australia is a great prowler, and his hairstyle alone makes it hard to get the ball past him. His captain, Ricky Ponting, is almost as good. But the best outfielder of recent times was **Jonty Rhodes** of South Africa, the man who made backward point such an important position. As the cricket writer Neil Manthorp said, Rhodes could leap like a salmon, throw down the stumps when off balance, and prevent quick singles by reputation alone. He is now South Africa's fielding coach.

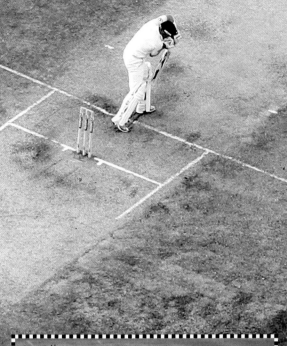

Bat-pad catching

When a ball from a spinner takes the edge of the bat, it often hits the pad as well, and pops up towards the man at silly point or short leg. These positions are in front of the bat, so they demand courage – and helmets, and shinpads – as well as lightning-fast reflexes. David Boon, who played for Australia in the 1990s, was a great bat-pad catcher, even though he looked like he had just wandered in from a pub in the outback.

Boundary fielding

Traditionally, fielding in the deep was a job for fast bowlers looking for a rest. They would amble round the boundary to collect the ball, keep their whites clean, and often bowl the ball back in to protect their shoulders. Not any more. Thanks to one-day cricket, even fast bowlers will slide, dive and ping the ball in to the stumps, flat and hard. And some teams use the relay throw, when the fielder in the deep throws the ball to a team-mate half-way to the stumps to send on. This, studies have shown, is quicker than one long, high throw – as long as the man in the middle gathers the ball cleanly.

Eight years ago, in Hollywood, a British theatre director called Sam Mendes started making his first film. A film crew is much bigger than a theatrical cast, and he found it very difficult. Two things got him through. One was having a very experienced cameraman; the other was re-reading a favourite book – *The Art of Captaincy* by Mike Brearley, one of England's best cricket captains. "I found myself reaching for this book, looking for insights," Mendes wrote later.

The film was called *American Beauty* and it was a big hit: Mendes ended up winning an Oscar for Best Director. He also played in the final of the National Village Cricket Championship at Lord's for Shipton-under-Wychwood (they lost). He is believed to be the best cricketer ever to win an Oscar.

Captaincy is massively important in cricket, far more so than football. At least, it is when your team are in the field. When they are batting, you won't notice the captain much – he will just sit on the balcony, watching the game and leading the cheers when a batsman reaches 50 or 100. The only decisions he will face are whether to send in a nightwatchman and, if things are going well, whether to declare. But when the team goes out in the field, the captain has to take dozens of decisions, large and small.

Who should open the bowling? Who is going to bowl into the wind? Is this a pitch where you have to be patient and apply pressure, or should we opt for all-out attack? Do we need a short leg, a fourth slip, a third man, or someone out at deep square leg for the hook? If I go for a third man, and a catch goes through the vacant fourth slip, does that mean I was wrong?

Should the big fast bowler who has just sprayed it around and conceded 20 runs from two overs be taken off? The umpire wants a word about someone's behaviour – should I take his point or defend my player? When are we going to bring the spinner on? And if he gets carted, what then?

A captain has all these questions bouncing around inside his head, yet he has to stay calm and in control. This takes a lot of different qualities. He needs to be decisive. He needs self-belief – he must trust his own judgement, or nobody else will. He must be able to inspire others. He needs intelligence, although it may well be a good cricket brain rather than the ability to pass exams: some players who never passed an A-level are very sharp when it comes to reading the game.

He needs to be able to talk to the media, a big part of the job which is still getting bigger. He needs to be able to get on with very different characters – some sociable, some more solitary, some domineering, some mousey, some confident, some nervous – and knit them together into a team. He needs to be prepared to gamble. And he needs to be tough: at some point he will have to put up with criticism from crowds and commentators, and he may have to give his closest friend a kick up the backside. It might be easier to make a film.

SEVEN TYPES OF CAPTAIN

THE THINKER

Current example
Stephen Fleming
New Zealand 1997-

TESTS	WON-LOST	%WON
80	28-27	35

Past master
▲ **Mike Brearley** ▲
England 1977-81*

TESTS	WON-LOST	%WON
31	18-4	58

THE SUPERSTAR

Recent example
Andrew Flintoff
England 2006-07*

TESTS	WON-LOST	%WON
11	2-7	18

Past master
▲ **Viv Richards** ▲
West Indies 1985-91

TESTS	WON-LOST	%WON
50	27-8	54

THE PLANNER

Current example
▲ **Mahela Jayawardene** ▲
Sri Lanka 2006-

TESTS	WON-LOST	%WON
11	6-3	54

Past master
Ray Illingworth
England 1969-73*

TESTS	WON-LOST	%WON
31	12-5	38

THE INNOVATOR

Current example
Michael Vaughan
England 2003-

TESTS	WON-LOST	%WON
36	22-6	61

Past master
▲ **Steve Waugh** ▲
Australia 1999-2004

TESTS	WON-LOST	%WON
57	41-9	72

THE SCRAPPER

Current example
▲ **Ricky Ponting** ▲
Australia 2004-

TESTS	WON-LOST	%WON
35	27-3	77

Past master
Allan Border
Australia 1984-94

TESTS	WON-LOST	%WON
93	32-22	34

Ponting has the best record of anyone who has captained in 20 Tests or more. He and his predecessor, Steve Waugh, have excellent win records because they played the game so fast, they almost eliminated the draw. Vaughan and Brearley have the best record among England's captains. Border has captained the most times, followed by Fleming, who has led his team to the most defeats – but is still much respected as a captain.

Dates show when the player was official captain, not just a stand-in.
* = these captains were replaced by other players for part of their time.
Figures to June 21, 2007

THE PRINCE

Recent example
Brian Lara
West Indies 1997-2007*

TESTS	WON-LOST	%WON
47	10-26	21

Past master
▲ **Imran Khan** ▲
Pakistan 1982-92*

TESTS	WON-LOST	%WON
48	14-8	29

THE PAIN IN THE REAR

Recent example
▲ **Sourav Ganguly** ▲
India 2000-05

TESTS	WON-LOST	%WON
49	21-13	42

Past master
Ian Chappell
Australia 1971-75

TESTS	WON-LOST	%WON
30	15-5	50

HOW TO SET A FIELD

The ground is big and flat and the ball zips across it as if on a giant pool table. So where does the captain put his fielders? Here are four examples, showing how to attack and defend with both fast and slow bowlers

BOWLING: FAST

Fine leg

SLIPS
2nd 1st
3rd
4th
Keeper

Leg gully

Gully

Cover point

Short leg

Mid-off
From 4th slip if another wicket doesn't fall

Mid-on from leg gully if another wicket doesn't fall

SCORE 20-2

The fielding side have started well and want more. They are happy to leave gaps to invite the drive, which could produce an edge to the slip cordon. This field is for a right-arm seamer bowling to a right-hand batsman. The ball is hard and shiny, and the pitch is offering some sideways movement: if it wasn't, one or two slips would move to catching positions in front of the bat, such as short extra and short mid-on. The pitch is also bouncy, so short leg is in, under the helmet, ready to pounce when the batsman fends off a rib-tickler. If the second wicket doesn't come, leg gully – the most unusual position here – will go out to mid-on, and soon afterwards 4th slip will drop to mid-off.

Third man
Fine leg

1st slip
Keeper

Gully
Square leg

Cover point

Extra cover
Mid-on

Mid-off

SCORE 200-3

The batting side have recovered well through a big partnership. The ball has gone soft, the pitch seems to have flattened out and the fielding captain has switched to the defensive, hoping to bore the batsmen out. He has just the one slip and a gully, and five of his nine fielders are in a ring, saving the single, to build the pressure. The only easy singles available are to third man and fine leg, who are protecting the boundaries against deflections – often the shots that go fastest off the bat, because the ball retains much of its pace.

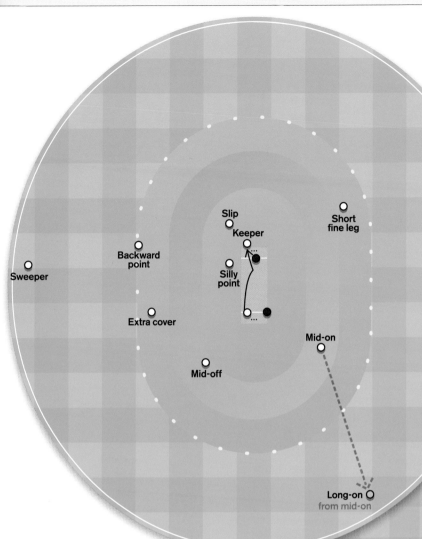

Slip
Keeper
Short
fine leg
Backward
point
Deep
square
Sweeper
Silly
point
Extra cover
Mid-on
Mid-off
Long-on
from mid-on

SCORE 250-5

The batting side are on top but not by much, with the tail only a wicket away. The spinner is on and he has what's known as an in-out field. There's a bit of turn, so he has a slip and one man at bat-pad, ready to snaffle an edge. But he is aware that the batsman wants to milk him, so he also has a ring of five and protection in the deep on both sides of the wicket. This field is for a slow left-armer like Monty Panesar, turning the ball away from the right-hander. The bat-pad man is at silly point and the ring is 3-2 (three on the off, two on the leg), with one man out for the sweep and another for the square drive or cut. If the bowler was an offspinner like Jamie Dalrymple, turning the ball in, the man under the helmet would jump across to short leg, and the ring would be 2-3. If a wicket doesn't fall for a while, mid-on might drop back to long-on to deter the lofted on-drive.

BOWLING: SLOW

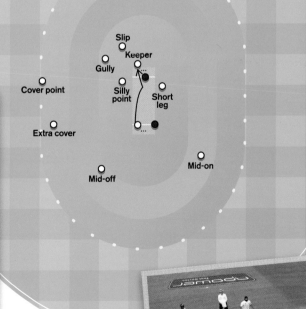

Slip
Keeper
Gully
Deep
backward
square
Cover point
Silly
point
Short
leg
Extra cover
Mid-on
Mid-off

SCORE 70-3

It's the fourth innings now and the pitch is breaking up. Monty is the main attacking weapon, and he already has a wicket or two. He crowds the batsman with four men round the bat, but he still wants some protection so as not to give away easy runs. He has one man out for the sweep, which leaves four fielders for the ring. These are divided 3-1 so that the off side, towards which his turn goes, is well patrolled. So the field ends up as 6-3, and Monty mustn't stray on to leg stump (that's OK – he seldom does). The batsman knows if he can thread it through that ring of three, he will probably get a four, but, equally, he could perish in the attempt, either by edging to slip or gully, or by playing too early and popping the ball up to one of the run-savers. The offspinner would push gully across to backward short leg, and the ring would be 2-2. All these plans can be tailored to individual batsmen. It makes you wonder, as the 1970s England spinner Derek Underwood once said, "Why do so many players want to be captain?"

▶ **Edged and gone**
Strauss catches Jerome Taylor off Panesar in the first innings at Old Trafford in 2007

SACHIN TENDULKAR
CRICKET'S BIGGEST STAR

The boy was 12, and this was his daily timetable: 7-9am, cricket; 9.30am-4.30pm, more cricket; 5.30-7pm, even more cricket. He played in the park near his home in Mumbai, India. When he batted, the coach would put a one-rupee coin on top of the stumps. Any bowler who dislodged the coin could keep it. Otherwise, the boy would keep it. He still has 13 of the coins.

Some great sportsmen are naturally gifted. Others are hard workers who make the best of their talents. Sachin Tendulkar is both. He has also needed a third quality: the ability to keep your head while all around are worshipping you. There are a billion people in India and their biggest hero is this small, quiet, modest man. India teems with life and noise, but it's said that when Tendulkar bats, India goes quiet. They call him Sachin, like a member of the family.

He scored his first century when he was 13. At 14, he batted in a schools semi-final with his friend Vinod Kambli. They came together at 84 for 2 and were still together at 748 for 2. Tendulkar made 326 not out and it wasn't even the top score, as Kambli got 349 not out. Tendulkar's average for the tournament was over 1000.

At 16, he played for India against Pakistan. He was too young to sign his own contract, so his father, a professor, signed it for him. He made only 15 in his first Test, but managed 59 in his second. He faced three great fast bowlers – Wasim Akram, Waqar Younis and Imran Khan – and was surprised to find Akram sledging him. "Why do you do that," he apparently asked, "when your bowling is so good?" Where many players would have gone down to Akram's level, Tendulkar rose above it, and paid him a compliment.

In his first two one-day internationals, he made 0. But his progress was unstoppable. In his second Test series, in New Zealand, he reached 88; then, in England, still only 17, he made his first Test hundred. Touring Australia, where Indian batsmen often struggle with the bounce, he made two more hundreds. His Test average was already 41.

How did he do it? By having what coaches call the three Ts: talent, technique and temperament. By applying himself, studying the conditions, seeing what was needed. By being strong – he is only 5ft 5, but chunky – and yet being able to caress the ball, the way some powerful men, like Andrew Flintoff, cannot.

In one-day cricket, he reached the top less directly. He kept getting fifties but went 78 matches without a single hundred. He was promoted to open the innings and finally, in Sri Lanka, against Australia, a hundred came along. Even then, he followed up with three ducks in a row. But the hundreds began to come at a steady rate, and now he has 41, far more than the next man (Sanath Jayasuriya with 25). That's Tendulkar: unbelievably steady.

For years there was a debate over whether he was the best player in the world. His contemporaries include two other all-time greats, Shane Warne and Brian Lara. Each has been the greatest in a different way. Warne has had the most impact on the game; Lara has been an exceptional entertainer, match-winner and record-breaker. Tendulkar has been the most gracious of the three, and it has been grace under phenomenal pressure: the burden of carrying a billion hopes. He has also shone in hand-to-hand combat, playing Warne quite comfortably. Tendulkar has seven hundreds against Australia, Warne only one five-for against India – and Tendulkar wasn't playing on that occasion.

He has been compared to Bradman by many, including Bradman, who said his style reminded him of himself. But he has also known failure. In the Test Ratings, he has never reached 900, a level Ricky Ponting, Mohammad Yousuf and Kevin Pietersen have all achieved in 2007 alone. As captain of India, in 25 Tests spread over two stints, he started well, only to end up with four wins, nine defeats and too many draws.

Tendulkar in 1990, playing for India at 17

But he has also been part of a new era of Indian cricket, tougher and more attacking than before. He has been central to several triumphs – beating Australia at home and drawing away, winning in Pakistan. He has broken Sunil Gavaskar's world record for the most Test centuries, and is the only man to make 25,000 international runs. He is in sight of Lara's Test career record. "Sachin is a genius," Lara once said. "I'm a mere mortal."

Off the field, he is a family man who likes driving and praying. He is so famous that both these activities have to be done in the middle of the night. He stays up late to drive fast cars in the deserted streets of Mumbai and to go to the Hindu temple. Along with the fame, and the fans, has come fortune. Tendulkar is probably the highest-earning cricketer of all time. His current deal with his agents is reported to guarantee him 60 crore a year, around £7m. He has been paid to promote cars, tyres, credit cards, televisions, shoes, biscuits, banks, cameras, Pepsi and Adidas.

So Tendulkar is one of the great success stories. But you may be wondering what happened to his friend Kambli. He played for India with Sachin, although it took him three years longer to get there. He was an instant hit, making 224 and 227 in consecutive matches. After seven Tests, he had an average of 113, but then the gods stopped smiling on him. The runs tailed off, he had trouble playing bouncers, and he became obsessed with his bat handle, which at one point had nine grips. When he was dropped, India had many other young batsmen, and he couldn't get back. His Test career was over at 23.

Tendulkar, meanwhile, just kept on going. Once, I watched India play Australia in Mumbai. Many of the crowd cheered when Rahul Dravid was out, even though it was a blow to India's hopes. They cheered because it meant they would see Tendulkar.

PLANET CRICKET

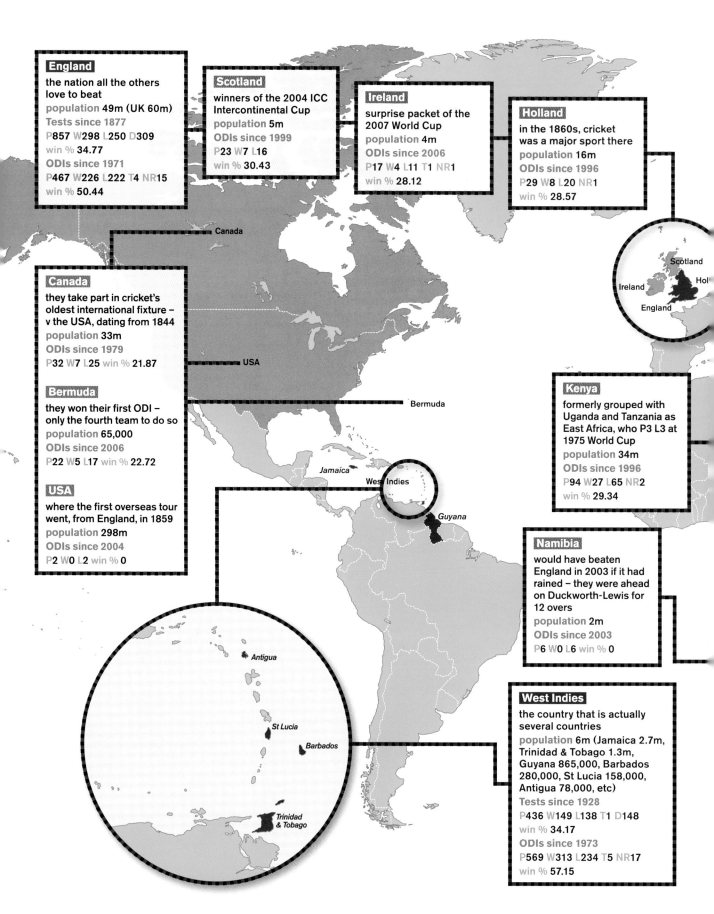

England

the nation all the others
love to beat
population 49m (UK 60m)
Tests since 1877
P857 W298 L250 D309
win % 34.77
ODIs since 1971
P467 W226 L222 T4 NR15
win % 50.44

Scotland

winners of the 2004 ICC
Intercontinental Cup
population 5m
ODIs since 1999
P23 W7 L16
win % 30.43

Ireland

surprise packet of the
2007 World Cup
population 4m
ODIs since 2006
P17 W4 L11 T1 NR1
win % 28.12

Holland

in the 1860s, cricket
was a major sport there
population 16m
ODIs since 1996
P29 W8 L20 NR1
win % 28.57

Canada

Canada

they take part in cricket's
oldest international fixture –
v the USA, dating from 1844
population 33m
ODIs since 1979
P32 W7 L25 win % 21.87

Bermuda

they won their first ODI –
only the fourth team to do so
population 65,000
ODIs since 2006
P22 W5 L17 win % 22.72

USA

where the first overseas tour
went, from England, in 1859
population 298m
ODIs since 2004
P2 W0 L2 win % 0

USA

Bermuda

Scotland
Ireland
England
Hol

Kenya

formerly grouped with
Uganda and Tanzania as
East Africa, who P3 L3 at
1975 World Cup
population 34m
ODIs since 1996
P94 W27 L65 NR2
win % 29.34

Jamaica
West Indies
Guyana

Namibia

would have beaten
England in 2003 if it had
rained – they were ahead
on Duckworth-Lewis for
12 overs
population 2m
ODIs since 2003
P6 W0 L6 win % 0

Antigua

St Lucia

Barbados

Trinidad
& Tobago

West Indies

the country that is actually
several countries
population 6m (Jamaica 2.7m,
Trinidad & Tobago 1.3m,
Guyana 865,000, Barbados
280,000, St Lucia 158,000,
Antigua 78,000, etc)
Tests since 1928
P436 W149 L138 T1 D148
win % 34.17
ODIs since 1973
P569 W313 L234 T5 NR17
win % 57.15

Overview: only **10 teams** have played Test cricket. Nine of them are countries, and the 10th is West Indies, a group of countries. All 10 are picked out in red here. You'll notice that they're very spread out, ranging from New Zealand (11-13 hours ahead of London time) to West Indies (five hours behind). And they're all on the edge of their continents. Why should cricket have landed up in such a scattered bunch of places? Because they were all part of the British Empire.

The countries picked out in **pink** are cricket's second division. They don't play Test cricket, but they do play one-day internationals. All of them have tasted victory, except Hong Kong, Namibia … and the USA.

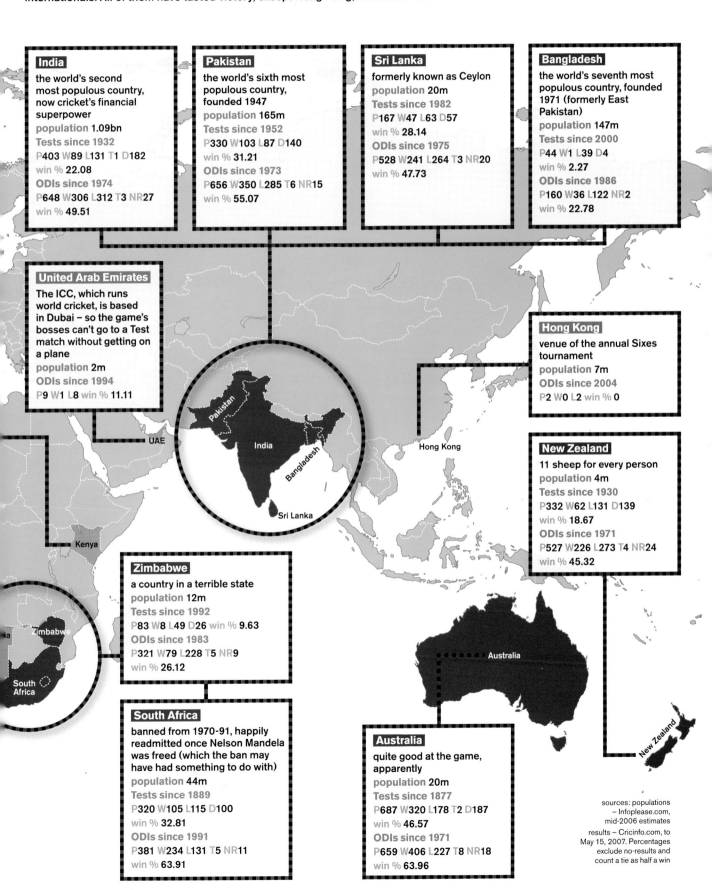

India
the world's second most populous country, now cricket's financial superpower
population 1.09bn
Tests since 1932
P403 W89 L131 T1 D182
win % 22.08
ODIs since 1974
P648 W306 L312 T3 NR27
win % 49.51

Pakistan
the world's sixth most populous country, founded 1947
population 165m
Tests since 1952
P330 W103 L87 D140
win % 31.21
ODIs since 1973
P656 W350 L285 T6 NR15
win % 55.07

Sri Lanka
formerly known as Ceylon
population 20m
Tests since 1982
P167 W47 L63 D57
win % 28.14
ODIs since 1975
P528 W241 L264 T3 NR20
win % 47.73

Bangladesh
the world's seventh most populous country, founded 1971 (formerly East Pakistan)
population 147m
Tests since 2000
P44 W1 L39 D4
win % 2.27
ODIs since 1986
P160 W36 L122 NR2
win % 22.78

United Arab Emirates
The ICC, which runs world cricket, is based in Dubai – so the game's bosses can't go to a Test match without getting on a plane
population 2m
ODIs since 1994
P9 W1 L8 win % 11.11

Hong Kong
venue of the annual Sixes tournament
population 7m
ODIs since 2004
P2 W0 L2 win % 0

New Zealand
11 sheep for every person
population 4m
Tests since 1930
P332 W62 L131 D139
win % 18.67
ODIs since 1971
P527 W226 L273 T4 NR24
win % 45.32

Zimbabwe
a country in a terrible state
population 12m
Tests since 1992
P83 W8 L49 D26 win % 9.63
ODIs since 1983
P321 W79 L228 T5 NR9
win % 26.12

South Africa
banned from 1970-91, happily readmitted once Nelson Mandela was freed (which the ban may have had something to do with)
population 44m
Tests since 1889
P320 W105 L115 D100
win % 32.81
ODIs since 1991
P381 W234 L131 T5 NR11
win % 63.91

Australia
quite good at the game, apparently
population 20m
Tests since 1877
P687 W320 L178 T2 D187
win % 46.57
ODIs since 1971
P659 W406 L227 T8 NR18
win % 63.96

sources: populations – Infoplease.com, mid-2006 estimates
results – Cricinfo.com, to May 15, 2007. Percentages exclude no-results and count a tie as half a win

AUSTRALIA

Test ranking 1 One-day ranking 1

Captain **Ricky Ponting**, age 30, 35 Tests in charge. Leader by example: batting average as Test captain is 65.

Coach **Tim Nielsen**, brand new. John Buchanan left in April 2007 after eight years: most successful coach ever – geeky but effective. They have never had a foreigner as coach.

Stars **Mike Hussey**, middle-order batsman – averages 79, plays the situation, gets them out of trouble. **Adam Gilchrist**, wicketkeeper and master blaster: best No 7 Test batsman of all time. **Stuart Clark**, seamer: looks like a lawyer, which he is, but his bowling asks questions which good players can't answer.

Traits Controlled aggression – dashing batting, miserly bowling. Almost invincible at home: won 46 Tests, lost three in last 10 years. Only a great performance, or their own arrogance, can beat them. Their cap, the **Baggy Green**, is rather like an Indian cow – sacred.

Test form Domineering. England (home) **won 5-0**, Bangladesh (away) **won 2-0**, South Africa (a) **won 3-0**, South Africa (h) **won 2-0**, West Indies (h) **won 3-0**, ICC World XI (h) **won 1-0**, England (a) **lost 1-2**.

One-day form Patchy, but perfect when it matters most. **Won World Cup** (in West Indies). **Lost 0-3** in New Zealand. **2nd in triangular series** v England and New Zealand (h). **Won Champions Trophy** in India. **Won triangular series** v West Indies and India in Malaysia. Bangladesh (a) **won 3-0**.

Good at preventing draws. Hitting sixes. Ground fielding (they use a baseball coach). Setting targets for themselves. Grinding opponents into dust. Singing in the dressing-room afterwards.

Not so good at Catching, since Mark Waugh retired and a few others have grown old. Defending big one-day targets. Keeping quiet on the field. Being modest.

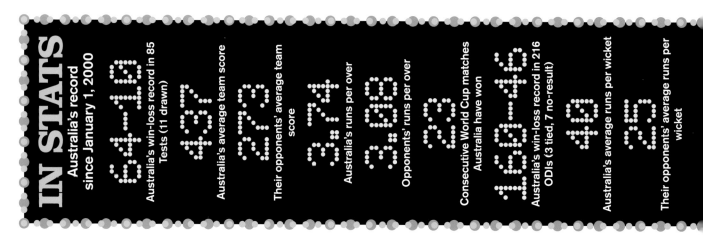

IN STATS

64-19 Australia's record since January 1, 2000

49-7 Australia's win-loss record in 85 Tests (11 drawn)

327 Australia's average team score

273 Their opponents' average team score

3.73 Australia's runs per over

3.68 Opponents' runs per over

21 Consecutive World Cup matches Australia have won

166-43 Australia's win-loss record in 216 ODIs (3 tied, 7 no-result)

49.4 Australia's average runs per wicket

28.5 Their opponents' average runs per wicket

5 REASONS WHY AUSTRALIA ARE THE BEST

1 The great outdoors
They have as much space as western Europe, and fewer people than south-east England. So there is a sports ground in every Aussie suburb and they are not about to turn it into luxury flats

2 Their whole system is competitive
Playing a game for a laugh, or to spend time with your mates, is a nice idea – but not an Australian one. Even grade teams (their equivalent of clubs) play hard

3 They've had several all-time greats at the same time
Warne, McGrath, Gilchrist, Ponting and Hayden are exceptional. Any team containing three of them would have been very good

4 The whole country is a fortress
The ground is hard, the bounce is high, the light is bright, the air is hot, and the cricket is intense. For a tourist, it's a great place; for a visiting cricket team, a daunting one

5 Being the best isn't enough for them
They want to better their own previous best

▲ **On top of the world** back, l-r **Michael Hussey, Brett Lee, Stuart Clark**; front, l-r **Matthew Hayden, Adam Gilchrist, Ricky Ponting and Shane Warne** after regaining the Ashes in 2006-07

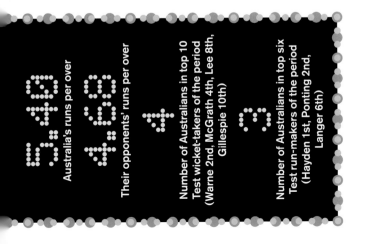

5.48 Australia's runs per over

4.14 Their opponents' runs per over

4 Number of Australians in top 10 Test wicket-takers of the period (Warne 2nd, McGrath 4th, Lee 8th, Gillespie 10th)

3 Number of Australians in top six Test run-makers of the period (Hayden 1st, Ponting 2nd, Langer 6th)

ENGLAND

Test ranking 2 One-day ranking 7

Captain Good question. In Tests, **Michael Vaughan**, age 32, 36 Tests (won 21), outstanding but often unfit. Understudies: **Andrew Strauss**, 29, 5 Tests (won 3), quiet but shrewd; **Andrew Flintoff**, 29, 11 Tests (won 2), straightforward leader from front. One-day capt: **Paul Collingwood** (new), 31, tough, combative character, untried as capt.

Coach **Peter Moores** (ex-Sussex), brand new: enthusiastic and respected, needs time to get used to international game. Replaced Duncan Fletcher (Zim), England's longest-serving (eight years) and most successful coach. Fletcher looked grumpy but lifted them from 9th to 2nd in Test table by being patient, backing strong characters and paying attention to detail. Didn't improve their one-day cricket, though.

Stars **Kevin Pietersen**, No 4/5 batsman – outrageous front-foot strokeplayer, brilliant against spin. **Flintoff**, big-hitting No 6/7 bat, 2nd slip, heartbeat of the team and superb 3rd seamer – fast and accurate, but injury-prone. **Monty Panesar**, left-arm spinner: huge hands, big turn, gets top players out, crowd favourite.

Traits Strong team spirit. Batting improving but stiff-wristed and still prone to collapse. Bowling rather depends on whether Steve Harmison is in the mood. Overworked – no country plays more Tests. Good at home: won 18 Tests, lost two from 2004 to June 2007. Wheels can come off overseas.

Test form Patchy. WI (h) **won 3-0**. Aus (a) **lost 0-5**. Pak (h) **won 3-0**. SL (h) **drew 1-1**. Ind (a) **drew 1-1**. Pak (a) **lost 0-2**. Aus (h) **won 2-1**.

One-day form Mostly poor. **Fifth in World Cup** 2007 in WI. **Won triangular series** v Aus & NZ in Aus. **Group stage of Champions Trophy** in Ind. Pak (h) **drew 2-2**. SL (h) **lost 0-5**. Ind (a) **lost 1-5**.

Good at Seam bowling, especially at home. Team spirit. Being given newspaper columns.

Not so good at Playing spin. Bowling mystery balls. One-day cricket.

PAKISTAN

Test ranking 3 One-day ranking 5

Captain **Shoaib Malik**, age 25, brand new; useful one-day finisher, but not fully established in team. Replaced Inzamam-ul-Haq, age 37, lordly and laid-back unless roused by opponents or umpires.

Coach Job vacant following the sudden death of Bob Woolmer (Eng) at the 2007 World Cup. An imaginative coach who had had great success with South Africa, Woolmer led Pakistan to victory over their biggest rivals, India, but results fell away as his influence waned.

Stars **Mohammad Yousuf** classical No 3 batsman who averaged 84 in his last 16 Tests with five scores over 190. **Younis Khan**, another stylist, averages 48. **Shahid Afridi**, one-day blaster – only batsman ever with career strike rate above a run a ball (among those with 1,000 Test runs). **Shoaib Akhtar**, fast bowler – explosive but moody.

Traits The word often used of them is mercurial – they're very up and down. Controversy follows them around like a demented fan.

Finest hour Winning 1992 World Cup in Australia from near-hopeless position. The captain, Imran Khan, said: "Fight like cornered tigers." And they did – assuming tigers can swing a cricket ball both ways.

Test form Good at home. SA (a) **lost 1-2**. WI (h) **won 2-0**. Eng (a) **lost 0-3** (really 0-2, one Test forfeited). SL (h) **won 1-0**. Ind (h) **won 1-0**. Eng (h) **won 2-0**.

One-day form Poor. **Failed to reach Super Eights in World Cup** in WI. SA (a) **lost 1-3**. **Group stage of Champions Trophy** in Ind. Eng (a) **drew 2-2**. Ind (in UAE) **drew 1-1**. SL (a) **won 2-0**. Ind (h) **lost 1-4**.

Good at Fast bowling, especially reverse swing. Dashing one-day batting. Bickering. Defying expectations.

Not so good at Travelling. Coping with bouncy pitches – in Aus they have won 1, lost 11 since 1983.

▲ **Majestic on their day** India's Harbhajan Singh left and Yuvraj Singh have something to sing about

INDIA

Test ranking 4 One-day ranking 6

Captain **Rahul Dravid**, age 34, 20 Tests (won 6), much liked and respected but has a tough job.

Coach Job embarrassingly vacant following resignation of Greg Chappell (Aus), who tried to change their ways but left them divided and demoralised.

Stars **Sachin Tendulkar**, master batsman and icon (see page 70). **Dravid**, just as good in a quieter way. **MS Dhoni**, flamboyant wicketkeeper-batsman. **Virender Sehwag**, explosive opener, struggling lately, and **Harbhajan Singh**, attacking offspinner known as The Turbanator, were both dropped for tour of England in 2007, but should return.

Traits Majestic on their day but often under-perform, perhaps feeling the pressure of intense media and massive support. Batting tends to collapse. Play too many one-day games, not enough Tests. Coaches have to fight a culture that places individual milestones above needs of team.

Finest hour Beating Australia 2-1 in 2000-01, when VVS Laxman batted like a god to grab victory from the jaws of near-certain defeat (see page 99).

Test form Mixed. SA (a) **lost 1-2**. WI (a) **won 1-0**. Eng (h) **drew 1-1**. Pak (a) **lost 0-1**. SL (h) **won 2-0**. Zim (a) **won 2-0**. Pak (h) **drew 1-1**.

One-day form Bad in big events. Bang (a) **won 2-0**. **Failed to reach Super Eights in World Cup** in WI. SL (h) **won 2-1**. WI (h) **won 3-1**. SA (a) **lost 0-4**. **Eliminated at group stage of Champions Trophy** in Ind.

Good at Batting, slow bowling, putting up with adulation, sitting on motorbikes in adverts.

Not so good at Fielding, going to the gym, saying "Yes coach – you're absolutely right".

▲ **That's huge** Kumar Sangakkara left and Mahela Jayawardene during their third-wicket stand of 624 against South Africa in 2006

SRI LANKA

Test ranking 5 One-day ranking 4

Captain **Mahela Jayawardene**, age 29, elegant batsman and crafty operator.

Coach **Trevor Bayliss** (Aus), brand new. He succeeded Tom Moody (Aus), who left to join Western Australia – less prestige but it's his old team, and easier for his family. Moody brought more professionalism and a sharper edge without stifling the players' exuberance.

Stars **Sanath Jayasuriya**, top-order blaster and one of the godfathers of modern one-day cricket. **Kumar Sangakkara**, wicketkeeper who is a good enough batsman to average 50. **Muttiah Muralitharan**, offspin wizard. **Lasith Malinga**, afro-haired fast bowler who slings it, and swings it, with textbook-defying accuracy.

Traits Elegant, wristy batting. Loads of spin bowling, some swing: Malinga is first real paceman. Spectators find them charming, opponents don't always agree.

Finest hour Winning 1996 World Cup in India. In the process, they reinvented one-day cricket, showing it was possible to do your big hitting at the start of the innings, not just the end.

Test form Mixed. NZ (a) **drew 1-1**. SA (h) **won 2-0**. Eng (a) **drew 1-1**. Pak (h) **lost 0-1**. Bang (a) **won 2-0**. Ind (a) **lost 0-2**.

One-day form Improving. **Losing finalists in World Cup** in WI. Ind (a) **lost 1-2**. NZ (a) **drew 2-2**. Topped qualifying group but **eliminated at group stage of Champions Trophy** in Ind. Eng (a) **won 5-0**. Pak (h) **lost 0-2**.

Good at Bowling. Middle-order batting. Smiling.

Not so good at Travelling, except to Pakistan. Coping with bounce – they tend to get rolled over in Aus and SA.

SOUTH AFRICA

Test ranking 6 One-day ranking 2

Captain **Graeme Smith**, age 26, 46 Tests as capt (won 19). Has improved after naïve start – understandable as he was only 22.

Coach **Mickey Arthur** (SA), age 38. Surprise choice when he took over in May 2005. Signed up for two more years in May 2007, so kept his job after the World Cup when most leading coaches were losing or relinquishing theirs.

Stars **Jacques Kallis**, run machine and useful swing bowler, sometimes accused of selfishness. **Makhaya Ntini**, big-hearted new-ball bowler. **Andre Nel**, fast bowler who hams it up like a pantomime villain, but takes key wickets.

Traits Tough, fit, but something missing – a deep self-belief, perhaps. They have yet to reach a World Cup final. Were labelled "chokers" by Steve Waugh, Australia's captain 1999-2004, which was harsh but, on recent evidence, fair.

Finest hour Test: topped Wisden World Championship (the unofficial forerunner of the ICC Test Championship) in 1998. One-day: pulled off biggest run-chase ever, making 438 for 9 against Australia in 2005-06 (see page 99).

Test form Good at home. Pak (h) **won 2-1**. Ind (h) **won 2-1**. SL (a) **lost 0-2**. NZ (h) **won 2-0**. Aus (h) **lost 0-3**. Aus (a) **lost 0-2**.

One-day form **Semi-finalists in World Cup** in WI. Pak (h) **won 3-1**. Ind (h) **won 4-0**. **Semi-finalists in Champions Trophy** in Ind. Zim (h) **won 3-0**. Aus (h) **won 3-2**.

Good at Fielding. Seam bowling. Two-team one-day series.

Not so good at Tests. Slow bowling. Big tournaments.

⋯➤

NEW ZEALAND

Test ranking 7 One-day ranking 3

Captain **Stephen Fleming**, age 34, 80 Tests as capt (won 28). Started as a young pup, now a wily old fox. Stepped down from one-day captaincy in May 2007.

Coach **John Bracewell** (NZ), age 49. Joined after turning Gloucestershire into a cup-winning one-day team.

Stars **Shane Bond**, the fast bowler with everything – pace, accuracy, swing – except reliable fitness.

Traits Shrewd, practical. Good at making best of slender resources: they have only 4m people to choose from, and the best sportsmen want to play rugby for the All Blacks. But attack is ordinary when Bond is on treatment table.

Finest hour 1985-86. Inspired by the great seam bowler Richard Hadlee, they beat Australia home and away before going on to win in England for the first time.

Test form Sketchy. SL (h) **drew 1-1**. SA (a) **lost 0-2**. WI (h) **won 2-0**. Zim (a) **won 2-0**. SL (h) **won 1-0**. Aus (h) **lost 0-2**.

One-day form Almost excellent. **Semi-finalists in World Cup** in WI. Aus (h) **won 3-0**. **Last in triangular series** v Aus & Eng in Aus. SL (h) **drew 2-2**. **Semi-finalists in Champions Trophy** in Ind. WI (a) won 4-1.

Good at Battling. Breeding allrounders. Playing rugby.

Not so good at Semi-finals – they have played five in World Cups and lost them all.

WEST INDIES

Test ranking 8 One-day ranking 8

Captain **Ramnaresh Sarwan** age 27, new in May 2007. Stylish batsman, and must be brave to take the job, but soon got injured and handed over to **Daren Ganga,** age 28, who showed promise in the field but flopped with the bat.

Coach **David Moore**, age 42, brought in from the Australian academy in May 2007. Has modest playing experience – one game for New South Wales – but playing and coaching are different things.

Stars **Chris Gayle**, opening batsman – bats like a pirate, looks like a rock star. **Shiv Chanderpaul,** adhesive batsman, crabby but effective. **Dwayne Bravo**, gutsy No 6 bat and useful seamer.

Traits Attractive but disorganised, divided and hopeless overseas. Problems appear to be structural: they keep having rows with their bosses. Decent one-day team – handy allrounders.

Finest hour 1976 to 1995: kings of the world. Recently: winning Champions Trophy, 2004.

Test form Dire. Pak (a) **lost 0-2**. Ind (h) **lost 0-1**. NZ (a) **lost 0-2**. Aus (a) **lost 0-3**. SL (a) **lost 0-2**. Pak (h) **drew 1-1**.

One-day form Not hopeless. **Sixth in the World Cup** in WI. Ind (a) **lost 1-3**. Pak (a) **lost 1-3**. **Finalists in Champions Trophy** in Ind. **Second in triangular** v Aus & Ind in Malaysia. Ind (h) **won 4-1**.

Good at Entertaining.

Not so good at Slow bowling. Travelling.

▲**Battlers** **New Zealand's Stephen Fleming** left and **Brendon McCullum at Auckland in 2005-06**

ZIMBABWE

Test ranking 9 One-day ranking 11

Captain **Prosper Utseya**, age 22, appointed July 2006 (23 ODIs as capt, won 4, all against Bangladesh). An economical offspinner, he has played only one Test as Zimbabwe suspended themselves from Test cricket in Jan 2006. This was because the country was in turmoil, suffering from extreme poverty and the rule of a vicious dictator, Robert Mugabe.

Coach **Kevin Curran** (Zim), age 47, former allrounder.

Stars **none**. Tatenda Taibu, sparky wicketkeeper-batsman and former captain, might be a star by now had he not fallen out with the administrators and left the country.

Traits Before most of their good players moved abroad, they were a mini-New Zealand, tough and resourceful, with one great player – the wicketkeeper, batsman and brilliant player of spin Andy Flower, who is now England's assistant coach. Since the good players left, they have been young, eager and hopelessly out of their depth.

Finest hour One-day: their very first match, in the 1983 World Cup, when they beat Australia with their captain, Duncan Fletcher (yes, that one), making 69 not out and taking 4 for 42. Test: 1998-99, when they beat India at home and Pakistan away – still their only Test series wins against anyone other than Bangladesh.

Test form Grim. Ind (h) **lost 0-2**. NZ (h) **lost 0-2**. SA (a) **lost 0-2**. Bang (a) **lost 0-1**. SL (h) **lost 0-2**. Bang (h) **won 1-0**.

▲ **Springing surprises** Aftab Ahmed left and Mohammad Ashraful celebrate a World Cup wicket

BANGLADESH

Test ranking 10 One-day ranking 9

Captain **Mohammad Ashraful** (brand new), age 22, ambitious strokeplayer, looks like an interesting choice.

Coach Job vacant as Dav Whatmore, the former coach of Sri Lanka, is stepping down after four years. He lifted their one-day results but found Tests more tricky.

Stars **Mohammad Rafique**, tidy slow left-armer who has been in the world top 20. **Mashrafe Mortaza**, classical away-swinger. **Aftab Ahmed**, extravagant strokeplayer, could be a star if he works out how to stay in for long enough to make a hundred.

Traits Young, keen, fervently supported.

Finest hour Beating Australia in a one-day game in Cardiff in 2005; beating India in the 2007 World Cup and qualifying for the Super Eights.

Test form Well, they've won one game … Aus (h) **lost 0-2**. SL (h) **lost 0-2**. SL (a) **lost 0-2**. Eng (a) **lost 0-2**. Zim (h) **won 1-0**. Ind (h) **lost 0-2**.

One-day form Better. Ind (h) **lost 0-2**. **Seventh in World Cup** in WI. Zim (a) **won 3-1**. Zim (h) **won 5-0**. **Third in qualifying group for Champions Trophy** in Ind. Kenya (a) **won 3-0**.

Good at Springing surprises in one-dayers.

Not so good at Test cricket.

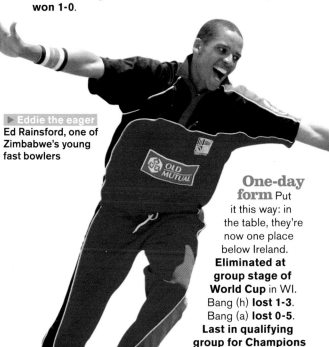

▶ **Eddie the eager**
Ed Rainsford, one of Zimbabwe's young fast bowlers

One-day form Put it this way: in the table, they're now one place below Ireland. **Eliminated at group stage of World Cup** in WI. Bang (h) **lost 1-3**. Bang (a) **lost 0-5**. **Last in qualifying group for Champions Trophy** in Ind. SA (a) **lost 0-3**. Bang (h) **won 3-2**. Against the top eight teams, since Jan 9, 2001, they have won 8 and lost 92.

Good at Soldiering on.

Not so good at Playing international cricket.

MY WORLD X1

Picking a World XI – to play against Mars, of course – is always fun. Who is the very best cricketer in the world in each position? If you can only have one allrounder, who do you pick: Andrew Flintoff or Jacques Kallis?

There is no guarantee that they would be a great team. A few near-world XIs have taken the field down the years – usually a Rest of the World, taking on Australia or England – and some of them have been hopeless. Last time one appeared, against Australia in the ICC Super Series of 2005, they were outplayed. But then they had the wrong captain (Graeme Smith of South Africa, still learning the trade), too little time to practise together, and two opening bowlers (Flintoff and Steve Harmison) who had just won the Ashes and needed to put their feet up. Plus, the Australians were playing at home, and were desperate to prove themselves after a rare defeat.

This team should do better. For one thing, it has four Aussies in its ranks – although none of them are bowlers, following the retirements of Glenn McGrath and Shane Warne. Also, it has been picked solely for Test cricket. It contains four of the top 20 Test run-scorers of all time and the second-highest wicket-taker in Murali. It has vast experience, with six men who have a hundred caps and five Test captains, past and present. If all these players perform according to their averages, they will make around 480 all out (allowing for a few extras), while their opponents will get about 280.

One problem with composite sides is that good players can be pushed out of position, as Steven Gerrard has tended to be in the England football team. Here, everybody is in his usual place except Mike Hussey, and he is well used to opening for Western Australia.

MATTHEW HAYDEN
1 Bats **left**
Born **29.10.1971** Team **Australia**
why **bats like a battering ram**
Tests **89**, runs **7739**, average **53**
deputy **Virender Sehwag** (India)
brilliant but struggling lately

MIKE HUSSEY
2 Bats **left**
Born **27.05.1975** Team **Australia**
why **cool, canny, seldom gets out**
Tests **16**, runs **1597**, average **79**
deputy **Graeme Smith** (South Africa)
bruising but limited

RICKY PONTING (capt)
3 Bats **right**
Born **19.12.1974** Team **Australia**
why **complete strokeplayer, burning desire**
Tests **110**, runs **9368**, average **59**
deputy **Mohammad Yousuf** (Pakistan)
fine stylist, shaky in Australia

RAHUL DRAVID
4 Bats **right**
Born **11.01.1973** Team **India**
why **classical technique, world's best blocker**
Tests **109**, runs **9366**, average **57**
deputy **Sachin Tendulkar** (India)
a fading genius at 34

KEViN PiETERSEN

5
Bats right
Born 27.06.1980 **Team** England

why explosive improviser
Tests 27, runs 2553, average 52
deputy **Mahela Jayawardene** (Sri Lanka)
elegant and wristy

ANDREW FLiNTOFF

6
Bats right **Bowls** right-arm fast
Born 06.12.1977 **Team** England

why grooved pace bowler, clean hitter, talisman
Tests 67, runs 3381, average 32
wickets 197, average 32
deputy **Jacques Kallis** (South Africa)
solid anchor, useful swinger

ADAM GiLCHRiST

7
Bats left
Born 14.11.1971 **Team** Australia

why decent keeper, marauding bat
Tests 90, runs 5353, average 48
deputy **Kumar Sangakkara** (Sri Lanka)
excellent but less daunting

WHiCH TEAM WOULD WiN?

A five-day match between this XI
and the players they pipped, listed
on each card, would be something
to see. Maybe you could stage it
on a computer game? Let me
know the result: send an email to
tim.delisle@gmail.com . Or tell me
if you disagree with my selection.

OFF YOU GO!

SHAUN POLLOCK

8
Bats right **Bowls** right, fast-medium
Born 16.07.1973 **Team** South Africa

why wily old seamer, stylish bat
Tests 107, runs 3781, average 32
wickets 416, average 23
deputy **Stuart Clark** (Australia)
similar skills, less experience

ANiL KUMBLE

9
Bats right **Bowls** legbreak googly
Born 17.10.1970 **Team** India

why probing, pressurising topspin
Tests 115, runs 2050, average 17
wickets 552, average 28
deputy **Stuart MacGill** (Australia)
more turn, less accuracy

MUTTiAH MURALiTHARAN

10
Bats right **Bowls** right-arm offbreak
Born 17.04.1972 **Team** Sri Lanka

why wizard offspinner
Tests 110, runs 1117, average 11
wickets 674, average 21
deputy **Harbhajan Singh** (India)
gifted but inconsistent

SHANE BOND

11
Bats right **Bowls** right-arm fast
Born 07.06.1975 **Team** New Zealand

why very fast and swings it too
Tests 16, runs 138, average 13
wickets 74, average 22
deputy **Makhaya Ntini** (South Africa)
less fiendish, huge heart

Figures from
Cricinfo.com,
to June 23 2007

ENGLAND TEAM PROFILES

The names are familiar, but what sort of players are they? What are their Test stats? And the highs and lows of their careers so far? You may know all this – if you do, get a friend to read bits aloud, and guess who they are about

Batsmen

Alastair Cook

age **22**, county **Essex**, nickname **Cooky**.
LHB, opener or No 3
Tests **18**, runs **1435**, ave **46**

Calm, well-organised left-hander who was thrown in the deep end, going straight from an England A tour of West Indies to a Test match in India. It was sink-or-swim, and he swam. Three years earlier he had been at Bedford School, breaking batting records and singing in the choir.

high **60 and 104 on Test debut, Nagpur, 2005-06**

low **Ashes 2006-07: only one score above 43**

Andrew Strauss

age **30**, Middlesex, Straussy.
LHB, opener
Tests **40**, runs **3012**, ave **41**

Easy-going accumulator who slotted in perfectly when called up in 2004. Made crucial hundreds against South Africa and Australia, and did well as stand-in captain, but by 2007 he was struggling to reach 50 and playing like a crab – everything was going sideways.

high **led England to 3-0 win over Pakistan, 2006**

low **Ashes 2006-07: kept getting out for 15 or 20**

Michael Vaughan

age **32**, Yorkshire, Virgil.
RHB, opener or No 3; OB
Tests **67**, runs **4846**, ave **43**
wkts **6**, ave **89**

Wonderful cover-driver and swivel-puller when fit and not distracted by the captaincy. Ropey fielder, useful part-time spinner, and one of England's best captains – commanding, imaginative, no-nonsense.

high **hitting three big hundreds in the Ashes 2002-03; winning the Ashes 2005**

low **missed 16 successive Tests through injury, Feb 2006 to May 2007**

Allrounder

Andrew Flintoff

age **29**, Lancashire, Fred.
RHB, No 6 or 7; RF, third seamer
Tests **66**, runs **3331**, ave **32**
wkts **190**, ave **32**

Fantastic when fit – a big, clean hitter with the bat, hostile and consistent with the ball, an excellent second slip and an inspiration to his team-mates.

high **Ashes 2005: he was the difference between the sides**

low **Ashes 2006-07: captained England to a 5-0 defeat**

Wicketkeeper

Matt Prior

age **25**, Sussex, MP.
RHB, No 7
Tests **4**, runs **324**, ave **64**

Punchy strokeplayer who made his Test debut in 2007, scored a rapid hundred, and looked like the answer to the selectors' prayers. But this was against West Indies, so it didn't prove a great deal. His keeping is more ordinary, but he makes up for it by talking a lot.

high **126no off 128 balls on debut**

low **12 one-day caps before that, six scores of 20+, no fifties**

Bowlers

Matthew Hoggard

age **30**, Yorkshire, Hoggy.
RHB, tail-ender; RMF, new ball
Tests **64**, wkts **240**, ave **30**
runs **444**, ave **7**

Admirable outswing bowler and general trouper. Has become England's best bowler abroad, and their biggest wicket-taker since Ian Botham. Bats as if holding a piece of concrete in his hand: possibly the worst regular No 9 in Test history.

high **Won a Test in Jo'burg with 12 for 205, 2004-05**

low **Ashes 2002-03: 6 for 375 in three Tests**

Steve Harmison

age **28**, Durham, Harmy.
RHB, tail-ender; RF, new ball
Tests **53**, wkts **201**, ave **30**
runs **631**, ave **11**

England usually have someone who is called an enigma, because he is mysteriously inconsistent. Currently, it's Harmison, who has it all – pace, lift, movement, hostility – but has only shown it occasionally since his annus mirabilis of 2004.

high **7 for 12 to blow West Indies away in Jamaica, 2003-04**

low **Ashes 2006-07, first ball: straight to second slip**

COMING UP ENGLAND'S NEXT 10 SERIES

away winter **2007-08**	Nov-Dec **Sri Lanka**	Feb-Mar **New Zealand**
home summer **2008**	May-June **New Zealand**	July-Sept **South Africa**
away winter **2008-09**	October **ICC Champions Trophy in Pakistan**	Nov-Dec **India** / Feb-Apr **West Indies**
home summer **2009**	May **Zimbabwe** / June **T20 World Cup in England**	July-Sept **Australia**

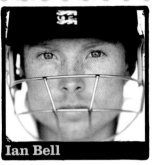

Kevin Pietersen

age **27, Hampshire, KP.**
RHB, No 4; OB
Tests **27**, runs **2553**, ave **52**
wkts **1**, ave **221**

Once a little-known South African offspinner, now a British celebrity and England's best batsman since Graham Gooch's heyday 15 years ago. Hits the ball like a bullet, invents new shots (reverse sweep for six, flamingo flick past mid-on) and often gets himself out.

high **Adelaide 2006-07: a majestic 158 out of 551**

low **Adelaide 2006-07: a gormless 2 as England collapsed to 129 all out**

Paul Collingwood

age **31, Durham, Colly.**
RHB, No 5; RM
Tests **24**, runs **1819**, ave **45**
wkts **2**, ave **158**

Gritty former one-day specialist who has turned himself into an effective Test regular, working the ball to leg with a strong bottom hand. Brilliant backward point or third slip, decent one-day bowler, and now one-day captain as well.

high **Adelaide 2006-07: an epic 206 as England piled up 551**

low **Adelaide 2006-07: a constipated 22 off 119 balls as England collapsed to 129**

Ian Bell

age **25, Warwickshire, Belly.**
RHB, No 6 or 3; RM
Tests **27**, runs **1845**, ave **43**
wkts **1**, ave **76**

Stumpy, stylish counter-attacker at No 6 with the best on-drive in the team. Less certain at No 3 or as a one-day opener, where he is apt to get bogged down. Fine fielder anywhere and an excellent short leg.

high **three hundreds in consecutive Tests v Pakistan, 2006**

low **out of his depth in 2005 Ashes – 171 runs in 10 innings**

Marcus Trescothick

age **31, Somerset, Trez.**
LHB, opener
Tests **76**, runs **5825**, ave **43**
wkts **1**, ave **155**

Powerful driver and puller who was a key figure for England until brought down by a stress-related illness in 2005-06. When fit, he opens the innings, sets the tone, polishes the ball and catches everything at first slip.

high **Ashes 2005: showed the way with some hard-hitting fifties**

low **Ashes 2006-07: left before the first Test with a recurrence of his illness**

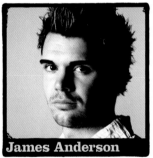

Simon Jones

age **28, Glamorgan, Horse.**
LHB, tail-ender; RFM, old ball
Tests **18**, wkts **59**, ave **28**
runs **205**, ave **15**

World's best fourth seamer when fit: quick, snaky, and gets reverse swing. Useful slogger.

high **third best player in the 2005 Ashes, behind Flintoff and Warne**

low **horrible knee injury when he slid to field the ball, Brisbane, 2002-03**

Monty Panesar

age **25, Northants, Monty (real name Mudhsuden).**
LHB, tail-ender; SLA
Tests **17**, wkts **65**, ave **28**
runs **107**, ave **8**

With his big hands, big heart, and taste for the big occasion, Monty is a crowd favourite. Great celebrator, with a fielding method every fan can relate to, and a gifted, accurate spinner.

high **8 for 93 v Pakistan at Old Trafford, 2006, including Yousuf in both innings**

low **being dropped for a rusty Ashley Giles for the first two Ashes Tests, 2006-07**

Liam Plunkett

age **22, Durham, Pudsy.**
RHB, No 8 or 9; RFM, new or old ball
Tests **9**, wkts **23**, ave **39**
runs **126**, ave **11**

On a good day, he has pace, bounce and outswing. On a bad day, he's cannon fodder. But young enough to get much better, and a handy lower-order biffer too.

high **bowling Adam Gilchrist first ball with the perfect yorker, Sydney 2006-07**

low **permanent drinks waiter, Ashes 2006-07**

James Anderson

age **25, Lancashire, Jimmy.**
LHB, No 11; RFM, new or old ball
Tests **16**, wkts **46**, ave **38**
runs **101**, ave **12**

An overnight sensation in 2002-03 with his pace and swing, he has struggled ever since, with the odd great day amid long spells of injury, non-selection and under-bowling. Still young enough to have a major career.

high **World Cup 2003: destroyed Pakistan with 4 for 29**

low **Ashes 2006-07: 5 for 413 in three Tests**

Figures from Cricinfo.com, June 22, 2007, and for England only – appearances for ICC World XI (by Flintoff and Harmison) not included. Ages to Oct 1, 2007

THE GREAT GROUNDS

Six of the best places to watch cricket: all spectacular and all different

Lord's London, England ▼

opened **1814** capacity **30,000** home of **MCC and Middlesex** lights **no** Tests **113** ODIs **42** on the side **archery for 2012 Olympics**

To some, it's a cathedral; to others, a stuffy old private club. But to almost everyone, it's the home of cricket, an oasis in the big city and a beautiful place in its own right. The field is a perfect green chessboard, the pavilion is a formidable Victorian edifice, and the newer stands are bold examples of modern architecture, while still being very usable. And then there are the quirks, like the eight-foot slope from one side to the other, which can befuddle both batsmen and bowlers. Take a tour on a non-match day to drink it all in, then go again when it's full. For more tips, see page 118.

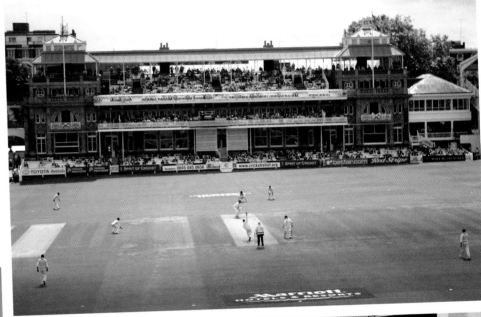

MCG Melbourne, Australia ▲

opened **1854** capacity **100,000** home of **Victoria** lights **yes** Tests **99** ODIs **123** on the side **Aussie Rules football**

For looks, you're better off at the SCG in Sydney, with its charming wrought-iron roofs. But the MCG, in the sports-mad city of Melbourne, is more of an experience. It's a colossal concrete coliseum. The Great Southern Stand alone, seating 48,000, is twice the size of most English grounds. The seats at the top are so high that they give a blimp's eye view and can cause vertigo. The pitch treats batsmen and bowlers more evenly than most grounds, while the weather is famous for its ability to lay on all four seasons in one day. The atmosphere is harsh and intimidating, with a gladiatorial edge, but it's exhilarating when your team is doing well – or so I'm told.

◀ Kensington Oval
Bridgetown, Barbados, West Indies

opened **1871** capacity **28,000** home of **Barbados** lights **no** Tests **43** ODIs **26**

The Kensington Oval has always had a sporty surface, a glorious climate and a buzzing atmosphere, with a crowd who seem to come equipped with just the right mixture of enthusiasm, expertise and laughter. But as a set of buildings, it used to be nothing special. Now that has been put right with a handsome new ground, built for the 2007 World Cup at a cost of $45m (£23m). The design is coolly futuristic: the 3Ws stand, named after the great Barbadian batting trio of Weekes, Worrell and Walcott, is like a more laid-back version of the Lord's media centre. The ends of the ground are now named after Malcolm Marshall and Joel Garner, who took the new ball here for Barbados only 20 years ago. For the World Cup final, the ground looked a picture. It was just a shame that the weather was wet, the umpires had a nightmare, and the last few overs were played out in virtual darkness.

◀ Eden Gardens Calcutta, India

opened **1864** capacity **90,000** home of **Bengal** lights **yes** Tests **34** ODIs **21**

The name suggests an innocent paradise, but the reality is a little different. Calcutta is a teeming city and its cricket ground – huge, plain and rudimentary – is all about the 90,000 people who stream into it. No cricket crowd is noisier or more passionate than this one. Sometimes the fervour bubbles over and there are riots; other times it inspires the Indian team to astonishing feats. In March 2001, India followed on there against Australia, 274 runs behind – and won. See page 98.

Newlands Cape Town, South Africa ▶

opened **1888** capacity **25,000** home of **Western Province** lights **yes** Tests **42** ODIs **30** on the side **rugby, round the corner**

Cricket leaves plenty of time to enjoy your surroundings, and there are none better than these. Cape Town is a spectacular city, dominated by the surreal beauty of Table Mountain – which looms over one side of the ground. It's hard to believe that something so steep could be such a close neighbour of something so flat. The mountain distracts you from the other surroundings, which include a brewery and a railway line. The pitch can be slow and the weather windy (which enabled the first official 100mph delivery to be bowled here – see page 56), but the atmosphere is lively, draws are rare, the ball turns, and the ground is a good size, big enough to have a sense of theatre, small enough to be intimate.

Pukekura Park
New Plymouth, New Zealand ▶

opened **1892** capacity **a few thousand** home of **Central Districts** lights **no** Tests **0** ODIs **1** on the side **rock concerts**

Its name is not encouraging, and it has hosted only one senior international, but this is a gem. No need to build a stand, as nature has provided one, in the form of a steep hill – all man had to do was carve some terraces into it for the spectators to sit on. If the cricket is a bit sleepy, which is not unknown in these parts, you can explore the park, which includes two lakes, a zoo, a waterfall, a racecourse and a 2,000-year-old tree. You may have seen the cricket field already: it appeared in the Tom Cruise film *The Last Samurai*, playing the role of a 19th-century army parade ground.

BOTHAM'S
ASHES

Some players take years to get used to Test cricket. Ian Botham took about three hours. It was 1977, the year of Star Wars. He was picked at 21, as England's third seamer, to play a Test at Trent Bridge, in the middle of an Ashes series. Australia had a strong batting line-up led by their captain, Greg Chappell, and by mid-afternoon on the Thursday they were nicely placed at 131 for 2, with Chappell on 19, playing himself in carefully. Botham, normally a full-length swing bowler, offered him a long hop, short and begging to be hit. Chappell missed it, it thudded into his pad, Botham went up, and so did the umpire's finger. Botham was away: soon, one wicket became five.

He carried on like that for two years, taking stacks of wickets and also making centuries as a crowd-pleasing No 7 batsman. Beefy, as his team-mates called him, was England's best all-rounder since WG Grace. He was shrewdly handled by the captain, Mike Brearley, who was 14 years older and a kind of father figure. But then Brearley stepped down. He recommended Botham as his successor, and the selectors agreed, even though he had little experience. Another of his father figures, the Somerset captain Brian Close, said to him: "You'll have the most miserable time of your life." And he did.

He lost form with the bat, became more expensive with the ball, and while he did his best as captain, he was a different person from the boisterous gambler he had been before. It was his bad luck to start with two series against West Indies, the world's best team, who Brearley had managed to avoid. But even when England faced Australia, who were more beatable then, Botham struggled. Back at Trent Bridge in June 1981, England lost the first Test, a strange, low-scoring affair. The second, at Lord's, was drawn, but it was a personal nightmare for Botham, who made 0 in both innings. As he walked back into the pavilion, the MCC members greeted him with a frosty silence. He resigned as captain, and the chairman of selectors, Alec Bedser, revealed that he would have been sacked anyway.

For the third Test at Headingley, Brearley was persuaded to return as a stop-gap captain. He was 39 now, a pensioner in cricket terms. But his skill lay in getting the best out of other people and that doesn't fade with age. Freed from the cares of captaincy, Botham immediately found his old self. He took six wickets and stopped the Aussies getting more than 400.

England's top order then collapsed, and although Botham made 50 off only 54 balls, they were all out for 174 and had to follow on. They collapsed again, to 135 for 7, with only Botham left of the main batsmen. Anyone else would have considered it a hopeless cause. Perhaps Botham did too, because he threw the bat as if playing in a village match. The force was with him: even some of his mis-hits went for four.

He hooked and drove and pulled and slogged his way to 149 not out off 148 balls. At the other end, two tail-enders, Graham Dilley and Chris Old, made 56 and 29. England reached 356, which gave them a little to play with. Australia had to get 130 to win.

Botham took a early wicket, but the Aussies cruised to 56 for 1. The situation was just as hopeless as it had been the day before. Then Brearley wound up his fastest bowler, Bob Willis, by saying he wasn't bowling very fast. Willis ran in like a demented buffalo (with long legs and big hair). He took 8 for 43, and England won by 18 runs. It was the greatest comeback in Test history.

The fourth Test was at Edgbaston. Botham was turning back into a pumpkin with only one wicket and scores of 26 and 3. Again it came down to a modest run chase for Australia: 151 to win. Again they were comfortably placed, at 87 for 3. And again they were blown away, this time by Botham, who took five wickets for one run in a spell of 28 balls. Lightning had struck twice.

In the next Test, at Old Trafford, Botham cracked a fabulous hundred, making 118 off only 102 balls, with six sixes. The pundits agreed that it was a more polished innings than the 149, if not so dramatic. England set Australia 506 to win and steadily chipped away to bowl them out for 402. The series stood at 3-1: with only one Test left, the Ashes had been won back.

Treating a Test like a village match: Botham hits another four in his famous 149 not out

Botham had many ups and downs after that. He never made a hundred against the fearsome West Indian attack, he became overweight, and his performances tailed off after the age of 30. But he remained the hammer of the Aussies. He destroyed them with his bowling in 1985 and his batting in 1986-87, and even won one last match against them, with both bat and ball, in the 1992 World Cup.

He was a great player, and he remains England's highest Test wicket-taker, with 383 – which is pretty amazing given that he also made 5,200 runs, and held 120 catches, standing closer than most at second slip. He had a touch of magic that stats cannot convey. When England came back from 1-0 down to pull off a dramatic Ashes win in 2005, everyone who was old enough to remember kept comparing the series to 1981, and saying Andrew Flintoff was the new Botham.

The old Botham was still going as a commentator on Sky and as a phenomenal charity fund-raiser, generating millions for Leukaemia Research with a series of walks around Britain. In 2007, he was knighted, and the papers said: "Arise, Sir Beefy!".

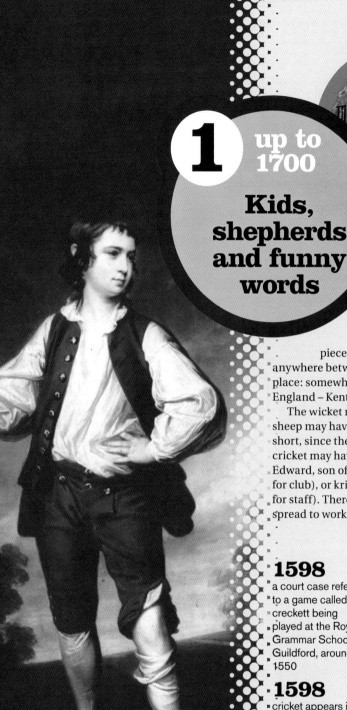

1 up to 1700

Kids, shepherds and funny words

Why is cricket like life itself? Because its origins are lost in the mists of time. It seems to have evolved from games played in the fields by shepherds or children, in which one player had a club or stick and tried to hit an object thrown or rolled by another. The object may have been a stone, a piece of wood, or a matted lump of wool. The time: anywhere between the ninth century and the 15th. The place: somewhere in northern Europe, most likely southern England – Kent, Surrey or Sussex.

The wicket may have originally been a wicket gate, and sheep may have been needed to make sure the grass was short, since the mower had yet to be invented. The name cricket may have come from creag (a game played by Prince Edward, son of Edward I, in Kent in 1300), or criquet (French for club), or kricke (Flemish for stick), or crycc (Old English for staff). There is a theory that it started as a children's game, spread to working men, and then to the gentry.

1598
a court case refers to a game called creckett being played at the Royal Grammar School, Guildford, around 1550

1598
cricket appears in an Italian-English dictionary as "cricket-a-wicket"

1610
first* "cricketing" match in Kent: the Weald v the Downs at Chevening

1611
two men from Sidlesham, Sussex, are caught missing church on Easter Sunday to play cricket, and are fined 1 shilling (5p) each

1622
first reference to a "cricket batt", in a court case

1624
first cricket fatality, in Sussex: one Jasper Vinall, a fielder hit by a batsman trying to avoid being caught

1640
Puritan clerics in Kent denounce cricket as "profane", especially if played on a Sunday

1652
a court case in Kent refers to "a certain unlawful game called cricket"

1658
first reference to a "cricket ball" by the lexicographer Edward Phillips

1666
a letter refers to a game on Richmond Green, south-west of London

1676
first reference to cricket being played abroad, by Britons living in Aleppo, Syria

1680
first reference to "wickets" in a cricket context, scribbled in an old bible and mentioning Marden in Sussex

1697
"a great match" is held in Sussex, between two sides of 11 men, for a prize of 50 guineas (£52.50)

[*first means first recorded]

THE 8 AGES OF CRICKET

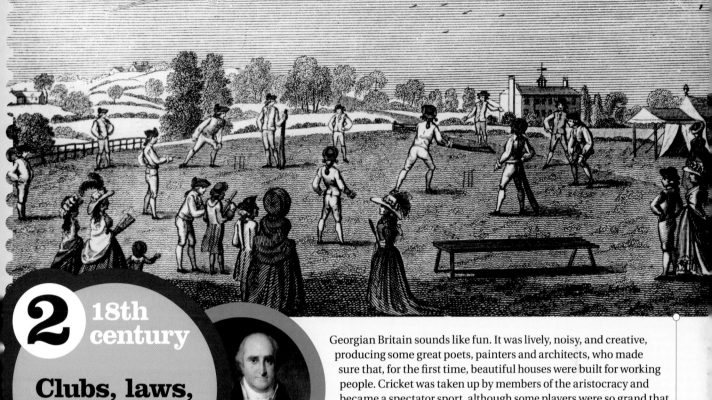

2 18th century

Clubs, laws, toffs and London

Georgian Britain sounds like fun. It was lively, noisy, and creative, producing some great poets, painters and architects, who made sure that, for the first time, beautiful houses were built for working people. Cricket was taken up by members of the aristocracy and became a spectator sport, although some players were so grand that they actually disliked being watched. The game was often played for money, and there was betting – and probably match-fixing. A match in 1751 between the Old Etonians and England was played for £1,500, with "near £20,000" wagered on the result. Cricket became entrenched in the southern counties and then moved into London. Islington and the City Road were briefly the centre of the cricket world, then Hambledon in Hampshire, before **Thomas Lord** led the way to Marylebone.

1702
match played at the Duke of Richmond's house, Goodwood in Sussex, now more famous for sports involving horses and cars

1706
the first match report – in Latin and in verse, written by William Goldwin, an old Etonian

1709
first county match: Kent v Surrey

1710
cricket pops up at Cambridge University

1718
controversial match at **White Conduit Fields**, Islington (then a village just north of London), between London Cricket Club and the Rochester Punch Club. London were winning, so Rochester walked off in a bid to save their stake money. A judge orders them to finish the next year. London win

1727
the first Articles of Agreement – laws, in effect – for matches between the Duke of Richmond's team and a Mr Brodrick's

1730
match played in central London at the Honourable Artillery Company, City Road, which still hosts cricket today

1739
first All-England team, meaning an XI chosen from everybody not available to the other side. They play Kent, who beat them by "a very few notches"

1744
first Laws of Cricket, saying the pitch has to be 22 yards, issued by the London Club

1744
first match recorded in *Scores & Biographies*, a series of books: Kent v All-England at the Artillery Ground

1751
a match is played in New York, "according to the London method"

1767ish
founding of the Hambledon Club in Hampshire, the leading club for the next 30 years

1769
first century, by John Minshull for Duke of Dorset's XI v Wrotham

1771
width of bat limited to 4¼ inches – still the rule today

1774
LBW law invented, possibly by a bowler

1775
first first-class century, by John Small, father of the straight bat, for Hambledon against Surrey

1775ish
third stump added

1776
first scorecards, at the Vine Club, Sevenoaks, Kent

1780
first ball with a seam, made by Dukes, who still make cricket balls today

1780ish
White Conduit Club founded in Islington

1787
Thomas Lord, a 31-year-old bowler, opens a ground in Dorset Square, Marylebone, for members of the White Conduit Club of Islington, who are fed up with playing on public ground because they don't like the rowdy opinions of the spectators. Lord receives financial backing from two earls and founds the Marylebone Cricket Club (MCC)

1788
White Conduit play their last game against MCC

1788
MCC revise the Laws

1777
Noah Mann, father of swing bowling, dies aged 33 after partying hard and "falling upon the embers"

1794
first school match: Charterhouse v Westminster

3 19th century

Proper bowling, writing and touring

▼ **Making waves** England's cricketers on board the ship waiting to depart from Liverpool for the first overseas tour to America. In the team are **John Wisden** and **John Lillywhite**

Georgian England gives way to Victorian England, which was more formal, less fun, but very good at getting things done. Round-arm bowling got going, and soon the batsmen decided they needed pads. Annual fixtures were set up between schools and universities. By the middle of the century, the railways had come along, so a team like the All-England XI could travel widely. The first foreign tour followed soon afterwards – with an unlikely destination. Two famous sporting brand-names cropped up: Lillywhite and Wisden. And round-arm turned to over-arm.

1805
first Eton-Harrow match: Lord Byron, later more famous as a poet, plays for Harrow

1806
first annual match between the Players (who get paid) and the Gentlemen (rich enough to play for fun). The Players usually win

1807
first round-arm bowling, by John Willes of Kent

1809
Lord's ground moves to its second site, at North Bank, St John's Wood

1811-14
cricket rudely interrupted by the Napoleonic War

1814
Lord's ground moves to its present site

1827
first annual match between Oxford and Cambridge universities, at Lord's

1828
round-arm allowed by MCC

1833
John Nyren, an ex-player, publishes the first famous cricket book, *The Young Cricketer's Tutor*, helped by a Shakespearian scholar called Charles Cowden Clarke – the game's first ghostwriter

1834
Alfred Mynn, "the Lion of Kent", makes his debut. A 23st giant who bowled fast round-arm, he was probably the first great player

1836ish
pads invented

1830s
the first bowling machine, the catapulta, is designed by Felix, artist, cricketer and schoolmaster, who uses the nickname in case parents disapprove of a teacher playing cricket

1839
first formal county club – **Sussex CCC**

1846
first match at the Oval in Kennington, south London

1846
William Clarke's All-England XI start touring the country, often playing against 20 or 22 local men

1848
Fred Lillywhite, of the sports-shop family, launches his *Guide To Cricketers*

1849
first Roses match – Yorkshire v Lancashire

1850
wicketkeepers start wearing gloves

1850
John Wisden, a leading fast bowler, opens a sports shop

1859
first overseas tour – of the US and Canada

1864
overarm bowling allowed

1864
Wisden launches his *Almanack*

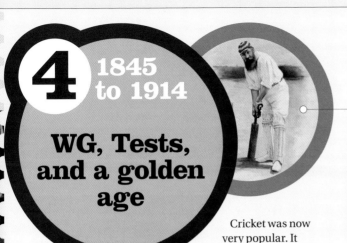

4 1845 to 1914

WG, Tests, and a golden age

Cricket was now very popular. It had its first superstar, a Gloucestershire doctor called William Gilbert Grace. He was grasping, crafty, pleased with himself and dishonest, claiming to be an amateur (unpaid) while trousering vast fees. But he was an exceptional cricketer and crowds went to see him play. At some grounds, the ticket price doubled if he was playing, and he was said to be the second best-known Englishman "after Mr Gladstone" (the prime minister).

An England team sailed to Australia, and the first Test match took place: you can guess who won. Then the Australians toured Engand. Losing away was one thing, but losing at home… Some English cricket lovers were so horrified, they put a mock death notice in the paper, and the legend of the Ashes was born.

Cricket began to take the shape we know today, with a county championship, a handsome red-brick pavilion at Lord's, a third team playing Tests, and an organisation called the ICC to supervise things. Batsmen developed stylish stroke-play and bowlers had to be clever, which led to the years leading up to the First World War being labelled the golden age. A book called *The Players* by Ric Sissons shows that for the professionals, it wasn't golden at all: some of them were so poor, they were sleeping three to a bed.

5 1918 to 1949

More countries, and Bradman

A sport with only three full members isn't much of a sport – especially if one of them is far too good for the others. In the 1920s, England and Australia saw the need to make the club a little less exclusive, so India, New Zealand and West Indies all joined in. West Indies made their mark quickly, inspired by the great George Headley; the others took 20 years or more to win a Test. But the period was dominated by one man – Don Bradman, the white Headley, the greatest run machine there has ever been.

1865
WG Grace starts playing for the Gentlemen v the Players: now the Gentlemen win more often than not

1877
first Test match – Australia v England

1882
England's first home defeat by Australia. Death notice for English cricket

placed in *Sporting Times*, which leads to tradition of the Ashes

1889
South Africa join Test cricket

1889
work begins on the present Lord's pavilion

1890
County Championship officially launched

1897
the googly invented by BJT Bosanquet

1903
MCC starts running England's overseas tours

1907-08
Jack Hobbs, arguably England's greatest player, makes his Test debut

1909
ICC founded to oversee the international game. Originally the Imperial Cricket Conference, it later changes its name to the International Cricket Council

1910
six runs awarded for a hit over

the boundary. Previously, you had to hit the ball out of the ground

1914
golden age comes to abrupt end with the First World War

1921
Australia beat England 5-0 – uniquely (until 2007)

1926
India, New Zealand and West Indies become full members of ICC

1927
first radio commentary on cricket, on the BBC

1928
West Indies' first Test

1928
Don Bradman's first Test

1929-30
West Indies' first victory, over England. George Headley, "the black Bradman", makes a hundred in each innings

1930
New Zealand's first Test

1930
Jack Hobbs's last Test

1932
India's first Test

1932-33
Bodyline affair: England bowlers target Australian batsmen's bodies, with several catchers on leg side

1935
Bodyline outlawed by MCC

1938
the BBC televises Test cricket for the first time, from Lord's

1940-44
cricket largely shuts down for the war

In Affectionate Remembrance
OF
ENGLISH CRICKET,
WHICH DIED AT THE OVAL
ON
29th AUGUST, 1882,
Deeply lamented by a large circle of sorrowing friends and acquaintances.

R.I.P.

N.B.—The body will be cremated and the ashes taken to Australia.

6 1950s and 60s

Professionalism and caution

Straight after the Second World War, cricket was glamorous and colourful, as people enjoyed themselves again after the sacrifices of wartime. But after that, it became greyer and less entertaining. The game was **televised**, but it was in black and white. Batting tended to be safety-first and although there were some famous feats, like Jim Laker's 19 wickets in a match, the atmosphere was staid. With the coming of rock 'n' roll in 1956, and then the **civil-rights** movement and the hippie movement in the Sixties, the world was changing. Cricket wasn't.

7 1970s and 80s

Pizazz, pace and Packer

Two great Australian fast bowlers, Dennis Lillee and Jeff Thomson, demolished England and West Indies – but West Indies fought back by picking four fast bowlers. Cricket began to catch up with modern life. One-day internationals arrived at last, invented almost by accident after an Australia-England Test was washed out and some light entertainment was required. They caught on instantly and a World Cup was devised. But the game was still being run high-handedly: the players were poorly paid and seldom consulted. **Kerry Packer**, an Australian media mogul, boldly offered them more money to play for him. Most of the leading Aussies and West Indians signed up, along with a few Englishmen, and the cricket world split in two. Packer pioneered coloured kit and floodlights, drew big crowds, and staged some thrilling matches. To many fans, they weren't the real thing – but nor were the so-called Tests that went ahead with less good players. After two years, peace broke out. Packer got the TV rights to Australia's home matches, and the national boards got their stars back.

1948
first five-day Tests in England

1948
Bradman's last Test

1951-52
India's first victory, over England: Vinoo Mankad takes 12 for 108

1952
Pakistan's first Test

1952-53
Pakistan's first victory, over India: Fazal Mahmood 12 for 94

1955-56
New Zealand's first victory, over West Indies, after 25 years

1957
Test Match Special launched on BBC radio

1962
last Gentlemen v Players match

1963
the end of the amateur

1963
first major one-day competition – the Gillette Cup (60 overs a side), contested by the English counties

1968
MCC hands over the running of the game in England to the Test & County Cricket Board

1970
South Africa banned from international sport because they would only pick white players

1970-71
first one-day international

1975
first World Cup, in England, won by West Indies

1976
West Indies become dominant team, playing four fast bowlers

1977
Kerry Packer signs many of the world's leading players to join a breakaway circus, leaving several Test countries fielding second-rate teams

1978
helmets arrive in Test cricket

1979
peace treaty between Packer and Australian board

1979-80
floodlights and coloured kit come into official ODIs

1980
Australia drops the eight-ball over

1982
Sri Lanka's first Test

1983
India win World Cup – first winner other than West Indies

1987
First World Cup outside England – held in India and Pakistan, won by Australia

◄▲ The fast and the fiery West Indies quick bowler Michael Holding cleans up England's Allan Knott at The Oval in 1976 above. England legend Fred Trueman left signs autographs for a couple of fans

source: Cricinfo

8 1990 to now

Small world, big money

Pace gave way to guile as Shane Warne showed that even a slow bowler could rule the world. Australia toppled the West Indies and took the game to a new level with their fast scoring. The cricket world was expanding. The seven Test teams became nine as South Africa returned and Zimbabwe joined in. The international programme ballooned, and nearly all of it was televised. Satellite TV came along to pay huge sums for the rights. India, with the most viewers, became the game's financial powerhouse. ICC grew rapidly from four people in a corner of Lord's to something like a multinational company, based in Dubai, with a vast turnover. But when an equally big development came along on another kind of screen, the administrators barely noticed. Cricinfo, one of the first sports websites, quickly became one of the biggest and best. It ran on enthusiasm, with a huge database built up largely by fans typing in old scorecards. It unearthed 1m cricket lovers in the US whose existence had been a well-kept secret. When it started publishing news and comment as well, fans had a single global noticeboard for the first time. This led to many arguments, but also to wider understanding. The cricket world had become a global village.

HOW INTERNATIONAL CRICKET HAS BALLOONED

2000s 1152 projection **1530**

2000s 350 projection **470**

1990s **983**

1990s 347

1980s 366

1980s 277

1970s 198

1970s 82

ODIs

1960s 186

1950s 164

Tests

1990
Sky TV broadcast their first England tour, to West Indies

1991
South Africa readmitted as apartheid crumbles

1992
South Africa play in World Cup for first time, in Australia and New Zealand. Cup won by Pakistan

1992
Zimbabwe's first Test

1993
Cricinfo, the first cricket website, launched by Simon King, a British scientist working temporarily in USA

1993
ICC become independent of MCC

1996
Sri Lanka win World Cup and reinvent one-day game by scoring fastest in opening overs

1997
Test & County Cricket Board replaced by England and Wales Cricket Board (ECB)

1999
ICC sell TV rights to next two World Cups and three Champions Trophies for $550m (£340m), to Rupert Murdoch's Global Cricket Corporation

1999
BBC TV loses rights to home Tests to Channel 4

2000
Cricinfo valued at $150m (£90m)

2000
Hansie Cronje, captain of South Africa, banned for life for taking bribes from bookmakers in match-fixing scandal

2000
Bangladesh's first Test

2002
Cricinfo bought by Wisden, owned by Sir Paul Getty, for a reported £1m

2003
Twenty20 cricket launched in England: first form of professional cricket that doesn't include a meal break

2005
ICC leave Lord's for Dubai

2006
Channel 4 loses TV rights to Sky

2006
Indian board announce their sponsorship and media-rights deals now worth US$1bn (about £500m)

2006
ICC sell audio-visual rights to next two World Cups, two Twenty20 World Cups, and 14 other events for a reported $1.1bn (£550m), to ESPN-Star Sports

2007
World Cup held in West Indies for first time, won by Australia for third time in a row

2007
first Twenty20 World Cup, held in South Africa

main source: *Wisden Cricketers' Almanack 2007*, pages 1440-44

◀ **Fan power**
Audiences in India are now a major force

THE GREATEST

FAST BOWLER

When *Wisden* invited 100 experts to name their Five Cricketers of the Century, no fast bowler made the final five – which was curious, because most series are won by the side with the better fast bowlers. The nearest miss was Dennis Lillee of Australia, a magnificent bowler. But he struggled in the Indian subcontinent and in my book he wasn't quite as great as **Malcolm Marshall** of West Indies, a bowler for all seasons and surfaces – very fast, very hostile, very accurate and able to swing the ball both ways. His average was among the very best (20) and so was his strike rate (46). Marshall died aged only 41, but had found time to become a leading coach and to pass on his secrets to Shaun Pollock of South Africa, who has even more Test wickets (416) than his mentor (376).

SLOW BOWLER

Anyone who thinks Murali's action is dodgy would say **Shane Warne**. But Murali's action either is dodgy or it isn't, and the game has decided that it isn't. He is not the first bowler to arouse suspicion on certain types of delivery. I'd put them equal. Warne's control is more remarkable, coming from a leg-spinner; **Murali** is more consistent on different surfaces and takes more wickets. Both have their weak spots – Warne didn't do well against India, and Murali has struggled in Australia.

BATSMAN

It has to be **Bradman**. In the Five Cricketers of the Century vote, all 100 members of the panel voted for him. See page 50.

ALLROUNDER

Not much argument about this one either. With 90 votes in Five Cricketers of the Century, it's **Garry Sobers**. See page 60 for some supporting stats.

PAIR OF BROTHERS

Until 1990, it was the Chappells – Ian, a formidable captain of Australia, and Greg, a class batsman who also captained his country. But then along came **Mark Waugh**, first replacing, then joining his twin **Steve** in the Australian team. Steve, the elder by four minutes, was a gutsy percentage player, tough as old boots and eventually a great captain. Mark was a stylish touch player, a forceful one-day opener and a scintillating slip fielder. They became two of the most capped players in Test history, with Steve playing 168 times and Mark 128, and played more than 100 Tests together. Steve's Test batting average was 51 to Mark's 41, but in all first-class cricket, their figures were virtually identical – Mark 52.04, Steve 51.95.

▼**Two sticks** Steve left and Mark Waugh right are given birthday cakes and walking sticks on their 36th birthday at Worcester, June 2, 2001

PERSONALITY

Shane Warne has to be in with a shout, but most experts would say **WG Grace**. A huge draw as a batsman, bowler, captain, showman and rogue, he was the game's first superstar.

PLAYER FROM EACH COUNTRY

COUNTRY	PLAYER	REASON?	DOUBT?	NEAREST RIVAL?
Australia	**Bradman**	best batsman ever	no	Shane Warne, leg-spin king
England	**WG Grace**	allrounder and colossus	some	Jack Hobbs, great opener
India	**Sachin Tendulkar**	78 international hundreds	some	Kapil Dev, punchy allrounder
New Zealand	**Richard Hadlee**	immaculate seamer	no	Martin Crowe, class batsman
Pakistan	**Imran Khan**	ace allrounder + captain	no	Wasim Akram, swing bowler
South Africa	**Graeme Pollock**	left-handed genius	some	Shaun Pollock, his nephew
Sri Lanka	**Murali**	best off-spinner ever	no	Sanath Jayasuriya, master blaster
West Indies	**Viv Richards**	domineering batsman	some	George Headley, great opener
Zimbabwe	**Andy Flower**	top batsman + keeper	no	Heath Streak, swing bowler

Bangladesh haven't played enough Tests to have a player worthy of this company – so far

OPENING BATSMAN

Herbert Sutcliffe of England has the highest Test average – 60. But he didn't have to face the great West Indian fast bowlers of the 1970s. **Sunil Gavaskar** of India did, and made 12 hundreds against them, averaging 65. He is also the highest-scoring Test opener with 9607 runs, although Matthew Hayden of Australia (7739) may yet catch him.

TEST BATTING AVERAGE (among those who have played 10 Tests)

No, it's not Bradman. It's not even a man. It's **Jo Broadbent** of Australia, who played 10 Tests in the 1990s and finished with an average of 109.25 from eight innings with four not-outs. She is now coach of Queensland Fire.

COACH

The most successful is John Buchanan, who stepped down as Australia coach after winning another World Cup in 2007. But he had such good raw materials to work with – Warne, McGrath, Gilchrist, Ponting, Hayden, the Waughs – that it is hard to know what value he added. The late **Bob Woolmer**, whose sudden and baffling death overshadowed the 2007 World Cup, may have been the best coach of all. He was an exceptional person, always bubbling with enthusiasm, knowledge and imagination. He steered South Africa almost to the top of the tree and Warwickshire to a string of trophies, and he helped everyone from Ian Bell to Pakistan and Scotland. Some of his former charges have already become effective coaches themselves, including Allan Donald (England's consultant bowling coach in summer 2007) and Jonty Rhodes (South Africa's fielding coach at the World Cup).

TAIL-ENDER

Of all the batsmen who have gone in regularly at No 9 to 11 (and made at least 500 runs), the one with easily the best average is **Shaun Pollock** of South Africa – 41.07 from 24 Tests as a tail-ender, with two hundreds. Only one other player averages over 30. Pollock is good to watch too, with the elegant strokes of a No 6.

WICKETKEEPER

Alan Knott of England just pips his 1970s contemporaries, Rod Marsh of Australia and Bob Taylor, also of England. Knott was eccentric, bendy and always had a handkerchief or two about his person, but nobody kept more neatly or nimbly, and he also made five Test centuries.

ONE-DAY NURDLER

The art of working the ball around for ones and twos is thought to have been first perfected by **Javed Miandad** of Pakistan. He was short, moustachioed, combative and forever annoyed about something, usually the fact that he had been replaced as captain because Imran Khan had decided to return to the team. But for nurdling the ball around, he was your man.

RUN-UP

You may know **Michael Holding** as a commentator with a great voice, once memorably compared to burnt molasses. But he used to be a fast bowler, one of the great West Indian attack of the 1980s, and his run-up was worth watching on its own – long, silky, rhythmic and almost silent.

WICKETKEEPER-BATSMAN

Adam Gilchrist of Australia, the greatest No 7 batsman in Test history, just pips Andy Flower of Zimbabwe, a brilliant player of spin who is now England's assistant coach.

FIELDER

In the modern age, which has been the era of athletic fielding, it's **Jonty Rhodes** of South Africa. See page 65.

GREAT RIVALRIES 1

THE ASHES

When Britain goes to war, Australia usually joins in – on the same side. But you wouldn't know it from the way they treat each other on the cricket field. This is the greatest rivalry in international cricket, because:

It's the oldest. It began in 1877, in the very first Test match, and has been going ever since, when not rudely interrupted by some other old foes – the Germans.

It's the one that is played most. England and Australia have met in 316 Test matches, twice as many as any other pair of teams. Next comes England v West Indies on 138. Most Test series are now only three matches long, but the Ashes is nearly always five or six.

It has the best name, trophy and story. As a name, the Ashes is short, vivid and memorable. As a trophy, it's lovable – tiny, plain, no airs or graces or bling. As a story, well, read on …

In 1882, England lost at home to Australia for the first time. It was quite an achievement after bowling the Aussies out for 63. Needing just 85 to win, England were suffocated by FR Spofforth, known as The Demon, who bagged 14

10 EPiC ASHES BATTLES

1920-21
Aussie whitewash
Australia win all five Tests. Their captain, Warwick Armstrong, is nicknamed the Big Ship. England's captain, JWHT Douglas, is nicknamed Johnny Won't Hit Today.

1930
Bradman's summer
A young Australian batsman, barely 22, makes 974 runs, still a world record for any Test series. Australia win 2-1. See page 50.

1932-33
Bodyline
The England captain, Douglas Jardine – actually a Scotsman – comes up with a dastardly plan to thwart Bradman: bowling at the batsman's body, with a ring of short legs to catch the ball as he fends it off. It works, but at a heavy cost. Most cricket-lovers disapprove and Australia almost breaks off diplomatic relations with Britain. See page 50.

1948
The Invincibles
England are at home, and have a powerful side, and Bradman is now 40. Somehow, Australia win 4-0. They are nicknamed The Invincibles. See page 50.

1953
Hutton's triumph
A dour series begins with four draws but sputters into life at the Oval as first Bedser and Trueman, then Laker and Lock bowl the Aussies out. England regain the Ashes after 19 years.

1970-71
Illingworth's triumph
After a tedious decade, the Ashes flicker into life again. England are captained by the canny Ray Illingworth, who deploys John Snow, a moodily brilliant fast bowler, to rip through the Aussies. England win 2-0.

1974-75
Lillee and Thomson
Australia now have a great pair of fast bowlers – one classical, the other a slinger. They terrorise an elderly England line-up and Australia win 4-1.

1981
Botham's Ashes
Australia get on top and England's captain resigns after only two Tests. Then he bounces back and plays like a superhero as England win 3-1. See page 86.

2005
Flintoff's finest hour
Australia arrive in England as firm favourites after dominating the Ashes for 16 years. At first

wickets in the match. In his last 11 overs, he took a staggering 4 for 2, as Australia squeezed home by seven runs. One spectator was reported to have dropped dead and another bit chunks out of his umbrella handle. A mock death-notice appeared in the *Sporting Times* (see page 91). The writer was a journalist, Reginald Brooks. The papers took up the phrase and England's next tour of Australia, in 1882-83, was described as a "quest to regain the ashes of English cricket". The quest was successful. The term then rather vanished in England, until, in 1904, Plum Warner of England wrote a book called *How We Recovered the Ashes. Wisden's* first mention of the Ashes followed in 1905.

In 1882-83, an urn had been presented to the England captain, Ivo Bligh. What it contained, nobody has ever established – maybe a bail, maybe a veil. When Bligh died in 1927, his widow gave it to MCC. It has been the official Ashes urn ever since. It is not technically a trophy, as it is not presented to the winning captain – he gets a replica. So as well as being small and plain, it is somewhat hypothetical. But you can see it in the Lord's museum and it's well worth a visit, if only to say, "Wow! It's so small!"

---

they win easily, but then England fight back through the cool captaincy of Michael Vaughan and some great all-round feats from Andrew Flintoff. A series of cliffhangers ends in a 2-1 win for England. Shane Warne takes 40 wickets and finishes on the losing side. See page 40.

 2006-07
Ponting's revenge
Australia keep faith with their defeated captain, Ricky Ponting. He leads them on a mission: not just to win back the Ashes, but to destroy England. They succeed, winning 5-0. England, captained by Flintoff as Vaughan is injured, are hopeless. From the heights of 2005, they have gone all the way back to square one – or 1921.

YORKSHIRE v LANCASHIRE

Another great name. Any meeting between Yorkshire and Lancashire is called the Roses match, after the white rose of Yorkshire and the red rose of Lancashire. It all started on the battlefield, in the Wars of the Roses (1455-85). The first Roses match was in 1849 and according to Wikipedia there had been 617 of them by June 2007 – although that was counting 2nd XI games, which was stretching a point.

The matches attract big crowds, who are often bored senseless, as the teams are so desperate not to lose that they forget about trying to win. The classic example was 1926, when 78,217 people piled into Old Trafford, only to watch a mind-numbing, high-scoring draw in which the second innings never even arrived. But every so often, the pattern is broken, usually by an Aussie …

 1924 **Headingley** On a spicy pitch, a Yorkshire side packed with big names (Holmes, Sutcliffe, Rhodes) bowl Lancashire out for 113 and 74, so they need only 58 to win. They are all out for 33.

 1927 **Old Trafford** In a bid to liven things up after a few draws and one heavy defeat, Lancashire get their tearaway Australian fast bowler, Ted McDonald, to attempt an early version of Bodyline, aiming at the batsman with four men in a leg trap and no conventional slips. He takes 11 for 135 and Lancs win by eight wickets.

 2001 **Headingley** Darren Lehmann of Yorkshire and Australia hammers 252 off only 288 balls. Many old pros turn in their graves. Yorkshire go on to win the County Championship.

 2004 **Headingley** In a Roses Twenty20 match, Andrew Flintoff opens for Lancashire and blasts 85 off only 48 balls. But Lancs' innings falls away and then **Ian Harvey** of Yorkshire and Australia goes one better with 108 off 59 balls. Yorks cruise home by eight wickets.

INDIA v PAKISTAN

These two used to be one – Pakistan began life only in 1947, when India became independent of Britain. They have a spiky political relationship, often clashing over the disputed territory of Kashmir. Sometimes it stops them playing cricket; other times it stops them playing good cricket.

When they have managed to play each other, the matches have been Roses-like – too cagey to be entertaining. In the 1980s and 1990s, there were 15 draws in 16 Tests, but lately there have been only three in 12. In 2003-04, India won a Test in Pakistan for the first time and went on to a famous series victory. Many Indian fans who went to watch were astonished to find a warm welcome and to see that the two nations had far more in common than they had been led to believe.

 1952-53 **Delhi** Vinoo Mankad, a slow left-armer (and opening batsman), settles the first Test between the two sides by taking 8 for 52 and 5 for 79. India win by an innings.

 1952-53 **Lucknow** Pakistan take instant revenge as the starring role switches to Fazal Mahmood, a seamer who was Pakistan's first great bowler. He takes 5 for 52 and 7 for 42.

 **1979-80** **Madras** Kapil Dev, India's greatest allrounder, has an incredible match against a powerful Pakistan side. He takes 4 for 90, then wallops 84, then takes 7 for 56.

2003-04 **Multan** Virender Sehwag hits 309 off only 375 balls – the first triple century for India. Unlike many huge scores, it leads to victory as Anil Kumble takes 6 for 72.

 **2005-06** **Karachi** After two Tests in a three-Test series, it's 0-0 as the teams revert to their drawing habit. Pakistan change all that with a fantastic team effort. After collapsing to 39 for 6, they recover to 245 through a sustained wag of the tail. They restrict India to 238 and then their top seven make up for the first innings by all passing 50, which is extremely rare. They declare on 599 for 7 and win by 341 runs.

extreme MATCHES

THE TiED TEST

Brisbane, December 1960. In an era of sleepy cricket, the captains of Australia and West Indies, Richie Benaud and Frank Worrell, made a pact that they would try to entertain. West Indies won the toss in the first Test and rattled up 359 for 7 on the opening day with Garry Sobers stroking 132. When they were all out for 453 off only 100.6 overs, Australia replied in the same vein with 505 off 130.3 overs. Sobers conceded almost as many as he had scored – 115.

West Indies then made 284 as Alan Davidson, a rather cool left-armer seamer, took six wickets to make 11 in the match. Australia needed only 233 to win, but low targets can be tricky and time was tight. Wes Hall, a great fast bowler smarting from being hit for 140 in the first innings, ripped through the top order. Australia collapsed to 92 for 6, and a leading commentator, Alan McGilvray, left at tea to catch a flight home. But Davidson was determined to make it his match. He hit 80 and at the other end Benaud reached 50. At 226 for 6, Australia needed only seven more runs with four wickets left. They couldn't lose – but they could panic. Davidson was run out, beaten by a brilliant throw from Joe Solomon.

Two balls later, at the end of the over, it was 5.54pm and there was time for only one more over. Australia needed six runs with three wickets left. And these were eight-ball overs, so the run-rate was quite manageable. But the bowler was Hall, fast, scary and charged-up. He hit Wally Grout, the Australian wicketkeeper, in the midriff. Grout doubled up in pain, but Benaud had set off for the run and they both scrambled in for a leg bye. Five needed off seven. Then Hall dropped

short, Benaud's eyes lit up, he went for a pull, and edged to the keeper. Hall bowled a dot ball, then Grout was so desperate to regain the strike, he ran a bye to the keeper. Four needed off four. Grout top-edged a pull. It was in the air so long that people said four players could have caught it. Hall raced over to claim it himself – and dropped it.

The batsmen had run one so it was three off three. Hall bowled yet another bouncer: Ian Meckiff, an Australian fast bowler, swished, connected, ran two and went for the third to win the match, but Grout was run out by a scorching throw in to the keeper from Conrad Hunte. Australia were 232 for 9: one run needed, one wicket left, two balls to go. Their No 11, Lindsay Kline, who had been in bed with tonsillitis, came in to face the music. "If you bowl a no-ball now," Worrell told Hall, "don't go back to Barbados." Hall delivered the ball from a foot behind the line, to be on the safe side. Kline poked the ball towards midwicket, where Joe Solomon was waiting. He dashed in, aimed for the stumps and hit. Meckiff became the third man to be **run out** in the space of eight balls. The West Indians celebrated as if they had won, but the scores were level: it was the first tied Test.

THE TiMELESS TEST

Durban, March 1939. There were many timeless Tests but this, the last of them, is the one that has been remembered – partly because, in the end, it wasn't timeless. England were touring South Africa and were 1-0 up in a five-Test series with one to play. So it was agreed that the last one should be timeless. The groundsman prepared a suitably flat pitch and South Africa made 530 off 200 overs. England, captained by the legendary Wally Hammond, replied with a disappointing 316. South Africa piled up another 481 to get past 1000 for the match, so England needed 696 to win. By now, a week had gone by – six days' play and one rest day.

England, with a mountain to climb, put on their hiking boots and got going. **Bill Edrich**, who had played eight Tests and done nothing, found his feet with 219 and added 280 for the second wicket with Paul Gibb. The eighth day was lost to rain, but on the ninth England bored on to 496 for 3. Now they needed just 200 more. They managed 158, to reach 654 for 5, by tea. But then it rained again and, after $43\frac{1}{4}$ hours' play, the game was called off – because England's boat was leaving. They missed out on completing the greatest run chase of all time. Wouldn't they have been better off missing the boat?

THE MOST DRAMATIC COMEBACK

Calcutta, March 2000. Australia, desperate to win a series in India for the first time in 31 years, are 1-0 up with two to play. They cruise to 214 for 2, but Harbhajan Singh, the offspinner known as The Turbanator, takes a very starry hat-trick (Ricky Ponting, Adam Gilchrist and Shane Warne) and pegs them back to 269 for 8. The Australian captain, Steve Waugh, makes a battling 110 and adds 133 with Jason Gillespie, so the Aussies still manage 445. They then bowl clinically and get India out for 171, with only one man passing 30 – the No 6, VVS Laxman, who makes a swashbuckling 59. India follow on

and, at 115 for 3, they are staring down the barrel of an innings defeat and a series loss.

Their captain, Sourav Ganguly, boldly promotes Laxman to No 3, swapping him with the more defensive Rahul Dravid. Laxman adds 117 with Ganguly (48) and finishes the third day on 109 not out, with Dravid just getting going. The two of them put together an epic partnership, batting through the whole of the fourth day to take India from 254 for 4 to 589. Laxman amasses a sparkling 281, a new record for a Test score by an Indian; Dravid makes a more sober 180, and their stand

is a monumental 376. India are in charge now.

Ganguly declares on 657 for 7, setting Australia 383 to win. Harbhajan twirls his way to another six wickets, Gilchrist gets a king pair (out first ball both times) and India win easily, by 171 runs. In the final Test, Harbhajan takes even more wickets (15) and spins India to a great series win. Laxman's parents, who wanted him to be a doctor rather a cricketer, realise that he may have made the right decision.

▼ **Day to remember**
VVS Laxman left and Rahul Dravid leave the field at the end of the fourth day, having batted through all three sessions

◄ **Last word**
Harbhajan Singh gets the final wicket of Glenn McGrath lbw and India win the match after following on, 274 behind

THE HIGHEST-SCORING ONE-DAYER

Johannesburg, March 2006. Australia and South Africa, old one-day foes, are 2-2 in the series with one match to go. For years, 300 has been a very good score in a one-day international. Australia win the toss on a spanking pitch and pile up an outrageous 434 for 4. Their captain, Ricky Ponting, hammers 164 off only 105 balls with nine sixes, while Mike Hussey, normally an accumulator, bashes 81 off 51 balls. Together they add 158 off only 15.4 overs. Jacques Kallis goes for 70 off his six overs. The only question is whether South Africa will lose by 100, 200 or 300 runs.

But they have nothing to lose and it shows. "Come on guys," Kallis tells them, "It's a 450 wicket. They're 15 short!" Graeme Smith

and **Herschelle Gibbs** rattle along at nine an over. Smith makes 90 off 55 balls, while Gibbs matches Ponting with 175 off 111. Wickets fall regularly but never in quick succession. When Gibbs is out, another old hand, Mark Boucher, runs the show and sees South Africa home to 438 for 9 with a ball to spare. There have been 872 runs in the day, smashing the old record of 693. Mick Lewis, an Aussie seamer, finishes with the most embarrassing figures in one-day international history: 0 for 113 off his ten overs. "It's not like I bowled a heap of pies," Lewis says. "I actually bowled quite well."

AUSTRALIA		18:58	S AFRICA		TOTAL	**438**
＊LEE	7.5	68 1	SMITH	90	WICKETS	**9**
BRACKEN	10	67 5	DIPPENAAR	1		
CLARK	6	54 0	GIBBS	175	OVERS	**49**
LEWIS	10	113 0	deVILIERS	14	BATSMAN – :	
SYMONDS	9	75 2	KALLIS	20		
CLARKE	7	49 1	＊BOUCHER	50	BATSMAN ×	50
			KEMP	13	PARTNERSHIP	5
Keeper: GILCHRIST			VD WATH	35	RUNS TO WIN	
EXTRAS BALLS LEFT		TO WIN	TELEMACUS	12	OVERS LEFT :	
			HALL	7	RATE ACH'D	8.8
20		1	NTINI	1	RATE REQ'D	

► **Chase of a lifetime** Mark Boucher and Makhaya Ntini celebrate the winning runs

WISDEN
FROM A TINY FAST BOWLER TO A FAT YELLOW BOOK

T he boy was short, slight, and very good at sport. Nowadays, he would probably have ended up as a jockey. But this was back in the 1820s. He was born in Brighton in Sussex, one of the few places where cricket had caught on. His father, a successful carpenter, died young, and perhaps that left the boy more determined to make his mark. To help support his six brothers and sisters, he found work as a pot-boy at a pub – what we would now call a barman – and earned sixpence an hour (2½p) as a long-stop at James Lillywhite's cricket practices. The pub was owned by the Sussex wicketkeeper, Tom Box, who taught the boy to play cricket. He was so good at it that, on his 12th birthday, he played for a team called Eleven Youths of Brighton. Height was not so important for bowlers in those days because the arm was not allowed to be raised above the shoulder. So John Wisden, who weighed only 7 stone and was somewhere between 5ft 4 and 5ft 6, became the most shrimp-like of all the famous fast bowlers.

He didn't just bowl fast: he bowled straight. He played for Sussex at 18 and took six wickets in his first bowl for them. In 1850, aged 23, he played for the South against the North at Lord's, and in the second innings he took 10 wickets, all bowled. One of his victims was Tom Box. This is still the only time that anyone has ever got all 10, all bowled, in a first-class innings. Historically, any bowling average under 20 is exceptional; Wisden's average was a third of that, 6.66. He loved taking wickets and in 1850, in only 38 matches, he took 340 of them. His deliveries were described as "very fast and ripping". He became known as the Little Wonder.

John Wisden could bat, too: he played with a straight bat, was strong on the leg side, and in 1855, he made 148 for Sussex against Yorkshire, the only century scored in the whole first-class season. Fuller Pilch, another great player, rated him the best allrounder of his day. And as well as an eye for a ball, Wisden had an eye for business. In 1849 he and another star player, George Parr, levelled a field in Leamington Spa, Warwickshire, to stage cricket matches, and in 1850 he started selling sports equipment there. In 1855 he went into partnership with a friend and fellow player, Fred Lillywhite, running a sports outfitter in central London. The shop sold something else too, which seems fairly strange now: tobacco.

The mid-19th century was a great time to be a cricketer. The game was growing rapidly and, thanks to the arrival of the railways, sportsmen were able to travel. Wisden appeared for the All-England XI, which played matches up and down the country, and then, when

he tired of being treated arrogantly by the captain, he helped found the United England XI, of which he was joint secretary. Wisden was known for treating people well, and even started a benevolent fund to help cricketers who were struggling to make ends meet.

In 1859, he was one of the organisers of the first England tour overseas – to America and Canada, of all places. He went on it as a player and helped the English team win all eight of their matches. But touring can put a strain on relationships and something seems to have happened between him and his friend Fred on this trip, as their joint venture came to an end soon afterwards.

Wisden, bowling medium-pace by now, was still taking plenty of wickets, but, like many ageing bowlers, he was playing through the pain. He had rheumatism – constant pain in his bones and joints – and it was made worse by a sprain picked up playing racquets, which caused him to miss the whole 1860 season. In 1863, aged 36, he gave up the game. The decision is usually put down to the rheumatism, but he had a new project: launching a cricket yearbook.

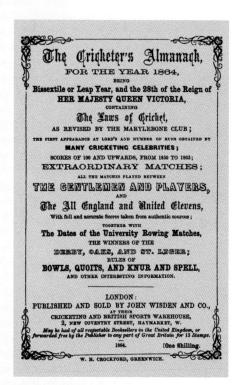

He called it *The Cricketer's Almanack* (the apostrophe moved later) and it first appeared in 1864, price one shilling (5p). It was a funny little book, only 112 pages long, with a fair amount of padding – it even included random facts like the dates of the English Civil War and the rules of other games, such as quoiting. It wasn't the first cricket annual: Wisden's old friend Fred Lillywhite had been publishing his *Guide to Cricketers* once or twice a year since 1849, and since 1851 this had included a review of the previous season. But Lillywhite's book had been controversial because it included comments, some of them negative, on the leading players. Wisden decided not to do that, and that may have been one reason why his *Almanack* took off – which is ironic, as it later became famous for expressing fearless opinions.

John Wisden is said to have "suffered greatly" late in his life, as many sportsmen do. He died of cancer in 1884, at the age of only 57, and was buried in Brompton Cemetery in London.

He had no children, but his brainchild was destined to grow and grow. In 1889, the *Almanack* started naming its Cricketers of the Year (see panel, right). In 1891, a new editor was appointed – Sydney Pardon, who was in charge for 35 years and became one of the fathers of modern sportswriting. The book began to express opinions and to have an influence as well as recording the previous year's cricket. Pardon started the Notes by the Editor (see panel, right).

The *Almanack* kept on appearing through both world wars, and one battered copy of the 1939 edition was passed round endlessly in prisoner-of-war camps in the jungle in Thailand, much to the bemusement of the Japanese guards. At one camp, it was in such demand that borrowers were limited to 12 hours. This copy, which belonged to the cricket writer EW Swanton, was stamped by the prison authorities "Not subversive". It was so heavily thumbed that it fell apart and had to be re-bound by two prisoners using rice paste as glue. It is now in the Lord's museum.

Wisden has long been a collector's item. Rare editions, from the very early years or from the wars, are worth thousands of pounds on their own, and complete sets are much sought after. If you want one, you will need a load of cash and some long shelves, as there have been 144 editions and lately they have tended to be around 1700 pages long. In 2005, a set of the first 52 *Wisdens* was sold for £150,000 – but they had another famous name attached. They had once belonged to WG Grace, who crossed out some of the scores next to his name and replaced them with bigger ones.

In 1963, John Wisden and Co. celebrated its centenary in publishing by launching the Wisden Trophy, to be awarded to the winners of Test series between England and the West Indies. Wisden is now owned by Mark Getty, head of the picture agency Getty Images, who inherited it from his father, the cricket-loving philanthropist Sir Paul. It is the world's oldest continuously published sports annual. In cricket, it is an institution with two distinct roles, acting as the game's chronicle and its conscience. It is also a surprisingly good read – see page 122 for tips on where to begin.

SOME WISDEN TRADITIONS

The Five Cricketers of the Year

The editor always chooses the Five Cricketers of the Year, a tradition that dates back to 1889. Nobody can be chosen twice, and the choices tend to be biased towards the English summer. The five chosen in 2007 were Paul Collingwood and Monty Panesar of England, Mahela Jayawardene of Sri Lanka, Mohammad Yousuf of Pakistan, and Mark Ramprakash, formerly of England, now a phenomenal run-maker with Surrey. Ramprakash was probably the first Cricketer of the Year to be a ballroom-dancing champion (see p49).

The Leading Cricketer in the World

Since 2004, the *Almanack* has named the world's leading player, based on performances in the previous year. This award can be won twice, although it hasn't been yet. The winners so far have been Ricky Ponting (2004 edition) and Shane Warne (2005) of Australia, Andrew Flintoff of England (2006) and Muttiah Muralitharan of Sri Lanka (2007). Also in the 2007 edition, the idea was backdated to 1900, which meant lots of extra mentions for DG Bradman.

The cover

The famous yellow jacket first appeared in 1938. Before that, it was sometimes salmon pink. The two men in top hats, a woodcut by the well-known artist Eric Ravilious, also made their debut in 1938. The first photograph appeared on the cover in 2003. It was a black-and-white shot of Michael Vaughan, of England, who had made seven Test centuries in a year.

Notes by the Editor

Started by Sydney Pardon in 1901, the notes are the first thing in each edition. They express strong views on the state of the game, from an independent point of view, and are reported throughout the cricket world. When they take issue with the game's bosses, it's a bit like having someone walk into school and give your head-teacher a good telling-off.

400

● ● ● **(not out)** the highest individual score in a Test, also by **Brian Lara**. You wait ages for a record-breaking score, then several come along at once. Garry Sobers' record of 365 not out for West Indies v Pakistan in 1957-58 stood for 36 years. Then Lara pinched it with 375 for West Indies v England at St John's, Antigua in 1993-94. Within ten years, the record had fallen into Australian hands, when Matthew Hayden made 380 at Perth in 2003-04 – but as it was against Zimbabwe, a weak team further weakened by terrible political problems, nobody outside Australia got very excited. A few months later, Lara grabbed the record back, again in Antigua, again against England, by becoming the first man to reach 400. Vast scores usually require certain conditions – a flat pitch, a small ground or fast outfield, and feeble or unmotivated bowlers (both Lara's Test records came in dead matches, with the series already settled). But they are still quite something. There's a reason why Lara breaks records and most batsmen don't: he is a fast scorer with an enormous appetite (for runs).

501

● ● ● **(not out)** the highest individual score ever made in a first-class match, by **Brian Lara**, for Warwickshire v Durham at Edgbaston in 1994. It was an astonishing feat, especially as Lara had set a new Test record of 375 only two months before. The 501 contained a record 72 boundaries – 62 fours and ten sixes. But the match still petered out into a draw. A big score can be a big bore.

19

● ● ● the most wickets ever taken by one bowler in a Test or first-class match, by **Jim Laker**, for England against Australia at Old Trafford, Manchester, in 1956. In theory somebody could take 20 in a match, but nobody ever has. Laker, an offspinner with a silky action, had a lot of help from the pitch, which was sticky at first, then dusty. The groundsman, Bert Flack, was under instructions to prepare a turning pitch, and he certainly obliged. Some of the Australian batsmen felt that they should have gone down in the scorebook as "bowled Flack". But it was still a staggering achievement by Laker, especially as there was a very capable spinner wheeling away at the other end – the slow left-armer Tony Lock. Poor old Lock took just one wicket. "Well bowled, you bastard," he said to Laker as yet another wicket fell. "Now give me the bloody ball!"

how the record has grown over 100 years

287	**RE Foster,** Eng v Aus, Sydney, 1903-04
325	**Andrew Sandham,** Eng v WI, Kingston, 1929-30
334	**Don Bradman,** Aus v Eng, Leeds, 1930
336	not out **Wally Hammond,** Eng v NZ, Auckland, 1932-33
364	**Len Hutton,** Eng v Aus, The Oval, 1938
365	not out **Garry Sobers,** WI v Pak, Kingston, 1957-58
375	**Brian Lara,** WI v Eng, St John's, 1993-94
380	**Matthew Hayden,** Aus v Zim, Perth, 2003-04
400	not out **Brian Lara,** WI v Eng, St John's, 2003-04

the magic

952

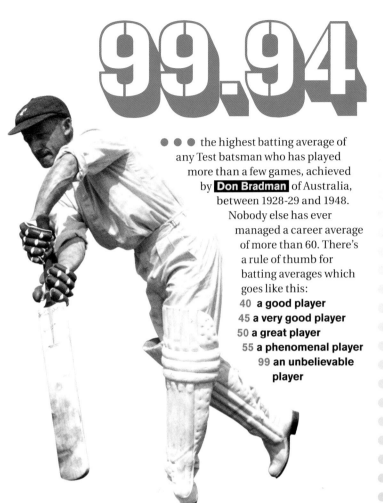

● ● ● **(for six declared, off 271 overs)** the highest team score in a Test, by **Sri Lanka** v India, at the Premadasa Stadium, Colombo, in 1997. India batted first and made 537 for 8 declared. The declaration came late on the second day, which is a normal thing to do – you pile up enough runs to have a chance of an innings victory, and then ask your opponents, who are dog-tired from two long days in the field, to bat for an hour or so. Sri Lanka finished that day on 39 for 1. The next day they didn't lose a single wicket, cruising to 322 for 1. They didn't lose a wicket the next day either, reaching 587 for 1. By now there was only one day left. Instead of trying to win, Sri Lanka just batted on and on, adding another 365. The term "bore draw" has never been more appropriate. They say records are made to be broken, but let's hope this one never is.

99.94

● ● ● the highest batting average of any Test batsman who has played more than a few games, achieved by **Don Bradman** of Australia, between 1928-29 and 1948. Nobody else has ever managed a career average of more than 60. There's a rule of thumb for batting averages which goes like this:

40 a good player
45 a very good player
50 a great player
55 a phenomenal player
99 an unbelievable player

708

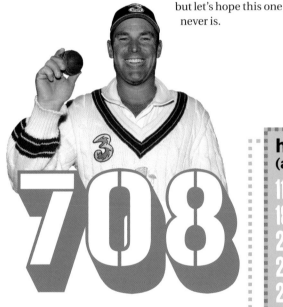

● ● ● the most wickets taken in a Test career, by **Shane Warne**, of Australia, between 1991-92 and 2006-07. When he retired, in January 2007, Warne made it clear that he expected to be overtaken soon by Muttiah Muralitharan – the man he pinched the record from in 2004.

how the record has grown over 100 years
(and the year each player broke it)

118 **Johnny Briggs,** England, slow left-arm, in 33 Tests (1899)	**355** **Dennis Lillee,** Australia, pace, in 70 Tests (1981)
189 **SF Barnes,** England, seam, in 27 Tests (1914)	**383** **Ian Botham,** England, swing, in 102 Tests (1986)
216 **Clarrie Grimmett,** Australia, legspin, in 37 Tests (1936)	**431** **Richard Hadlee,** New Zealand, seam, in 86 Tests (1988)
236 **Alec Bedser,** England, seam, in 51 Tests (1953)	**434** **Kapil Dev,** India, swing, in 131 Tests (1992)
252 **Brian Statham*,** England, seam, in 70 Tests (1963)	**519** **Courtney Walsh,** West Indies, pace, in 132 Tests (2000)
307 **Fred Trueman,** England, pace, in 67 Tests (1963)	**527** **Muttiah Muralitharan,** Sri Lanka, offspin, in 90 Tests (2004)
309 **Lance Gibbs,** West Indies, off spin, in 79 Tests (1976)	**708** **Shane Warne**,** Australia, legspin, in 145 Tests (2004)

* Statham held the record for a month before it was grabbed by his own opening partner.
** Murali held the record for five months before Warne overtook him. By the time Warne retired, Murali had 674 wickets from 110 Tests. Source: mainly BBC.co.uk

numbers

All records as at April 10, 2007. For updates, go to the records section on Cricinfo – www.cricinfo.com/db/STATS/

4.07

●●● the lowest batting average of any Test cricketer who has played at least 50 matches, by **Bhagwat Chandrasekhar** of India. Known as Chandra to save time, he had a withered arm from a childhood bout of polio. This was no problem for his bowling: he was an excellent legspinner with a whippy, befuddling action, who helped turn India into a team that could win Test matches abroad. But the arm may have made a difference to his batting, which was magnificently inept. He played 58 Tests between 1964 and 1979 and only managed to collect 167 runs, at the rate of just under one a month. His highest score was 22. His typical score was 0: of his 41 completed innings, 23 ended in a duck. He is well adrift at the bottom of the table of those who have played 50 Tests. The next worst batsman is Lance Gibbs of the West Indies (6.97), just behind Glenn McGrath of Australia (7.36) and Matthew Hoggard of England (7.53). All of them are career number 11s except Hoggard, who, amazingly, has often appeared at No 9.

6

●●● the lowest team score in a first-class match, made by a team called **the Bs** against England at Lord's in 1810. One man was absent, and the rest may as well have been. The lowest since 1900 is 12 all out by Northamptonshire v Gloucestershire at Gloucester in 1907 (batsmen all present … and incorrect). The lowest in the 21st century is 19 all out by Matabeleland v Mashonaland, Harare, 2000-01. They may have succumbed to boredom as much as anything else: some years, Matabeleland and Mashonaland are the only teams in the first-class competition in Zimbabwe, so they see a lot of each other. I like to think the Mashonaland supporters sang "Oh dear, what can the Matabe?"

26

●●● the lowest team score in a Test – by **New Zealand** v England, Auckland, 1954-55. New Zealand batted first and made 200, which wasn't bad for them at the time: after 25 years of trying, they had yet to win a Test match. They then bowled England out for 246 and were probably entertaining hopes of that elusive first victory when they reached 6 for none. But then they collapsed like a house of cards in a high wind. England, playing under Len Hutton for the last time, were so ruthlessly efficient they didn't even concede any extras. The New Zealand captain, a former fighter pilot called Geoff "Boney" Rabone, was LBW to Brian Staham for seven, although he thought he had edged the ball. "It was very unfortunate," he said later. "We might have made 30 if I hadn't been given out." Curiously, the five lowest Test scores were all made against England. And all rather a long time ago.

◄ **Nought again**
Bhagwat Chandrasekhar is out for another duck during India's tour of England in 1967

► **Top score**
Bert Sutcliffe's 11 was the highest of the innings

35

● ● ● the lowest team score in a one-day international, by **Zimbabwe** against Sri Lanka at Harare in 2004. Lucky they were playing at home – otherwise it could have been really disastrous. Nobody reached double figures: the highest score was 7 by Dion Ebrahim, equal with Extras. The innings occupied 18 overs and was over inside an hour and a half. Sri Lanka knocked off the runs in 39 minutes for the loss of one wicket. The previous record, also set against Sri Lanka, was 36 by Canada in the 2003 World Cup.

▲ **It's all over** Farveez Maharoof (3 for 3) dismisses Zimbabwe's last man Tinashe Panyangara

79

● ● ● the lowest team score in a Twenty20 international, by **Australia** against England at the Rose Bowl in 2005. Chasing 179, the Aussies collapsed to 31 for 7 in the face of some unexpected aggression from the England bowlers, led by the old warhorse **Darren Gough**. Funny how the shortest form of the game has produced the highest of the lowest scores. It's partly because it hasn't been around for long – only three years. Australia made up for it the next time they met England in a Twenty20 match, at Sydney in January 2007, by setting a new record for the highest score in this form of the international game: 221 for 5, at a rollicking rate of 11 an over. By the time you read this, both records may well have been broken, as the first Twenty20 World Championship will have been held in South Africa in September 2007.

▼ **Aggression** Darren Gough squares up to Andrew Symonds

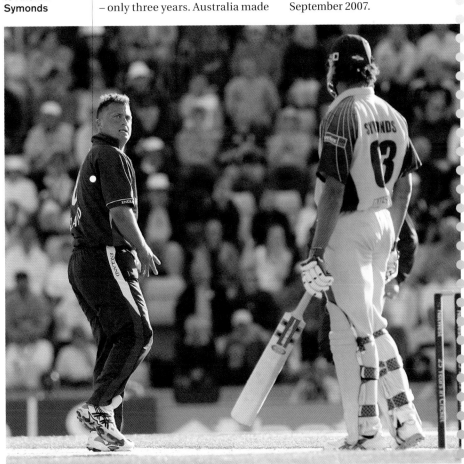

numbers

All records as at April 10, 2007. For updates, go to the records section on Cricinfo – www.cricinfo.com/db/STATS/

STATISTICS

Cricket loves its stats. Averages get flashed up on the television screen and are much quoted by the pundits. So it's worth knowing a bit about them

How averages work

A batting average is calculated like this: the total number of runs the batsman has made, divided by the number of times he has been out. So if he makes **30, 60, 0 and 10**, his average is **25 (100 ÷ 4)**. But if one of those scores was not out, his average would be **33.33 (100 ÷ 3)**. And if two of them were not out, he would have an average of **50**, even though he had only passed 50 once.

A batting average is usually presented like this:

	mat	inns	NO	runs	HS	ave	100/50
Brian Lara	131	232	6	11,953	400*	**52.88**	34/48

The abbreviations stand for **matches, innings, not-outs, highest score, average** and **hundreds and fifties**. The fifties don't include the hundreds, and the asterisk means that the 400 was not out.

A bowling average is calculated like this: the total number of runs the bowler has conceded, divided by the number of wickets he has taken. So if you take **3 for 60**, your average is **20**. If you then take **0 for 30**, **2 for 70** and **3 for 80**, you'll have a total of **8 for 240**, and your average will be **30**. The lower, the better: for Test bowlers, an average of 20 is phenomenal, 25 great, 30 good, and 35 OK as long as they make runs as well.

A bowling average is usually presented like this:

	mat	balls	runs	wkts	ave	5/10w
Brett Lee	59	12,279	7300	231	**31.60**	7/0

The abbreviations stand for **matches, wickets, average** and **five-wicket innings and ten-wicket matches.**

With both batting and bowling, you need to be clear whether the average is for a career, a series, a season or a period, and whether it is for Test cricket, or first-class, one-day internationals or all professional one-day games (List A, as they're known). Averages are usually given to two decimal places (99.94), although goodness knows why: even Bradman didn't have the ability to score 0.94 of a run.

What's good about them

Averages are clear-cut, easy to work out for yourself, and they tend to even out over time. Look at how **Graeme Smith**, the South African captain, did in England in 2003:

Test	score	total	ave so far
1st	277	277	**277**
	85	362	**181**
2nd	259	621	**207**
3rd	35	656	**164**
	5	661	**132.20**
4th	2	663	**110.50**
	14	677	**96.71**
5th	18	695	**86.87**
	19	714	**79.33**

In the first two Tests, he was a superhero. But after that, the England bowlers worked him out, going round the wicket to cramp him on his off stump, just as they would with Adam Gilchrist in the Ashes two years later. Smith picked up two single-figure scores, as opening batsmen are always liable to, facing a new ball and fresh bowlers. And his average, so huge early on, went down with every innings – although it still ended up very high. So it reflected his series pretty well.

Heading for 277 Smith sweeps past Alec Stewart

Strike rates

Averages are not the only statistical measure. There are also strike rates, and again, there is one for batting and one for bowling.

A batsman's strike rate is the number of runs he makes per hundred balls, so high is good. Here are the Test strike rates for five current players:

	mat	runs	balls	SR	note
Shahid Afridi (P)	26	1683	1954	**86.13**	fastest scorer ever
Adam Gilchrist (A)	90	5353	6505	**82.29**	amazing for a long career
Virender Sehwag (I)	52	4155	5485	**75.75**	hot stuff for an opener
Kevin Pietersen (E)	25	2448	3666	**66.77**	world's fastest middle-order batsman
Rahul Dravid (I)	109	9366	22,040	**42.49**	cautious but effective

Fast scorers help win matches by giving their bowlers more time to take 20 wickets. But sometimes the slowcoaches are vital too, holding up an end, preventing collapse, and tiring the opposition out. Dravid wins matches in his own way.

What's not so good about them

Averages can be random. In 1953, Bill Johnston toured England with the Australians. He was a good fast bowler and a hopeless batsman, but he kept collecting not-outs – 17 of them in 18 innings. He scraped 102 runs, so his average was **102**. Which was amusing, but hardly accurate, as his average innings (completed or not) was **5.66**. Today's not-out king is Jacques Kallis of South Africa, whose Test batting average in Zimbabwe is **503**.

Also, averages treat all runs or wickets as equal. "I'm not that into averages," Andrew Flintoff told me in 2005, "because you can make a hundred in a dead game and average 50 for the series, so they're not that representative. It's more about whether you have a good series – did you turn a game?" Which can be done with a gutsy 40, or a timely 2 for 20.

Cricket's love of averages forces players to cart their whole careers around, like emotional baggage. Flintoff is a top player who started poorly in Tests, and although that's ancient history now, it still dents his figures. After 11 Tests, late in 2001, his batting average was **14** and his bowling average **58**. Since then, he has averaged **36** with the bat and **31** with the ball, but his career averages are **32** for both.

Bowlers' strike rate

A bowler's strike rate is the number of balls he needs for each wicket, so low is good. This is an excellent measure because great bowlers are wicket-takers. Here are the best of all time in Tests among those with 200 wickets:

	mat	balls	wkts	SR	note
Waqar Younis (P)	87	16,224	373	**43.4**	king of the reverse-swinging toe-ball
Malcolm Marshall (WI)	81	17,584	376	**46.7**	master of pace and swing
Allan Donald (SA)	72	15,519	330	**47.0**	nicknamed White Lightning, struck often
Fred Trueman (E)	67	15,178	307	**49.4**	probably England's best fast bowler
Joel Garner (WI)	58	13,169	259	**50.8**	yorker ace, and Marshall's Bajan partner

The best current bowler is a surprising one: Makhaya Ntini of South Africa, on **51.3**. Neither Shane Warne nor Murali features here. Spinners need more overs to take their wickets, so Murali is 17th on the list with **54.4** and Warne 25th with **57.4**. And even the best bowlers need at least seven overs per wicket. Getting Test batsmen out isn't easy.

Bowlers' economy rate

This is the number of runs per over that the bowler concedes – crucial in one-day cricket. Again, low is good. Here are the best of all time in ODIs, among those with 200 wickets:

	mat	balls	runs	econ	note
Curtly Ambrose (WI)	176	9353	5429	**3.48**	tall and extremely accurate
Shaun Pollock (SA)	285	14,794	9153	**3.71**	swing and control with the new ball
Kapil Dev (I)	225	11,202	6945	**3.71**	India's best fast bowler, also a big-hitter
Courtney Walsh (WI)	205	10,822	6918	**3.83**	Curtly's partner, angling it in awkwardly
M Muralitharan (SL)	297	16,094	10,321	**3.84**	terrific economy for a spinner

THE LG WORLD RATINGS

Since 1990, there has been a world rating system similar to that used in tennis or golf. Unlike averages, it's impossible to work out for yourself, as it's all done with a complicated algorithm that takes into account the total number of runs in the match and the quality of the opposition. But it is still interesting. Here are the ratings as they stood in June 2007:

TEST BATSMEN — points
1 Ricky Ponting (A) 936
2 Mohammad Yousuf (P) 915
3 Kevin Pietersen (E) 909
4 Kumar Sangakkara (SL) 857
5 Mike Hussey (A) 842
6 Matthew Hayden (A) 828
7 Jacques Kallis (SA) 820
8 Rahul Dravid (I) 801
9 Younis Khan (P) 789
10 Ashwell Prince (SA) 755

TEST BOWLERS
1 Muttiah Muralitharan (SL) 913
2 Makhaya Ntini (SA) 856
3= Anil Kumble (I) 730
3= Shaun Pollock (SA) 730
5 Shane Bond (NZ) 722
6 Stuart Clark (A) 720
7 Mohammad Asif (P) 710
8 Matthew Hoggard (E) 708
9 Shoaib Akhtar (P) 698
10 Andrew Flintoff (E) 694

TEST HUNDREDS AT LORD'S – ENGLAND

Members of the board
Alastair Cook far left and Monty Panesar with the honours boards at Lord's

HUNDREDS FIVE-FORS
PLAY AND DUCKS

Cricketers do love a round number. A hundred may be only a few runs better than a 90, but it means far more. You can see this by the way some players act when they get close – into the so-called nervous nineties. Their fluency dries up and they bat like beginners again. But if they make it to a hundred, joy is unconfined. It looks great on the scorecard, sticking out further than all the other scores. It brings a warm round of applause from the crowd and the chance for the batsman to wave his bat wildly. And it gets him on to the **honours board**, if there is one, with his name embossed in gold leaf, never to be rubbed out.

The Lord's honours boards

There are honours boards in each dressing-room, and you can tell they mean a lot to the players because they are always talking about them. Everybody who gets a hundred or a five-for in a Lord's Test is up there. A duplicate set, not quite so handsome, is in the Film Theatre at the back of the Lord's museum, so you can see if your favourite player is up there.

England have added lots of names lately. There were six in the first Test of 2007 alone – **Alastair Cook**, Paul Collingwood, Ian Bell, Matt Prior and Kevin Pietersen made centuries, and Monty Panesar picked up a six-for. But it's just as interesting to spot who isn't there. Shane Warne isn't; nor is Brian Lara, or Sachin Tendulkar. Visiting players may only play a Test or two at Lord's and not all are at their best.

Hundreds aren't everything – many a match has been won by a 70 or 80 – but you can tell a lot about a batsman by how often he makes one. Here are some examples …

A HUNDRED EVERY …

	Player	
1.8 TESTS	Don Bradman (Aus)	29 in 52
2 TESTS	Barry Richards (SA)	2 in 4
2.2 TESTS	George Headley (WI)	10 in 22
2.9 TESTS	Clyde Walcott (WI)	15 in 44
3 TESTS	Alastair Cook (E)	6 in 18
3.3 TESTS	Mohammad Yousuf (P)	23 in 75
	Graeme Pollock (SA)	7 in 23
	Ricky Ponting (A)	33 in 110
	Matthew Hayden (A)	27 in 89
3.4 TESTS	Kevin Pietersen (E)	8 in 27
3.6 TESTS	Garry Sobers (WI)	26 in 93
3.7 TESTS	Sachin Tendulkar (I)	37 in 137
3.9 TESTS	Brian Lara (WI)	34 in 131
4 TESTS	Andrew Strauss (E)	10 in 40
4.1 TESTS	Michael Vaughan (E)	16 in 65
5.3 TESTS	Adam Gilchrist (A)	17 in 90
7.2 TESTS	Mike Atherton (E)	16 in 115
8.9 TESTS	Alec Stewart (E)	15 in 133
9.7 TESTS	Chris Gayle (WI)	7 in 68
11 TESTS	WG Grace (E)	2 in 22
11.5 TESTS	Stephen Fleming (NZ)	9 in 104
13.4 TESTS	Andrew Flintoff (E)	5 in 67
17 TESTS	MS Dhoni (I)	1 in 17
22 TESTS	Douglas Jardine (E)	1 in 22
25.5 TESTS	Mark Boucher (SA)	4 in 102
34 TESTS	Geraint Jones (E)	1 in 34
36.5 TESTS	Daniel Vettori (NZ)	2 in 73
53.5 TESTS	Shaun Pollock (SA)	2 in 107
71 TESTS	Jason Gillespie (A)	1 in 71

To June 23, 2007. Figures rounded to one decimal place

Worth the wait

Some very good players take a long time to reach three figures in a Test innings. **Steve Waugh**, a great captain of Australia, went 26 Tests without a hundred. Then he hammered 177 not out against England, and followed up with 152 not out in the next Test. His career average shot up from 30 to 40 in two matches. He added 30 more hundreds in the next 15 years, eventually overtaking Bradman as Australia's biggest ton-maker.

▶**Late developer** Steve Waugh salutes the crowd as he reaches 100 in his last Test in England at The Oval in 2001. He went on to score 157, all with a calf strain

Doubles

Players who reach 100 are often exhausted. Many get out soon afterwards. The average century made for each country in Tests ranges from 122 (Bangladesh) up to 144 (Sri Lanka), which is quite low when you consider that some go much higher, like Brian Lara's 400. So a double century is quite something. Only 270 of them have been made in 130 years of Tests. Australia lead the way with 61. Bangladesh haven't got one yet. The king of the 200 is Bradman, inevitably, with 12, followed by Lara with nine. Ricky Ponting, undoubtedly a great batsman, only has four.

Triples

A triple hundred should be a very rare thing. It takes about three hours to make a single Test hundred, so you can work out how long it takes to make a triple. Until recently, it WAS very rare. In the first 113 years of Test cricket, up to 1990, there were only 11 individual scores above 300. Then the England captain Graham Gooch hit 333 against India, the highest score ever recorded at Lord's, and started a fashion. In the 17 years since, there have been 10 more Test triples, including the four biggest scores ever made. There have been more triples in county cricket too – most of them made by Australians, desperate to attract the Test selectors' attention.

Five-fors

The bowler's equivalent of a hundred is a five-wicket haul, known as a five-for. Five-fors are harder to come by than hundreds – you never get three of them in the same innings, for a start – but for some reason they often go less celebrated. A bowler will tell you this is because bowlers are down-to-earth professionals who do the job without fuss, unlike those preening characters with a bat in their hand.

The king of the Test five-for is **Muttiah Muralitharan**, who has a staggering 57 of them. Next, way behind, is Shane Warne with 37, and Richard Hadlee of New Zealand with 36. Murali has taken 10 wickets in a match 19 times, which is as many as Warne and Hadlee put together. But Murali and Hadlee have had the advantage of being the only great bowler in their team. As Gooch once said of facing New Zealand, "It's the World XI at one end and Ilford 2nds at the other."

Warne has had to share the wickets with another of the great destroyers – Glenn McGrath, who took 29 five-fors. He and Warne played 104 Tests together and took 1001 wickets between them. They even retired from Tests together, on January 5, 2007.

◀**King of the five-for** Murali leads the Sri Lanka team off the pitch in the Trent Bridge Test of 2006, after bagging 11 wickets in the match, eight in the second innings

▼**The dreaded pair** Geraint Jones is run out by Ricky Ponting to make two ducks in his last Test, at Perth in 2006-07

Ducks

What's the most common score in top-class cricket? No score at all. It's called a duck, because the big 0 once reminded someone of a duck's egg and the name stuck. And egg is what it leaves on the batsman's face. No sooner has he arrived at the wicket than he has to go back again. Or maybe he stayed a while – but that can be just as mortifying, if he missed several chances to score.

The king of the ducks is Courtney Walsh with 43. Next are two old friends – McGrath, with 35, and Warne, with 34. And fourth is Murali with 30. The top two specialist batsmen in the duck league are Marvan Atapattu of Sri Lanka and Steve Waugh of Australia, both on 22. And they are a strange pair to find here, because Atapattu is fourth equal on the list of players with the most double hundreds, with four, and Waugh, as mentioned above, is Australia's biggest maker of hundreds. Funny game, cricket.

The worst thing that can happen to a batsman, short of serious injury, is two ducks: the dreaded pair, so-called because it once reminded someone of a pair of specs. Gooch got one in his first Test, Andrew Flintoff in his second. Ian Bell got one as England won the Ashes at The Oval in 2005; Ian Botham got one in his last Test as captain in 1981.

No fewer than 48 players got one in their last Test, including **Geraint Jones** of England, the Australian captain Kim Hughes, and WG Grace's brother Fred. It was his first Test too. He probably thought things couldn't get any worse, but then he slept on a damp mattress, caught pneumonia, and died at the age of 30. The only consolation was that he had taken a brilliant catch, holding on to a ball that had been in the air so long, the batsmen had already turned for a third run.

SIXES!

The biggest and the best

A six isn't just the biggest shot a batsman can play, it's often the best. It means taking a big risk, because he could be caught. In many cases, he could be stumped as well, since the shot often involves launching himself out of his crease, so if he misses it or mis-hits it, he will feel a bit of a fool. But then people who never risk making a fool of themselves don't go very far.

More than any other stroke, a six draws the crowd into the action. The ball is heading for them, and it is usually travelling in a great arc, which gives them time to spot it, follow it and enjoy the suspense. As the ball hangs in the air, time stands still. Is it going to be the best possible result for the batsman from one ball – six runs – or the worst – being caught? Is it going to hit someone in the crowd (in 1976, a woman watching England play the West Indies at Lord's had her arm broken by a six from Gordon Greenidge), or are they going to catch it, take a bow and get seen on telly by all their friends?

Where you fit in

You're lucky: you've come along at a time when some of the best six-hitters of all time are playing the game. Nobody has hit more sixes in Tests than Adam Gilchrist, Australia's No 7. He has 97 sixes and soon after this book is published he will surely become the first person to make 100 of them.

Only 17 other men have managed as many as 50 sixes. Eleven of those 17 have played Test cricket in the 2000s. Matthew Hayden, also of Australia, has 79 sixes, and Andrew Flintoff of England was on 77 going into the English summer of 2007. Shahid Afridi of Pakistan has 50 in just 26 Tests, so he is the only man ever to get close to two sixes per Test through a decent career. Kevin Pietersen hit 36 sixes in his first 27 Tests, so he may one day overtake Flintoff as England's biggest six-hitter.

Six-hitter supreme

But the biggest hero in this list is someone else: **Chris Cairns** of New Zealand. He retired from Tests in 2004 with 87 sixes, which was then a world record. He was an allrounder, often batting as low as No 8, and his 87 sixes came out of only 3,320 runs, so about one-sixth of all his runs were heaved over the boundary. The man whose record he broke, Viv Richards of the West Indies, hit 84 sixes in a total of 8,540 runs. And Viv was known as the Master Blaster.

The trend for more six-hitting is partly because bats are heavier and boundaries shorter. But there has also been a change of attitude, with more batsmen taking risks. Don Bradman hit only six sixes in his Test career, Mike Atherton four, WG Grace one.

Six sixes in an over

Some batsmen have managed as many as Bradman in a single over – though not (yet) in Test cricket. One day in 1969, the great West Indian allrounder Garry Sobers was playing for Nottinghamshire against Glamorgan at Cardiff. He was facing Malcolm Nash, a gentle left-armer. The over went like this: 6, 6, 6, 6, 6, 6. Sobers mostly played the pull shot, with a huge follow-through. You can see him do it, looking very smart with no helmet, on YouTube.

Sobers' feat was matched by Ravi Shastri, the Indian allrounder (normally rather a snail), in a domestic match in 1984-85, but nobody got very excited about that. It had never been done in international cricket until the 2007 World Cup, when **Herschelle Gibbs** of South Africa hit six sixes in an over from Daan van Bunge of Holland in St Kitts. Gibbs said it felt "quite nice". Before the game, the Dutch captain had said to his team, "Let's make history!" Afterwards, he said, "Well, we made history!"

Personally, I think a six should be worth more – eight, probably. It's harder to pull off than a four and two singles. But in a way, it already is worth more. It lifts the batting side, deflates the bowlers, and thrills the crowd, whose enthusiasm then feeds back to the batsman.

BANG! POW! CRACK! SMASH! CRASH! WOW!

HAT-TRICKS!

The bowlers' equivalent of a six, only rarer still, is a hat-trick – taking three wickets in three balls. The three balls can be interrupted by an over from the other end, or even a whole innings, but they have to be consecutive deliveries from the same bowler in the same match.

In Tests, a hat-trick comes along about once every four years. There have been 36 of them in 130 years of Test history. England have managed three in recent years, all by swing bowlers – Dominic Cork, Darren Gough and Matthew Hoggard. Hat-tricks by spinners are extremely rare, but Shane Warne got one against England (and one of his victims was Gough). Wasim Akram of Pakistan, a magnificent, fast, snaky, reverse-swing bowler, took two Test hat-tricks. Nobody has taken three.

In one-day internationals, hat-tricks are almost common. There have been 24 of them in 36 years, two by Wasim, who therefore has a world-record four international hat-tricks. In the 2007 World Cup, for the first time in any international, somebody took four wickets in consecutive balls – **Lasith Malinga** of Sri Lanka, against South Africa in Guyana, with his round-arm slingers. Funnily enough, there isn't a special name for four in four. Perhaps, in honour of Malinga, it should be called a hair-trick.

▼**WWWW**
Lasith Malinga gets four wickets in four balls; Shaun Pollock bowled, Andrew Hall caught by Upul Tharanga, Jacques Kallis caught by Kumar Sangakkara and Makhaya Ntini bowled

BOWLED! CAUGHT! CAUGHT! BOWLED!

strange
BUT TRUE

One of the best bits in *Wisden* is the Index of Unusual Occurrences, introduced in 1996. Here are some choice examples – and a few from earlier times

In 1899, in a junior house match at Clifton College, a 13-year-old boy called AEJ Collins scored 628 not out. Collins, an orphan, treated the bowling with "lordly contempt", although the bowlers defeated him a few times: he was dropped on 80, 100, 140, 400 and 556. The drop on 80 may be the most expensive mistake ever made on a cricket field. Once Collins reached 400, word spread, and crowds came to watch, along with a correspondent for *The Times*, who kept getting his name wrong, calling him AEG not AEJ. The match was timeless and eventually, after six days, Collins's team, Clarke House, won by an innings and 688 runs. So, strictly speaking, they didn't need his runs. But they did need his wickets – he took 11. After school, he went into the Army, and he was killed in action early in the First World War. The field where the game was played is known as Collins's Piece, and 628 is still the highest score ever recorded in cricket.

In 2006, two brothers opened the batting in a one-day international – on different sides. The match was Ireland v England in Belfast. **Ed Joyce**, an Irishman, was making his England debut after qualifying for them through playing for Middlesex. His younger brother Dominick was playing for Ireland. Ed made 10, which was 10 more than Dominick, although they each held a catch. Two of their sisters, Isobel and Cecelia (who are twins), and another brother, Gus, have also played for Ireland.

Until March 2005, only one set of twins had played Test cricket – the Waugh brothers. Steve Waugh had played more Tests than anyone else (168); Mark Waugh, whose debut came when Steve was dropped, was ninth on the same list with 128 Tests. But then New Zealand picked **James Marshall**, whose twin, **Hamish**, was already in their team. And these two had something the Waughs didn't: they were identical. They were playing against Australia, whose captain, Ricky Ponting, said that if they batted together, he wouldn't be able to tell them apart. This was hardly surprising as their own father said he found it difficult, too, when the twins were wearing whites. James opened the batting, while Hamish was down at No 3, and sure enough, they found themselves batting together after half an hour of the match. They added 38 before Glenn McGrath removed James. But they made it easy for the Aussies to tell who was who: James wore an arm guard. Or was it Hamish?

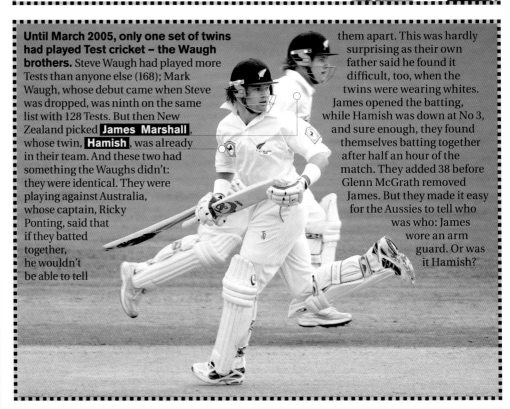

On May 16, 2007, a boy in Swansea turned 17, and his mum booked him a driving lesson as a present – but she had to cancel it because he was chosen to play for Glamorgan against Gloucestershire. The boy was **James Harris**, an allrounder who bowls medium-fast. He proceeded to take 12 wickets, breaking the record for the youngest person to take 10 wickets in a county championship match. He had to miss the next game, though, to sit his A-levels. "I've got to get my head in my books for the exams," he told reporters. "But then hopefully it will be cricket, cricket, cricket."

In a Twenty20 match at Edgbaston in 2004, Warwickshire's **Neil Carter** hit the ball high in the air. Somerset's Keith Dutch was bracing himself to catch it when the ground announcer, George Gavin, shouted "Wooooooooooh!" Dutch held on. Warwickshire apologised.

On their tour of India in 1951-52, England were fielding in a warm-up match at Poona when they were joined by a monkey, who wandered on to the field and stood at point, just to the left of cover. It was chased off by a member of the ground staff wielding a stick. Not to be deterred, the monkey reappeared the next day and went to stand at gully. The same member of the ground staff again chased it away. The story is told in *The Reduced History of Cricket*. "Disgusted at this harassment," say the authors, "the monkey jumped on the pavilion roof and refused to speak to the media at the end of play."

During the First World War, British soldiers held a cricket match at Versailles, "in an enclosure between some houses out of observation from the enemy," according to the poet Robert Graves, who was one of the players. The match was Officers v Sergeants. "Our front line is three-quarters of a mile away," Graves wrote in his book *Goodbye To All That*. "I made top score, 24; the bat was a bit of a rafter, the ball a piece of rag tied with string; and the wicket a parrot cage with the clean, dry corpse of a parrot inside. Machine gun fire broke up the match." It is not known whether this was the inspiration for the dead-parrot sketch in Monty Python.

On their tour of England in 2002, India picked a 17-year-old reserve wicketkeeper called **Parthiv Patel**. He was quite short and when he led the team out on to the stage at an awards ceremony, some people assumed he was the team mascot. Then the first-choice keeper got injured and Patel found himself in the Test team. The England and Wales Cricket Board had just brought in a rule that players under the age of 18 had to keep wicket in a helmet, unless they had a note from their mother or father giving permission for them not to. The board decided not to insist that Patel produce a note.

In a Second XI game against Derbyshire at the Oval in 2003, the Surrey openers, **Scott Newman** and **Nadeem Shahid**, reached 500 for no wicket in only 74 overs. The international umpire Billy Bowden, who was warming up before standing in a Test match, whipped out a camera and stopped play to take a picture of the two batsmen, grinning broadly, in front of the scoreboard. They were eventually parted at 552, whereupon Bowden handed the camera to the other umpire, Bob McLeod, and posed in front of the scoreboard himself, giving a thumbs-up.

In a one-day game against Glamorgan at Headingley in 2003, **Ryan Sidebottom** of Yorkshire and England finished with the bizarre figures of 0.1–0–11–0. He started with two wides, then bowled a short ball which was hooked for six. After sending down three more wides, he retired with a tight hamstring. He later joined Nottinghamshire, won a Championship medal, and received a surprise recall by England in May 2007.

In 1994-95, the double world-record holder Brian Lara played in a charity match in Sydney and faced the bowling of an Australian Test allrounder called Zoe Goss. Visibly alarmed by the prospect of getting out to a woman, Lara played scratchily for a few minutes. Then he charged down the track, had a swing, edged the ball, and was caught behind. In case the umpire hadn't heard the nick, the keeper stumped him as well. So Lara ended up getting out twice to a woman off the same ball.

Sources: *Wisden Cricketers' Almanack*, Cricinfo, *The Daily Telegraph*, and *The Reduced History of Cricket*, by Aubrey Ganguly and Justyn Barnes (Andre Deutsch, 2005); *A Social History of Cricket* by Derek Birley (Aurum, 1999). For more occurrences, turn to the back page of any recent *Wisden*.

FAMOUS QUOTES

Cricket – a game which the English, not being a spiritual people, have invented in order to give themselves some conception of eternity.

Lord Mancroft, politician

I tend to believe that cricket is the greatest thing that God ever created on earth.

Harold Pinter, playwright

This is great. When does it start?

Groucho Marx, comedian, after half an hour's play at Lord's

Of course it's frightfully dull! That's the whole point!

Character played by **Robert Morley** in *The Final Test*, a 1953 film about cricket

What do they know of cricket, who only cricket know?

CLR James, author

It's hard work making batting look effortless.

David Gower, England batsman of the 1980s

These people haven't come to watch you bowl, they've come to watch me bat.

WG Grace, to a furious bowler, after he had been bowled first ball, and the umpire allegedly called "not out"

Ninety per cent of cricket is played in the mind.

Richard Hadlee, great New Zealand bowler

Captaincy is 90 per cent luck and 10 per cent skill. But don't try it without that 10 per cent.

Richie Benaud, a very good Australian captain and an even better commentator

He's got a degree in people, hasn't he?

Rodney Hogg, Australian fast bowler, on **Mike Brearley**, England's captain, in about 1979. Brearley later qualified as a psychotherapist

▲ **Psyching them up**
Brearley was a master at getting the best from his players, like Bob Willis at Headingley in 1981 (see page 87)

Warnie's idea of a balanced diet is a cheeseburger in each hand.

Ian Healy, Australian wicketkeeper, on **Shane Warne**

6 CELEBRATED SLEDGES

Sledging, as you know, is a mean, sad thing to do, but it sometimes redeems itself by being quite funny. Health warning: some of these tales may be apocryphal (a fancy word meaning not strictly true), but they are part of cricket's folklore.

During the Bodyline series of 1932-33, the England captain, **Douglas Jardine**, was batting. He complained to his Australian counterpart, **Bill Woodfull**, that a slip fielder hadv sworn at him. Woodfull solemnly addressed his team-mates: "All right, which one of you bastards called this bastard a bastard?"

When India toured Pakistan in 2003-04, **Shoaib Akhtar** (fast and often furious) was bowling to **Virender Sehwag** (brilliant but hot-headed). Shoaib kept firing in bouncers and Sehwag kept letting them go past him. Shoaib, exasperated, asked: "Why don't you hit one for a change?" Sehwag imperiously replied: "Are you bowling, or begging?"

Matthew Fleming, an allrounder who went on to play one-day cricket for England, was making his county debut, for Kent, against Yorkshire. Fleming had an unusual background for a cricketer – he was a member of the banking family and the great-nephew of Ian Fleming who wrote the James Bond books. His first scoring shot was a six. So was his second. The wicketkeeper, the late **David Bairstow**, said: "I'd bat like that too if I had your money."

Ian Botham went in to bat against Australia in the early 1980s. **Rod Marsh**, a great wicketkeeper and conversationalist, asked him: "How's your wife and my kids?" Botham replied: "The wife's fine. The kids are retarded."

Ian Healy, another excellent Australian wicketkeeper, was in temporary charge of Australia in an Ashes Test while the captain was off the field. He moved a fielder to a position several yards from **Nasser Hussain's** bat, saying: "Let's have you right under Nasser's nose."

Jimmy Ormond, a seam bowler then playing for Leicestershire, was making his Test debut for England at The Oval in 2001. When he went in to bat, **Mark Waugh** said to him: "Mate, what are you doing out here? There's no way you're good enough to play Test cricket." Ormond replied: "Maybe not, but at least I'm the best player in my own family."

PLAYER SPEAK

You might say ...	They will say ...
pitch or wicket	track or deck
good shot	shot
edge	nick
sledging	banter or verbals
cricket bag	coffin
century	hundred or ton
score of 150+	daddy hundred
score of 100–120	baby hundred
do well	come to the party
outswing	shape
line and length	good areas
take control	put your hand up
tall order	big ask
turning pitch	Bunsen (rhyming slang: Bunsen burner)
five-for	Michelle (Pfeiffer, film star)
well bowled, Shane	bowling, Warney

GO

AND SEE A GAME

Watching on the telly is great, but for atmosphere, and a feel for the pace of the game, there's nothing like going to a big match. It can be a long day, but follow these tips to make sure it's an enjoyable one

Cricket is quite an odd sport to go and watch. It lasts all day, unless it's a Twenty20 game. It stops for meals, and also (boo) for rain or bad light. And the action happens in a series of little flurries which can be hard to follow with the naked eye.

That's the bad news. The good news is:

- the whole scene is quite something, from the perfect grass to the groups of male fans who come dressed as nuns
- there's usually a great atmosphere, with singing, dancing and flag-waving
- you get a strong sense of how fast the ball travels
- one or two players will field near you
- there's plenty of space, and it's safe, so the grown-ups can be persuaded to let you go off by yourself or with a friend
- there are ice-creams to eat, bats to

drool over in the shop, and famous faces to spot
- and if you do miss a crucial moment, there's always the replay on the big screen or the highlights on telly when you get home.

There are two dangers – getting burnt or bored. Deal with the first one by going Slip, Slap, Slop as they say in Australia (slip on a shirt, slap on a hat, slop on some sunscreen), and don't mess around because the damage that leads to skin cancer is usually done in childhood. Deal with the boredom by watching selectively and taking breaks (see below). And if you're not sure you can face a whole day, just go for the afternoon, or start with a Twenty20 game – they're fast-moving and great fun. Whatever you do, remember the point is to enjoy it.

5 TIPS FOR BIG GAMES AT LORD'S

1 go to the museum (behind the pavilion)

Admission for kids is only £1 and although it's quite old-fashioned, it's full of intriguing things, from WG Grace's boots (a bit grubby) to the Ashes (unbelievably tiny). Don't miss the film theatre at the back, or the sparrow in a glass case on the ground floor – it was stuffed after being killed by a ball in 1936

2 check out the real-tennis court (behind the pavilion)

Real? More like surreal. A weird mixture of tennis and squash, with a sloping roof to bounce your serve off. During Tests, the viewing area turns into a champagne bar, but you can sneak in there for a gawp

3 have a bacon sandwich and a smoothie (in the food court, behind the big screen)

The permanent bars don't serve great food, but the temporary stalls set up for big matches do. You can have an Indian, fish and chips, an Aussie pie, or, best of all, a Helen Browning's organic bacon sandwich. Ask for a Butty Marvellous, squirt on some sauce, and wash it down with a smoothie from the little stall in the top right-hand corner. Then tell your parents that as you've been so healthy, you've clearly earned a visit to the old-style sweet stall behind the Tavern

6 MOMENTS TO PAY ATTENTION

1 at the start
Each day is a new beginning. You never know how the pitch will play and who will get on top, so watch closely for the first half-hour

2 when KP comes in
Some players just make things happen. Kevin Pietersen is one of them. Get ready to wave your 4 or 6 sign – especially if he is joined by Andrew Flintoff or Matt Prior

3 straight after lunch, tea or drinks
A wicket often falls in the first over after a break, or the first ball after drinks

4 after 80 overs in a Test
The bowlers can take a new ball, which acts like a can of Red Bull – the bowling gets quicker, wickets may fall, and often runs flow

5 when the tail-enders come in
Bad batsmen are good to watch. Look out for some slogging, and see the fielders' heads go down, as if tail-end runs count double

6 when Monty Panesar bowls
His bowling is a joy, and his celebrations are unmissable –

does he not know the point of a high five is to clap the other person's hand? Or is he just very bad at it?

3 MOMENTS TO GO FOR A WANDER

1 half an hour before lunch
When the players go off, the shops and stalls get ridiculously crowded. Go early and get back to your seat to eat your lunch, then you can watch the highlights of the morning on the big screen

2 after 20 overs in a one-day international
In the 50-over game, the middle overs are the dullest. The field is spread, the bowlers are just trying to contain, and the batsmen milk them for singles. Go for a stroll, and ask someone to text you if the powerplay starts

3 when Matthew Hoggard is batting
He's a great character – tough and tireless with a nice dry wit. But watching him bat is like watching grass grow. On average he stays in for 23 balls, making 7, so you can take half an hour off

THE BARMY ARMY
Some people like to watch cricket very quietly, wearing a jacket and tie, as if sitting in church. And some don't. If you see a fellow spectator singing a song, doing the conga, wearing a nun's outfit and carrying a tray of 24 beers, he's probably a member of the Barmy Army. The Barmies were founded in Australia in 1994-95, when England were so hopeless, you had to be barmy to spend a whole winter watching them. They get mixed reviews. Are they admirably dedicated, tireless, and quite funny, or tediously repetitive, tiresome and witless? Go along and decide for yourself. Your opinion may depend on how close you are sitting to them. Meanwhile, for a collection of their chants, go to www.barmyarmy.com/baharm_lyrics_eplayers.cfm

HOW TO GET TICKETS

1 Ask a member
Got an uncle or grandpa (or aunt or granny) who's a member at Lord's or one of the other Test grounds? Don't be shy about asking them to take you along. They'd love to. They may even turn into a small child before your eyes

2 Get your parents to join the mailing list
Or even the England Supporters' Club. Details at www.ecb.co.uk/fans/tickets/

3 Go along on the day
It's easier to get in than you might think. Often a few hundred tickets will be held back for sale on the day – turn up about 9am, queue up, get your tickets and then go for breakfast. Sometimes there are fans with spares to sell too. On the fifth day of a Test (usually a Monday in England), all the tickets are held back and they are often reduced. The snag is that the game can fizzle out, but still, you'll have been to a Test match

DO
- take binoculars
- take water
- stroll round behind the stands
- take a mobile if you have one
- wear sunscreen
- applaud both sides
- take a tennis ball

DON'T
- move behind the bowler's arm
- ask who's winning
- shove your autograph book under a player's nose without saying anything
- snore too loudly
- laugh if Monty drops a catch

4 take the rules with a pinch of salt (everywhere, within reason)
Lord's is a magical place, but it does have an awful lot of fussy rules. As you go to your seat, a notice says "The use of portable telephones is not permitted." And then you notice that everyone is on their mobile anyway, making plans to meet up with friends or family. You also notice that there are adverts everywhere promoting mobile-phone companies – including on the England team shirts

5 play Count The Ties (round the back of the stands)
If you do find yourself on the concourse in an interval, progress is painfully slow. Amuse yourself by seeing how many MCC ties (orange and yellow, known as egg-and-bacon) you spot coming the other way. On the Sunday of the West Indies Test in 2007, my daughter Laura scored 51. Make the game more like cricket by scoring four for an MCC hat, six for a blazer, and 50 for a set of MCC pyjamas

THE MEDIA

Cricket was a multimedia experience before the term even existed. Because it takes a long time and the action happens in short bursts, the game is perfectly suited to television and radio. It's also the best sport to read and write about, and it has taken to the internet like a duck to a school scorecard. But there's now so much media coverage that it can be hard to find the good stuff, so here are some pointers

TELEVISION

Best live coverage Sky. (Also the worst, since it is the only channel with any live rights.) Strong on quantity: they show all England's matches, home and away, plus plenty of county one-dayers and Twenty20s, and the odd four-day game. Also good at camerawork, interviews, and detective gizmos like HawkEye, Snicko and HotSpot. Not so hot at commentary – they tend to think any old England captain can do it. Keep the sound turned up for Mike Atherton (calm and shrewd) and Nasser Hussain (excitable, but highly intelligent). Turn it down for Ian Botham and David Gower, two wonderful players whose commentary isn't quite so sparkling.

Best highlights Five. Smartly packaged, with Mark Nicholas presenting, and beautifully timed – during home Tests (May to September) they're on at 7.15-8pm, perfect for family viewing.

RADIO

Best live coverage Test Match Special (BBC Radio 4 198LW or 720 AM). Not just a commentary team but a national treasure, *TMS* has fans who don't even like cricket. The show has a special flavour, old-fashioned but full of character. There's genial jokiness from Jonathan Agnew, fruity exuberance from Henry Blofeld ("My dear old thing!"), relaxed earnestness from Christopher Martin-Jenkins, wry humour from Vic Marks, high-pitched expertise from Graham Gooch, immaculate stats from Bill Frindall, and delicious chocolate cake from Mrs Blenkinsop in Tunbridge Wells.

Best for news BBC 5 Live (909 AM). Obsessed with football – they think Chelsea v Bolton matters more than England v India. But they do cover home Tests and one-dayers, usually with a solid update from Pat Murphy and Mike Gatting, about once every 15 minutes.

INTERNET

Best for scores, stats and history Cricinfo. An amazing site. Their scorecards are fast, they do live averages, they always tell you the number of balls faced, and their text commentary is sparky, if not as good as *The Guardian's* (see below). They also have StatsGuru, a searchable database of the whole history of international cricket, so you can check out Ricky Ponting's Test average at home as captain (82) or Steve Harmison's average overseas since 2005 (48). Plus, they have good writers in India and around the world, fine columns like Ask Steven (you send in a question, he answers it), and the Wisden archive, which is in a league of its own. **www.cricinfo.com**

Best for basic news BBC.co.uk. Want to know who's in, who's out, who's injured and who's just resigned? The BBC site is the place to go – quick, efficient and easy to navigate. Plenty of lively comment too, but not so much authority. **news.bbc.co.uk/sport1/hi/cricket/default.stm**

Best for text commentary Guardian Unlimited. Not content with having several good writers in the paper, *The Guardian* has a couple more doing over-by-over coverage. They're wildly outspoken, often funny, and they even get good emails from readers, which is not something many blogs have yet managed. Look out for Rob Smyth, who is a riot but really knows his stuff. **sport.guardian.co.uk/cricket/**

NEWSPAPERS

Best all round daily
The Guardian. The only paper that has stylish writers all the way down the order. For England matches, they normally have a match report from Mike Selvey (former England bowler, good on technique and players' minds, with a nice line in similes), and sidebars from David Hopps (witty observer who famously likened Ashley Giles's bowling action to a wheelie-bin) and Lawrence Booth (rising star and author of *Arm Ball to Zooter*). Their other gifted contributors include Andy Wilson and Tanya Aldred, who are believed to be the first cricket writers ever to have married each other. Sample them all at **sport. guardian.co.uk/ cricket/**

Best all round Sunday
The Sunday Telegraph. The British tradition is to have different writers and editors on a Sunday. They spend the whole week thinking about their coverage and it shows. *The Sunday Tel* has Scyld Berry, the most experienced and wisest of the main correspondents, and Mike Atherton, one of the smartest ex-player writers, plus a county column from the former Glamorgan captain Steve James.

Best for comment
The Daily Telegraph, which has authoritative reporting from its two main men, Derek Pringle and Simon Briggs, plus three strong columnists. Geoff Boycott, who opened the batting for England in 100 Tests, is blunt and hard-hitting. He bangs on a bit about his own career, but he is right about most things: he was calling for Duncan Fletcher to step down as England coach six months before it happened. Mark Nicholas, who captained Hampshire before becoming a super-smooth TV presenter, is thoughtful and full of boyish enthusiasm. Simon Hughes, a seamer for Middlesex who became The Analyst on Channel 4, is perceptive and informed. Go to **www.telegraph.co.uk/ sport/**

Best for county cricket
The Times, which has a report on every match, usually at decent length. *The Telegraph* has almost as many match reports, but some are so short, there's barely room to say who won. The downmarket papers seldom bother with county cricket, but don't be put off because the upmarket papers are not half as daunting as they used to be – they are physically smaller, livelier, more colourful, and easier to read. Have a taste at **www.timesonline.co.uk/tol/ sport/cricket/**

MAGAZINES

Best for writing and design
The Wisden Cricketer (monthly). Now owned by Sky, not Wisden, which is quite weird, but the editor remains the same (John Stern) and Sky have promised him independence. He produces a smart, readable magazine with excellent interviews, photos and comment.

Best for a laugh
Spin (monthly). Hard to find, but worth seeking out: cheeky, imaginative and child-friendly.

7 TYPES OF CRICKET ARTICLE

News What just happened

Comment What the writer thinks about it

Match report What happened in the match

Sidebar Article next to the match report, usually more colourful or opinionated

Column Regular comment from the same writer or player

Feature Thorough look at a team, player or trend

Profile Feature about one person, usually involving an interview

BROADCAST LIKE BENAUD
6 tips from the man himself

The greatest cricket commentator is widely reckoned to be Richie Benaud, the voice of cricket on British and Australian television for more than 40 years. Now in his late seventies, he is only working for Channel 9 in Australia, but he remains the Bradman of the microphone. Here are his tips

1 Develop a distinctive style

2 Put your brain into gear before opening your mouth

3 Never say "we" if referring to a team

4 Concentrate fiercely at all times

5 Try to avoid allowing these past your lips:

"Of course ..."
"As you can see on the screen ..."
"You know ..."
"I tell you what ..."
"That's a tragedy ..." or *"a disaster ..."* (The Titanic was a tragedy, the Ethiopian drought a disaster, and neither bears any relation to a dropped catch.)

6 Above all, don't take yourself too seriously, and have fun

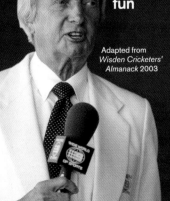

Adapted from *Wisden Cricketers' Almanack* 2003

CRICKET BOOKS A FIRST XI

Cricket is famous for producing good books. It has also produced plenty of bad ones – players' autobiographies, especially, should be approached with extreme care – but here are 11 books that can be enjoyed by children as well as adults, and the age at which you might try them*

These are just guidelines. Some people take to reading young, others don't, and it doesn't make much difference in the long run

 age **7**

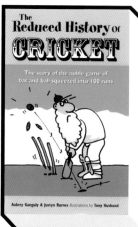

The Reduced History of Cricket

by Aubrey Ganguly and Justyn Barnes (Andre Deutsch, 2005)

Slim volume containing 100 entertaining stories and plenty of cartoons.

8

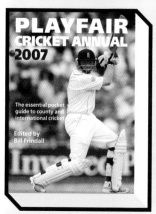

Playfair Cricket Annual

edited by Bill Frindall (Headline, every April)

Pocket-book of facts and figures on all the county players, plus scorecards from last year's Tests.

The Cricketers' Who's Who

edited by Chris Marshall (Green Umbrella, every April)

The details on every county player, from the exams he has passed to his views on the game.

 9

The Cricinfo Guide to International Cricket

edited by Steven Lynch (John Wisden, every November)

Pithy profiles of 200 current internationals, based on Cricinfo's player pages.

Stiff Upper Lips and Baggy Green Caps

by Simon Briggs (Quercus, 2006)

The story of the Ashes with all the rude bits left in, written by a bright young writer who is No 2 cricket correspondent on *The Daily Telegraph*.

10

One Hundred Greatest Cricketers

by John Woodcock (Macmillan, 1998)

Quick sketches of the all-time greats from an elegant writer who was *The Times*'s cricket correspondent for 33 years.

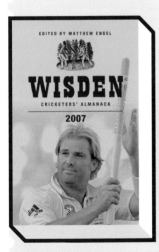

Wisden Cricketers' Almanack

edited by Matthew Engel (John Wisden, every April; 2008 editor Scyld Berry)

Punchy comment, chunky records, solid reports on all last year's internationals and county matches, and plenty of dry wit. Some kids find it hard going, but others lap it up – next year's editor, Scyld, started reading it when he was six. See panel, right.

11

Rain Men

by Marcus Berkmann (Abacus, 1995)

The first and funnier of two books about the same cricket club, the Captain Scott Invitation XI – probably the worst team ever to inspire one book, let alone two. The other one is **Penguins Stopped Play** (2006), by Berkmann's former co-captain Harry Thompson, and it's pretty funny too.

On and Off the Field

by Ed Smith (Penguin, 2004)

The diary of a good player's best season – 2003, when Ed Smith made so many runs for Kent, he played three Tests for England in an exciting series against South Africa. Honest and highly intelligent.

12

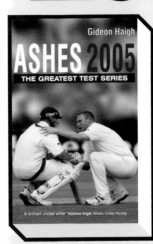

Ashes 2005: the Full Story of the Test Series

by Gideon Haigh (Aurum, 2005)

Most memorable of the many books about a classic series, written by an outstanding Anglo-Australian cricket writer.

The Art of Captaincy

by Mike Brearley (Hodder, 1985)

The best book about the most complex of all cricket's arts, expertly explained by one of England's most successful captains. Probably the only cricket book to have inspired an Oscar-winning film director (see page 66).

HOW TO READ WISDEN

Wisden is like a museum: it can be a bit daunting, but there's plenty of fun to be had if you know where to look. Here are five tips:

1 Start at the back, with the **Index of Unusual Occurrences** (page 1664 of the 2007 edition), which leads you into the book via some of the wackier stories (see page 114). When you see an entry like "Water bombs stop play", it's hard not to find out more.

2 Next, head for the **Wisden Forty** (page 196), which is a sort of school report on the top 40 players in the world.

3 Then find your **county** (arranged alphabetically from page 630 to 885) and remind yourself how well or badly they did last year.

4 Don't be afraid to **dip in at random**. There's always something interesting, especially in the boxes, which tend to be lighter than the main text. And it's amazing how often you go in to look up one thing and end up somewhere quite different.

5 Try the **articles** at the front, such as Mike Atherton's tribute to Shane Warne (page 27). A lot of people think Wisden is all stats, but once you find the articles, you'll know better.

HAVE A GO YOURSELF

STAGE ONE
PARK CRICKET

1 Persuade someone to play with you. Two is the bare minimum, three is fine, four or five is ideal. If grown-ups try to protest that they're no good at the game, gently point out that you're not exactly Kevin Pietersen either.

2 Get two tennis balls, preferably old (not too bouncy) and a cheap wooden bat (not plastic – they're noisy and useless). One of the balls is a spare. Take some water too. Stumps are optional: you can use other things for a wicket, like a thin tree, a shopping bag or a small child (well, the first two anyway). The second wicket can be a sweater. If there are only two of you, use inanimate objects as fielders – clothes, backpacks, etc. They won't be much worse than your friends.

3 Go to the park, unless you have a very big garden. Choose an area, about 20 metres square, that has short grass, no dog mess, and no irritable-looking people. Angle the pitch so that the sun isn't in the batsman's or bowler's eyes.

4 Agree on the rules beforehand. My preferred answers are in brackets.
● **the boundaries** (that line of trees over there)
● **whether you can be out first ball** (no)
● **whether it's tip and run** (yes, once the batsman has 10)
● **whether it's one-hand-one-bounce** (yes; half out)
● **who is deciding LBWs** (a grown-up, if they are competent to; if not, don't bother with it)
● **whether you have to say "walking" or "in" to show you don't want a second run** (yes – "walking" – it's clearer)
● **when the batsman has to retire** (at 20)
● **how many innings each player is going to get** (start with one and make sure everyone has the same number. Stomping off in a huff after you've batted is a grave crime)
● **whether to doctor the ball.** A ball that is half-taped will swing, so try that once you're more confident, and you may end up bowling for Pakistan

5 Decide who's batting first. If everyone wants to, toss for it. Announce which team or player you're going to be. Play like them if you can. If you can't, follow the basics …

Batting
Keep calm. Stand side-on. Grip the bat with two hands, wrong hand on top. Move your feet forward or back. Watch the ball right on to the bat. If the ball is heading for the stumps, keep it out. If not, whack it. Don't hit everything to leg.

Bowling
Take a short run-up. Keep your arm straight. Aim for accuracy first. Get the length right – the ball should bounce once before it reaches the batsman and head for the top of the stumps. Then the line – ideally off stump, certainly within the batsman's reach. Add spin or swing later.

Fielding
Pay attention. Get your body behind the ball as well as your hands. If you're bored, try harder. If that doesn't work, negotiate an earlier finish. Don't just sit down or stomp off.

Everyone
Try hard but not too hard. Games are only fun if you take them reasonably seriously, but if you take them too seriously, they're no fun at all.

DO SAY
Great shot. Good ball. My turn to get it.

DON'T SAY
You're rubbish. My average is 46.25. Shane Warne does it, so it must be allowed.

BEACH VARIATIONS
Find a strip of firm sand. Work out which way the tide is going. Give six if the ball is hit straight into the sea; six and out if it's lost.

▲ **Run-out!** every bit as exciting as a one-day international

STAGE FOUR
GETTING SOME COACHING

Cricket is quite complicated, so you'll be better at it if you have some coaching. It's not cheap but you can ask for it as a present. Try to home in on any cricket-loving uncle or grandparent – perhaps there's one who gave you this book. They will be keen to help and may even go with you to get a bit of a refresher course themselves. A creaky, aching, 50-year-old makes a reasonable match for a sprightly 12-year-old.

If you live near a county cricket club, ask your mum or dad to ring them (or ring yourself – phone calls are easier than you might think) and find out if nets can be booked. Book an hour if you can, and take along three friends, then you can bat for 15 minutes, bowl for 40 and spend five minutes getting changed and trying to work the vending machine. It's good exercise and good fun, especially in the middle of winter.

Anyone in reach of London can book a net at the MCC Indoor School at Lord's by ringing 020 7616 8612. You can choose to have a coach, a bowling machine (if you're 12+) or both. It's expensive – £36 per hour without a coach, £56 with – but good value, especially if you can split the cost. The nets are top-class and the coaches are gentle but effective.
www.lords.org/lords-ground/indoor-school/

REMEMBER ...

These stages can happen in any order. Some people first sample the game at school, others at club open days. The point is to get on and do it.

STAGE TWO
FINDING A CLUB

If you keep making 20 in the park, or taking wickets, you're ready for a step up. And here you're in luck. No generation in sporting history has had as much encouragement to have a go. The government wants you to. The England and Wales Cricket Board wants you to. Several charities want you to. You're in demand.

- If you're in England or Wales, you can find your nearest club at: **www.play-cricket.com**
- If you're in Scotland, go to: www.cricketeurope4.net/SCOTLAND/DATABASE/SCL/clubs.shtml
- A link to a list of Irish clubs had stopped working – maybe they were still celebrating their World Cup run – **so if you're in Ireland, get a parent to ring the Irish Cricket Union in Dublin on (01) 845 0710.**

STAGE THREE
PLAYING AT SCHOOL

If your school plays cricket, you're in luck. Sadly, most schools in Britain don't. But there are big efforts going on to make it easier for them. If your school doesn't play cricket, ask a teacher if you can. Ask them to get hold of a Kwik cricket set to get things going, and tell them there is a charity, Chance To Shine, set up to encourage cricket in state schools. It is trying to raise £25m, which the government says it will match. Within ten years, it aims to reach a third of all schools in England and Wales, with a coach going in for four hours a week in the summer term, and courses in the holidays as well.
www.chancetoshine.org

DO TRY THIS AT HOME

You can play in the corridor with a mini-bat and a ping-pong ball, but it soon gets frustrating. A better idea is to persuade a generous parent to give you a Crazy Catch. This is a rebound net, invented in New Zealand, which sends the ball back at you at unexpected angles. You have to take it outside to use a cricket ball, but there's a lot of fun to be had indoors with a tennis ball. You can play alone, unlike most forms of cricket, or with someone else; all ages can play together. Your catching will improve dramatically. Should you ever find yourself writing a cricket book, you'll find it's the perfect way to relax after a morning bashing away at the keyboard. **www.crazycatch.com**

INDEX

This index is selective, but aims to point you to anything more than a passing reference. For definitions of cricket terms, see page 26; for the main fielding positions, see page 64

A

Afridi, Shahid 76
Ahmed, Aftab 79
Akhtar, Shoaib 56, 76
Akram, Wasim 95
Allott, Geoff 25
Allrounders 60
Anderson, James 83
Art of Captaincy, The 66
Arthur, Mickey 77
Ashes, the 2005
    scorecard 14;
    origins 91, 96;
    epic battles 96
Ashraful, Mohammad 79
Atherton, Mike 53
Athleticism 43
Australia 73, 74;
    supremacy in stats 74; why the best 75;
    v England 96;
    Tied Test 98;
    v India 2000-01 99;
    v SA 2005-06 99;
Autographs 47

B

Baggy Green 74
Ball making and
    materials 20;
    tampering 23
Bangladesh 73, 79
Bat 20
Batting 40; attacking
    40; defensive 41;
    the four choices 42
Batting gloves 20
Batsmen qualities
    required 42
BBC 120
Beach cricket 124
Bedi, Bishan 59
Bell, Ian 83
Benaud, Richie 121
Berkmann, Marcus 123
Bermuda 72
Body shapes 44
Bodyline 50
Bond, Shane NZ star
    78; World XI 81
Books 122
Boon, David 65
Botham, Ian as
    allrounder 61;
    most amazing
    allround Test 61;
    his Ashes 86
Bowden, Billy 23, 115
Bowled 8
Bowlers qualities
    required 42
Bowlers, number of 14
Bowling, fast 56
Bowling figures 14
Bowling, round-arm 38
Bowling, slow 58
Box 20
Box, Tom 100
Bracewell, John 78
Bradman, Don life story
    50; place in history
    91; best batsman
    ever 94; Australia's
    best player 95;
    Test average 105
Brains 43
Bravo, Dwayne 78
Brearley, Mike 66, 86,
    123
Bridgetown 85
Briggs, Simon 122
Broadbent, Jo 95
Brown, Jack 24
Bucknor, Steve 23

C

Cairns, Chris 112
Calcutta 85
Canada 72
Cape Town 56, 85
Captains qualities
    required 42
Catching, bat-pad 65;
    slip 64
Caught 9
Chance To Shine 125
Chanderpaul, Shiv 78
Chandrasekhar,
    Bhagwat 106
Chest guard 20
Chinaman 59
Clark, Belinda 39
Clark, Stuart 74
Club, joining a 125
Coaching 125
Collingwood, Paul 83
Collins, AEJ 114
Connor, Clare 39
Control 57
Cook, Alastair 82
County Championship
    34
County cricket 34
Crazy Catch 125
Cricinfo 93, 120
Crowe, Martin 95
Curran, Kevin 79

D

Dar, Aleem 23
Dedication 43
Derbyshire 36
Dev, Kapil 95
Dhoni, MS 76
Dismissals 8
Double hundreds 111
Dravid, Rahul captaincy
    76; World XI 81
Draw 12
Ducks 111
Durham 36

E

Eden Gardens 85
Ends 18
England 72, 75;
    team profiles 82;
    v Australia 96
England and Wales
    Cricket Board
    (ECB) 37
Essex 35
Etiquette 22
Extras 14
Extreme matches 98
Eye 42

F

Fall of wickets 14
Faulkner, Aubrey 60
Field setting 64
Fielders qualities
    required 42;
    placing 68
Fielding 64
5 Live (radio
    station) 120
Five (TV station) 120
Five-fors 111
Fleming, Stephen
    captaincy 66, 78;
Fletcher, Duncan 40, 75
Flintoff, Andrew life
    story 40; his tips
    on fast bowling 57;
    as allrounder 60;
    type of captain 66;
    England star 75, 82;
    World XI 81
Flower, Andy 95
Focus 42
Friends Provident
    Trophy 34

G

Ganguly, Sourav 67
Gavaskar, Sunil 95
Gayle, Chris 78
Gibbs, Herschelle 113
Gilchrist, Adam
    Australia star 74;
    World XI 81;
    best wicketkeeper-
    batsman ever 95
Glamorgan 34
Gloucestershire 34
Goddard, Trevor 61
Going to a game 118
Grace, Martha 39
Grace, EM 39
Grace, WG 39, 91, 94,
    95
Graves, Robert 115
Gregory, Jack 61
Greig, Tony 61
Grounds 84
Guardian, The 120, 121
Guts 42

H

Hadlee, Richard as
    allrounder 61;
    NZ's best player 95
Haigh, Gideon 123
Hampshire 35
Handled the ball 10
Harmison, Steve 82
Harper, Daryl 23
Harris, James 114
Hat-tricks by Warne 59;
    in general 112

Hayden, Matthew 7;
    World XI 81
Headley, George 95
Heart 57
Helmet 20
Heyhoe-Flint, Rachael
    39
Highest Test score 104
History 88
Hit the ball twice 10
Hit wicket 10
Hobbs, Jack 95
Hogg, Brad 59
Hoggard, Matthew 82,
    119
Holding, Michael 95
Hong Kong 72
Hughes, Merv 57
100mph delivery 56
Hundreds 110
Hussey, Mike 74;
    World XI 81

I

ICC 93
India 73, 76; v Pakistan
    97; dramatic
    comeback 99
Ingleby-Mackenzie,
    Colin 38
International
    programme 93
Internet 120
Intimidatory bowling 23
Ireland 72

J

Jayawardene, Mahela
    67, 77
Jayasuriya, Sanath 95
Jones, Simon 83
Joyce, Dominick 114
Joyce, Ed 114

K

Kallis, Jacques 60, 77,
Kambli, Vinod 70
Kensington Oval 85
Kent 35
Kenya 72
Khan, Imran as
    allrounder 60;
    as captain 66;
    Pakistan's best
    player 95
Khan, Younis 76
Kit 20
Knott, Alan 95
Koertzen, Rudi 23
Kumble, Anil 59, 81

L

Laker, Jim 105
Lancashire 36;
    and women 38;
    v Yorkshire 97
Language, cricket 26
Lara, Brian as captain
    66; run records 104;
    dismissed by
    woman 115;
Laws 22
Laxman, VVS 99
LBW 9
Lee, Brett 114
Leg side (also known as
    on side), 18
Leg spin 59
Leicestershire 36
Lift 57
Light, bad 23
Lillywhite, Fred 100
Lillywhite, John 90
Lord, Thomas 89
Lord's 84, 89, 110, 119
Lynch, Steven 122

M

Maclagan, Myrtle 39
Malik, Shoaib 76
Malinga, Lasith 113
Marshall, Hamish 114
Marshall, James 114
Marshall, Malcolm 94
Marylebone Cricket
    Club (MCC) and
    Spirit of Cricket 23;
    and women 38;
    formation 89
MCC Cricket Coaching
    Book 54
MCG 84
Media 120
Mendes, Sam 66
Miandad, Javed 95
Middlesex 35
Miller, Keith 60
Money 89
Moore, David 78
Moores, Peter 75
Mortaza, Mashrafe 79
Most Test wickets 104
Movement 57
Muralitharan, Muttiah
    spin bowling 58;
    best offspinner today
    and ever 59;
    World XI 81;
    equal best slow
    bowler ever 94;
    most five-fors 111
Mynn, Alfred 90

N

Namibia 72
NatWest Pro40 34
Neilsen, Tim 74
Nel, Andre 77
New Plymouth 85
New Zealand 73, 78
Newlands 85
Newspapers 121
Nightwatchman 14
Noble, Monty 61
Northamptonshire 36
Nottinghamshire 36
Ntini, Makhaya 77
Numbers magic 104;
    tragic 106
Number of players 18

O

Object of the game 6
Obstructing the field 10
Occurrences, unusual
    114
Off side 18
Off spin 59
One-day internationals
    33
Outfielding 65
Overs 18
Over the wicket 19

P

Pace 56
Packer, Kerry 92
Pads 20
Pakistan 73, 76;
    v India 97
Panesar, Monty 75, 83
Park cricket 124
Partnerships 7
Patel, Parthiv 115
Patience 42
Pietersen, Kevin kit 20;
    England star 75, 83;
    World XI 81
Pitch 16
Planet Cricket 72
Player, day in the life
    of 46
Playing the game
    yourself 124
Playfair Cricket Annual
    122
Plunkett, Liam 83
Pollock, Graeme 95
Pollock, Shaun as
    allrounder 60; World
    XI 81; SA's second-
    best player 95; best
    tail-ender ever 95
Ponting, Ricky captaincy
    67, 74; World XI 81
Prior, Matt 82
Pukekura Park 85

Q

Queen, the 38
Quotes, famous 116

R

Radio 120
Rafique, Mohammad
    79
Ramprakash, Mark 46
Ratings, LG Test 108
Read, Chris 63
Reduced History of
    Cricket, The 122
Reflexes 43
Results, the four
    possible 12
Retired out 10
Reverse swing 57
Rhodes, Jonty 65, 95
Rhodes, Wilfrid 25
Richards, Viv 95
Richardson, Mark 53
Rivalries 96
Roses matches 97
Round the wicket 19
Running between the
    wickets 18
Russell, Jack 63

S

Sarwan, Ramnaresh 78
Scorecard, how to read
    14
Scotland 72
Seam bowling 57;
    fields for 68
Sehwag, Virender 76
Shastri, Ravi 25
Shepherds 88
Sidebottom, Ryan 115
Singh, Harbhajan 76
Sixes 112; six in an
    over 113
Sky TV 120
Sledging 22, 117
Slips 64
Slow bowling general
    58; fields for 68
Slow left-arm 59
Smith, Big Jim 24
Smith, Ed 123
Smith, Graeme 77, 106
Sobers, Garry 60; best
    allrounder ever 94;
    six sixes 113
Somerset 34
South Africa 73, 77, 99
Spin magazine 121
Spirit of cricket 23
Sri Lanka 73, 77
Statistics 108
Stoicism 43
Strauss, Andrew 75, 82
Streak, Heath 95
Strictly Come Dancing
    49
Strike rate, batting 53
Stumped 9
Substitutes 18
Surrey 35
Sussex 35
Swing bowling 57
Symonds, Andrew 7

T

Taibu, Tatenda 79
Taufel, Simon 23
Team, balance of 19, 60;
    v individual 19
Telegraph, The Daily
    121
Telegraph, The Sunday
    121
Tendulkar, Sachin
    career span 24;
    life story 70; India
    star 76; India's
    best player 95;
    most international
    hundreds 111
Test cricket 32
Test Match Special 120
Thigh pad 20
Tickets 118
Tie 12
Tied Test 98
Time 24
Timed out 10
Timeless Test 24, 98
Times, The 121
Toss 16
Trescothick, Marcus 83
Triple hundreds 111
Twenty20 Cup 34
Twenty20 internationals
    33

U

UAE 72
Umpires 22
Umpiring signals 23
USA 72
Utseya, Prosper 79

V

Vaughan, Michael 67,
    75, 82
Vettori, Daniel 59

W

Walking 22
Wardle, Johnny 59
Warne, Shane life story
    30; spin bowling
    58; hat-trick 59;
    best legspinner ever
    59; equal best slow
    bowler ever 94;
    Australia's second-
    best player 95; Test
    wickets record 104;
Warwickshire 36
Waugh, Mark 64, 94
Waugh, Steve 94
Weather who likes what
    16; umpires' role 23
West Indies 72, 78, 98
Wicketkeeping 63
Willes, Christina 38
Willes, John 38
Willis, Bob 87
Winning by runs 12; by
    wickets 12
Winning margins,
    widest and
    narrowest (by
    sides batting first
    in Tests) 13
Wisden, John 90, 100
Wisden Cricketer, The
    121
Wisden Cricketers'
    Almanack 123
Women's cricket 38
Woodcock, John 123
Woolmer, Bob 95
Wools, Rachael 41
Worcestershire 36

Y

Yorkshire 36; v
    Lancashire 97
Yousuf, Mohammad 76

Z

Zimbabwe 73, 79, 106

When you work for Wisden, you find yourself standing on the shoulders of giants. It's especially true of this book, which started life as an idea developed by Matthew Engel and Christopher Lane, editor-in-chief and publisher of the *Almanack*, about 10 years ago. I'm grateful to them for having the idea, and for not doing it themselves. This book has ended up being a different one, but it grew in the same soil.

The main difference is that this one is more visual. For that, most of the credit goes to Nigel Davies, who designed all the inside pages. Ten years ago, Nigel arrived at *Wisden Cricket Monthly* from the world of Manga comics. He took a bit of persuading to stay (thank you, John Brown), but he is still there as art director of *The Wisden Cricketer*, after surviving two changes of editor, two changes of owner, one change of name and two changes of address. He is the king of cricket designers, prolific, tireless and creative. Working with him, I felt like a journeyman batting with Kevin Pietersen. I just had to take the single, jog down the other end and enjoy the show.

While the concept came from Wisden, the execution has come from A&C Black, who distribute the *Almanack*. Nigel and I are grateful to Robert Foss, our editor there, for his easy-going enthusiasm. Among Rob's colleagues, thanks go to Jill Coleman for her trenchant leadership, to Terry Woodley and Jocelyn Lucas for their work on the cover, to Lucy Beevor for her hawk-eyed proof-reading, and to Rosanna Bortoli and Nicola Mann for the publicity.

Special thanks go to my agent, Araminta Whitley, for her relaxed expertise over 18 years, and to her assistant Lucy Cowie; to James Bunce, who did the repro with good humour; and to my former Wisden colleagues Steven Lynch and Simon Briggs, who read a lot of pages with tactful acumen. Any errors that remain are my fault, not theirs.

Big thanks to the seven sounding boards, Daniel de Lisle, Laura de Lisle, Tanya Aldred, Dileep Premachandran, Josie Robson, Robert Butler and Sam Butler-Sloss; and to those who helped with specific pages – Clare Skinner, Philip Brown, Rory Brown, Billy Bowden, Nathan Ross and Mark Ramprakash.

The main sources were Cricinfo.com, BBC.co.uk, *Wisden Cricketers' Almanack* and Wikipedia. I have also drawn on *What Is a Googly?* by Rob Eastaway, *One Hundred Greatest Cricketers* by John Woodcock, *Armball to Zooter* by Lawrence Booth, *A Social History of Cricket* by Derek Birley, *A Century of Great Cricket Quotes* by David Hopps, *All About Cricket* by Brian Johnston, *Freddie Flintoff: England's Hero* by Tanya Aldred, and *Barclays World of Cricket*, edited by EW Swanton et al. For inspiration, the main source was *Pick Me Up*, the superb neo-encyclopedia by David Roberts and Jeremy Leslie. The idea of telling a story at regular intervals came from *The Dangerous Book for Boys* by Conn and Hal Iggulden.

Behind every cricket-mad child lies a tolerant family. I've been lucky and had two. My parents, Everard and Mary Rose, gave endless loving support on this and every other front. They took me to matches, bought me kit and books, and, along with my sister, Rosie, calmly absorbed levels of cricket conversation that would have tested the patience of saints.

These days, my cricket habit is inflicted on my wife, Amanda, who knows more about sport than I do, my son Daniel, who knows more about American football than I do, and my daughter Laura, who knows more about riding than I do. They all put up with this project without losing their cool or their warmth. I have also watched many games with my in-laws, Clive and Gay Barford, whose hospitality is in proportion to their plasma screen.

But the central figure in my cricket life has been my brother, Charlie, who introduced me to the game, played it with me in our ropey old net, made interesting points about it, led the way into cricket writing, and treated me more sportingly than any younger brother had a right to expect. This book is dedicated to him.